*HOME- AND COMMUNITY-BASED
SERVICES FOR OLDER ADULTS*

Home- and Community- Based Services for Older Adults

AGING IN CONTEXT

By Keith A. Anderson,
Holly I. Dabelko-Schoeny,
and Noelle L. Fields

 COLUMBIA UNIVERSITY PRESS   NEW YORK

COLUMBIA UNIVERSITY PRESS
Publishers Since 1893
New York   Chichester, West Sussex

cup.columbia.edu
Copyright © 2018 Columbia University Press

Library of Congress Cataloging-in-Publication Data
Names: Anderson, Keith A., author. | Dabelko-Schoeny, Holly I., author. |
    Fields, Noelle L., author.
Title: Home- and community-based services for older adults : aging in context /
    by Keith A. Anderson, Holly I. Dabelko-Schoeny, and Noelle L. Fields.
Description: New York : Columbia University Press, [2018] | Includes bibliographical
    references and index.
Identifiers: LCCN 2017048967 (print) | LCCN 2017053510 (e-book) |
    ISBN 9780231546997 (E-book) | ISBN 9780231177689 (cloth) |
    ISBN 9780231177696 (pbk.)
Subjects: LCSH: Older people—Medical care—United States. |
    Older people—Care—United States. | Older people—Services for—United States. |
    Home care services—United States. | Community health services for older people—
    United States.
Classification: LCC RA564.8 (e-book) | LCC RA564.8 .A525 2018 (print) |
    DDC 362.19897/00973—dc23
LC record available at https://lccn.loc.gov/2017048967

Columbia University Press books are printed on permanent
and durable acid-free paper.
Printed in the United States of America

Cover design: Jordan Wannemacher
Cover image: © Jamie Heiden / Trevillion Images

CONTENTS

TWELVE

THIRTEEN

AFTERWORD

ACKNOWLEDGMENTS

I WOULD LIKE TO ACKNOWLEDGE the support and love of my father, George V. Anderson Jr., who is aging with grace, and my mother, Helen L. Anderson, who never grew old.

Keith A. Anderson

I would like to thank Steve Schoeny for helping me balance the demands of being an academic with being a mother to our sons, Geoffrey and Nate. I am grateful to my parents, Dr. David and Elaine Dabelko, for teaching me to love the process of discovery and to respect all people. Finally, I am thankful for Nana, Granddad, Grandma, and Zeddo, whose lives provide me with inspiration.

Holly I. Dabelko-Schoeny

Thank you to Justin and Libby Fields for all of the joy and love that you bring to my life. I am also grateful for my parents, Dr. Hap and Blakie LeCrone, for all of their support and for instilling in me a love and respect for older adults.

Noelle L. Fields

The authors also thank our doctoral student, KyongWeon "Kathy" Lee, for her assistance in the preparation of this book. Finally, the authors acknowledge the guidance of our friend and mentor, Dr. Virginia E. Richardson, who continues to inspire and shape our careers.

HOME- AND COMMUNITY-BASED
SERVICES FOR OLDER ADULTS

1

Introduction

Among the various places that become meaningful for us, home is the single most significant one. Beyond meeting the need for shelter, a true home is where we can be ourselves and be *at home*. Home sets the stage of our life experience; it is the psychological and emotional frame of reference from which we relate to all other places and life experiences. It is the space where we express ourselves and socially interact and where events of joy and sorrow take place. Home is where we grow old and become comfortable; it provides a setting where we can manage our daily lives in spite of physical frailty.

CHOUDHURY, 2008, pp. 7–8

THE POPULATION OF THE UNITED States is aging, and we have all heard the cliché references to the "Silver Tsunami" and the "Graying of America." As the baby boomer generation (born between 1946 and 1964) continues to move into old age, our already strained systems of care for older adults will face a monumentally increased burden. The aging of the population presents challenges, but we also see opportunities for creative approaches to caring for older adults and for supporting their family caregivers in their preferred setting—at home and in the community. Our homes and the communities in which we live have deep significance. This significance is magnified in later life and in illness. Home is where we find strength, support, and renewal. Nobody wants to be sick and to need care. But when we do, we want to be in our own homes and be cared for in our communities of family, friends, and neighbors. *Home- and community-based services* (HCBS) are exactly what the name implies—health care and support services delivered to the residences and the neighborhoods where older adults and their family caregivers live. HCBS are cost-effective and the preferred platform for service delivery to older adults and their families. Given the benefits and capacities to provide care, HCBS may hold the key to solving the challenges of our aging society. As such, HCBS merit the attention of researchers, policy makers, and practitioners.

This book introduces you to the policies, settings, services, successes, and challenges associated with HCBS. The target audience are students in the health professions, such as nursing, social work, and allied health services (for example, physical therapy or occupational therapy). Students in public health and health care management fields also may find this topic of interest, particularly in light of the policy-related and service-oriented challenges facing society as we care for a growing older adult population. Some of the topics may be familiar to you from prior learning or life experiences. For example, you may have a family member who is a resident in an assisted living facility. Other topics may cover new ground, such as the resurgence of home-based primary care ("house calls") or the ever-advancing technology of smart homes. As you read, we hope you will share our enthusiasm for the continued development of HCBS that are humane, holistic, and person- and family-centered.

Conspicuously, this book does not contain a chapter on nursing home care. This intentional omission directly reflects our firm belief that our systems of care will continue to move away from institutional care and toward HCBS. It may be surprising to learn that only 4.2 percent of older adults use nursing home care and that the number of nursing home residents has steadily declined from a high of 1,628,300 in 1999 to 1,369,700 in 2014 (Harris-Kojetin et al., 2016). This trend has occurred despite the growing number of older adults. Length of stay in nursing homes is also declining, indicating that older adults are either being discharged to home care or that older adults are using nursing homes for end-of-life care only, similar to hospice (Department of Health and Human Services [DHHS], 2016). Another factor to consider is the prohibitive cost of nursing home care. Nursing home care is 2 to 4 times more expensive than HCBS (Genworth Financial, 2016). Finally, the capacities of HCBS are growing, and we can now provide levels of care in the home and community that previously could only be provided in the nursing home setting. For all of these reasons, the nursing home is becoming an unwanted, outdated, and ineffective approach to caring for the overwhelming majority of older adults. Will nursing homes disappear in the future? Probably not; however, they may someday resemble inpatient hospices where older adults come only at the very end of their life.

We first need to establish a foundation for understanding the demographic characteristics and the biopsychosocial needs of the older adult population in the United States. The populations of those age 65 and older and 85 and older have risen dramatically and are projected to increase significantly in the future (figure 1.1). Currently, the older adult population is approximately 14 percent of the overall population, and it is expected to grow to 21 percent of the overall population by 2040. Given the lower life expectancy of men, women constitute 56 percent of those age 65 and older and 67 percent of those age 85 and older. The older adult population is not as diverse as the general population; however, diversity is projected to grow in the coming years. In 2012, approximately 86 percent of the older adult population was white and 14 percent were ethnic and racial minorities (for example, black, Hispanic, Asian). By 2050, it is projected that 23 percent of the older adult population will be ethnic and racial minorities (Ortman, Velkoff, & Hogan, 2014).

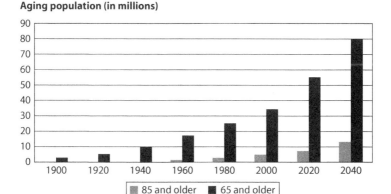

Aging population (in millions)

FIGURE 1.1 Population projections ages 65+ and 85+.
Source: U.S. Census Bureau, 2010.

Percentage of older adults with:

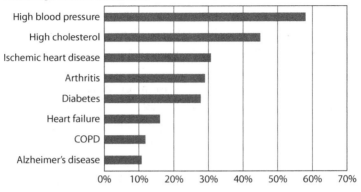

FIGURE 1.2 Chronic conditions among Medicare beneficiaries.
Source: CMS, 2012.

The growing number of older adults is not necessarily a problem. The problem lies in our ability to meet the biopsychosocial needs of this expanding and particularly vulnerable population. Addressing the physical health needs of older adults is a particularly vexing issue. Thanks to advances in medical sciences, older adults are living longer with chronic and costly health conditions (figure 1.2). The Centers for Disease Prevention and Control (CDC, 2017) report that 3 out of 4 older adults have multiple chronic conditions including Alzheimer's disease, diabetes, arthritis, cancer, and cardiovascular disease. Chronic conditions can persist over decades and cause disability and functional limitations. Chronic conditions, particularly multiple chronic conditions, are costly in terms of debilitation and quality of life and account for "approximately 71 percent of the total health care spending in the United States."

Aging is often accompanied by changes and increases in socioemotional health needs. Mental health has been identified as a priority concern for older adults. In 2008, the CDC reported that 20 percent of older adults (in this case age 55 and older) "experience some type of mental health concern." Approximately 5 percent of those age 65 and older reported current depressive symptoms and more than 10 percent had a lifetime diagnosis of depression. In addition, more than 7 percent of those over age 65 reported a lifetime diagnosis of an anxiety disorder. In this same report, approximately 1 out of 8 older adults reported that they "rarely or never received the social and emotional support they needed." Loneliness and social isolation have been identified as significant socioemotional concerns for older adults, increasing the risk for morbidity and mortality (Holt-Lunstad, Smith, Baker, Harris, & Stephenson, 2015). Loss is a natural part of aging, whether it be loss of abilities due to compromised health or the loss of loved ones through death. Grief is also a natural part of aging, but grief can take a toll on the overall well-being of older adults (for more on grief and complicated grief in later life, see Miller, 2012). Mental health issues, lack of social support, social isolation, loneliness, and loss and grief are problematic and affect the quality of life, well-being, and health care utilization of older adults.

Poverty is an issue for many older adults and affects 10 percent of those age 65 or older. Although the poverty rate for older adults is typically lower than for other groups (21 percent for those under age 18; 13 percent for those age 19 to 64), poverty disproportionately affects older women and people of color (Proctor, Semega, & Kollar 2016). In fact, poverty rates for older women are almost twice that of older men (12 percent versus 7 percent), 2.5 times higher for black older adults, and 3 times higher among Hispanic older adults (Cubanski, Casillas, & Damico, 2015). Financial insecurity has far-reaching negative consequences: lack of affordable and appropriate housing, higher risk of food insecurity, lack of access to quality health care, and disparities in health outcomes. This book focuses on home- and community-based services, and it is important to note that a significant number of lower-income older adults have far less access and far fewer options when it comes to selecting a service that best meets their needs.

Meeting the biopsychosocial and financial needs of older adults is costly, and expenditures are expected to skyrocket unless systematic changes are made to our health and financial support programs. Old Age and Survivors Benefits under the Social Security program, the primary income support and poverty prevention program for older adults, is projected to run short-falls and have solvency issues by 2037 (Social Security Administration, 2016a). Social Security provides at least half of the income for 61 percent of older adult beneficiaries (Social Security Administration (2016b). The costs of Medicare and Medicaid, the primary payer sources for the health care of older adults, have grown exponentially over the years (figure 1.3). Much of these costs are incurred near the end of life (Cubanski, Neuman,

Expenditures (in billions)

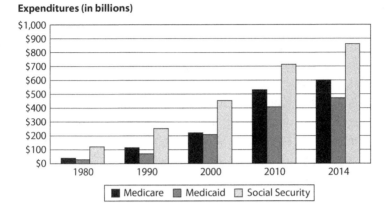

FIGURE 1.3 Expenditures in Medicare, Medicaid, and Social Security.
Sources: CMS, 2016; Social Security Administration, 2016b.

Griffin, & Damico, 2016). Unless changes are made in our approach to care and support for older adults, the future of these programs is precarious.

There can be no doubt that *challenges lie ahead as our society continues to age*. HCBS holds great promise for meeting some of these challenges. In each chapter, you will find descriptions, examinations, and discussions of care settings, professional roles, research findings, policies, and projections for the future for HCBS. Featured elements include case studies, interviews with researchers and practitioners, discussions about diversity, and discussion questions and exercises. We encourage you to use these resources and to continue to further explore topics related to HCBS. Learning is a lifelong process, and we hope this book ignites your curiosity in discovering more about later life.

CHAPTER SUMMARIES

Chapter 2. Policies Related to Home- and Community-Based Services

It is critically important to understand the policies that affect HCBS prior to discussing the services that are offered. In this chapter, we examine and discuss policies related to HCBS and efforts to help older adults age in place, such as the Social Security Act, Medicare, and Medicaid. As health care policies continue to evolve in the United States, so will the services that provide care to older adults.

Chapter 3. The Older Americans Act and the Aging Network

The aging network and an array of services currently provided to older adults have been established through the Older Americans Act. These services include Area Agencies on Aging, transportation, caregiver support, home delivered meals and congregate meal sites, adult protective services, long-term care ombudsman services, and senior centers. This chapter summarizes these important services and the impact of the Older Americans Act.

Chapter 4. Multidisciplinary and Interdisciplinary Practice Skills Across Home- and Community-Based Services Settings

Across HCBS settings, there are multidisciplinary and common interdisciplinary practice skills. These include individual and family assessment, care planning, monitoring, the referral process, family mediation, and discharge planning. In this chapter, we discuss these skills and provide exercises and applications to help you develop these skills.

Chapter 5. Family Caregiving

Family caregivers are the backbone of HCBS, providing the majority of the support for older adults and bearing most of the burden. In this chapter, we review the vast literature on family caregiving in the community and discuss strategies and interventions for supporting and partnering with family caregivers.

Chapter 6. Home Health Care Services

Home health care services are probably the most familiar kinds of services, but you may be surprised by the growing sophistication and the capacities of this care system in meeting the complex health needs of older adults. In this chapter, we review the variety of services offered in the home setting and highlight the growth of the home health care services industry.

Chapter 7. The Village Concept and Naturally Occurring Retirement Communities

The Village concept and naturally occurring retirement communities (NORCs) are organic environments in which older adults organize and advocate for services within their neighborhoods and communities. In this chapter, we explore the evolution of these efforts and evaluate existing and emerging evidence.

Chapter 8. Home-Based Primary Care

Physician house calls may seem like a relic of the past, but this mode of care delivery has recently emerged as a legitimate and potentially effective option within HCBS. In this chapter, we focus on the resurgence of interest in home-based primary care and how this seemingly outdated approach can help to meet the needs of older adults in their own homes.

Chapter 9. Assisted Living and Housing with Services

Assisted living is one of the most recognizable (and most misunderstood) community settings for older adults. In this chapter, we review the capabilities and limitations of assisted living and ponder the future permutations of this care setting. This chapter includes information on subsidized housing with services for lower-income older adults.

Chapter 10. Adult Day Services

Adult day services have evolved from church basement programs to comprehensive community care centers capable of delivering a range of complex services. We provide an overview of the adult day services sector, including recent data from national surveys and systematic reviews on effectiveness and outcomes.

Chapter 11. Hospice in Community Settings

Although often thought of as a place or an institution, in reality hospice is an approach to end-of-life care that is primarily delivered in home and community settings. In this chapter, we review the philosophy of hospice, the types of services offered, and current research. We also examine barriers to hospice use and the potential that hospice offers to increase the quality of care and to lower costs at the end of life.

Chapter 12. International Perspectives on Home- and Community-Based Services

We recognize that there are different and promising international approaches to caring for older adults. In this chapter, we highlight a select group of these novel international approaches to HCBS and explore the potential for bringing these programs to the United States.

Chapter 13. Technology in Home- and Community-Based Services

Technology has grown into a promising facilitator for the delivery of HCBS. From telehealth, to smart home innovations, to the development of caregiving robots, technology may be the future of care for older adults. In this chapter, we introduce you to these emerging technologies and explore what the future may hold.

Afterword: A Commentary on the Future of Home- and Community-Based Services

Joseph E. Gaugler, PhD, a leading scholar on HCBS for older adults, provides insight into what the future may hold for this important service sector.

REFERENCES

Centers for Disease Prevention and Control. (2008). *The state of mental health and aging.* Retrieved from https://www.cdc.gov/aging/pdf/mental_health.pdf

Centers for Disease Prevention and Control. (2017). *Multiple chronic conditions.* Retrieved from https://www.cdc.gov/chronicdisease/about/multiple-chronic.htm

Centers for Medicare & Medicaid Services. (2012). *Chronic conditions among Medicare beneficiaries.* Retrieved from https://www.cms.gov/Research-Statistics-Data-and-Systems/Statistics-Trends-and-Reports/Chronic-Conditions/Downloads/2012Chartbook.pdf

Centers for Medicare & Medicaid Services. (2016). *National health expenditures by type of service and source of funds, CY 1960–2015*. Retrieved from https://www.cms.gov/research-statistics-data-and-systems/statistics-trends-and-reports/nationalhealthexpenddata/nationalhealthaccountshistorical.html

Chaudhury, H. (2008). *Remembering home: Rediscovering the self in dementia*. Baltimore, MD: Johns Hopkins University Press.

Cubanski, J., Casillas, G., & Damico, A. (2015). *Poverty among seniors: An updated analysis of national and state level poverty rates under the official and supplemental poverty measures*. Retrieved from http://files.kff.org/attachment/issue-brief-poverty-among-seniors-an-updated-analysis-of-national-and-state-level-poverty-rates-under-the-official-and-supplemental-poverty-measures

Cubanski, J., Neuman, T., Griffin, S., & Damico, A. (2016). *Medicare spending at the end of life: A snapshot of beneficiaries who died in 2014 and the cost of their care*. Retrieved from http://kff.org/report-section/medicare-spending-at-the-end-of-life-findings/

Department of Health and Human Services. (2016). *2015 CMS statistics*. Retrieved from https://www.cms.gov/Research-Statistics-Data-and-Systems/Statistics-Trends-and-Reports/CMS-Statistics-Reference-Booklet/Downloads/2015CMSStatistics.pdf

Genworth Financial. (2016). *Genworth cost of care survey 2016*. Retrieved from https://www.genworth.com/dam/Americas/US/PDFs/Consumer/corporate/131168_050516.pdf

Harris-Kojetin, L., Sengupta, M., Park-Lee, E., Valverde, R., Caffrey, C., Rome, V., & Lendon, J. (2016). Long-term care providers and services users in the United States: Data from the National Study of Long-Term Care Providers, 2013–2014. *Vital Health Statistics, 3*(38). Retrieved from https://www.cdc.gov/nchs/data/series/sr_03/sr03_038.pdf

Holt-Lunstad, J., Smith, T. B., Baker, M., Harris, T., & Stephenson, D. (2015). Loneliness and social isolation as risk factors for mortality: A meta-analytic review. *Perspectives in Psychological Science, 10*(2), 227–237.

Miller, M. D. (2012). Complicated grief in later life. *Dialogues in Clinical Neuroscience, 14*(2), 195–202.

Ortman, J. M., Velkoff, V. A., & Hogan, H. (2014). *An aging nation: The older population in the United States*. Retrieved from https://www.census.gov/prod/2014pubs/p25-1140.pdf

Proctor, B. D., Semega, J. L., & Kollar, M. A. (2016). *Income and poverty in the United States: 2015*. Retrieved from https://www.census.gov/content/dam/Census/library/publications/2016/demo/p60-256.pdf

Social Security Administration. (2016a). *2016 annual report.* Retrieved from https://www.ssa.gov/OACT/TR/2016/tr2016.pdf

Social Security Administration. (2016b). *Facts & figures about Social Security, 2016.* Retrieved from https://www.ssa.gov/policy/docs/chartbooks/fast_facts/2016/fast _facts16.html

U.S. Census Bureau. (2012). *The next four decades: The older population in the United States: 2010 to 2050.* Retrieved from https://www.census.gov/prod/2010pubs /p25-1138.pdf

2

Policies Related to Home- and Community-Based Services

▶ AMANDA J. LEHNING, PHD, MSW,
UNIVERSITY OF MARYLAND

No greater tragedy exists in modern civilization than the aged, worn-out worker who after a life of ceaseless effort and useful productivity must look forward for his declining years to a poorhouse. A modern social consciousness demands a more humane and efficient arrangement.

PRESIDENT FRANKLIN D. ROOSEVELT, 1929

LEARNING OBJECTIVES

In this chapter, you will:

- Develop an understanding of the history and evolution of home- and community-based services policy.
- Learn about the provisions of major public policies that support HCBS.
- Examine the strengths and limitations of current HCBS policy.
- Identify barriers to the development, adoption, and implementation of more comprehensive HCBS policy.
- Explore future directions for HCBS policy.

A BROAD RANGE OF HOME- and community-based services (HCBS) are available to older adults and individuals with disabilities in the United States. HCBS include long-term services and supports (LTSS) provided to older adults and their families in a noninstitutional setting, including in the home (such as home health or personal assistance) and the community (such as adult day services and congregate meals). Approximately 10 million Americans receive HCBS (Kaye, Harrington, & LaPlante, 2010), and slightly more than half of those receiving assistance are over age 65 (Kassner, 2011). An estimated 70 percent of older adults will at some point need LTSS, including HCBS, institutional care in a nursing home or assisted living facility, or other supports such as assistive technology (Kemper, Komisar, & Alecxih, 2005). HCBS are critical to helping the most vulnerable older adults age in place and "live in their homes or communities as long as possible" (Yen & Anderson, 2012, p. 951). However, public policy has played a relatively limited role in the provision of HCBS, with the government primarily involved in financing care only for those without economic resources. In this chapter, we focus on major federal HCBS policies, some of which are jointly funded or administered at the state and local levels. The predominant approach to HCBS policy in this country reflects a residual model, in which the responsibility for accessing, coordinating, and paying for assistance falls mainly to older adults and their families until they are no longer able to manage on their own. More recently some innovative HCBS have emerged from both the public and nonprofit sectors. Relatively few older Americans can access these more integrated and comprehensive services today, but they offer promising approaches for the future of HCBS policy.

FACT OR FICTION?

Consider the following statements.

- Medicaid is the largest public source of funding for HCBS.
- Consumer-directed HCBS are less desirable and less effective for older adults when compared to other populations.
- Public long-term services and supports (LTSS) have an institutional bias.
- Older Americans now have access to a voluntary long-term care insurance program through the Community Living Assistance Services and Supports (CLASS) Act.
- The economic value of assistance provided by family caregivers is much higher than that provided through formal HCBS.

After reading this chapter, you will be able to affirm which statements are fact and which are fiction.

HISTORY OF HOME- AND COMMUNITY-BASED
SERVICE POLICY

Historically, families and other sources of informal support assumed the full costs and burden of assisting older adults with physical or cognitive limitations. Prior to the mid-twentieth century, the only public support was institutional care (referred to as "indoor relief" at the time) in almshouses, which often was financed by the local government and restricted to older adults who were poor, socially isolated, or disabled (Watson, 2009). It was not until 1965, with the creation of Medicare and Medicaid and passage of the Older Americans Act (OAA), that the federal government became involved in the provision of LTSS. However, these policies initially offered minimal support for services in the home or community. Medicare, a federal program funded mostly through payroll taxes, was designed to cover the costs of health care but not long-term care, and reimbursement was restricted to short-term skilled care following an acute health crisis (Robison, Shugrue, Fortinsky, & Gruman, 2014). Medicaid, a joint federal–state means-tested program, limited eligibility to older adults living in poverty and included an institutional bias by mandating that states, not the community, cover care in nursing homes. Finally, the federally funded OAA created an "aging network" that now includes fifty-six State Units on Aging, 629 Area Agencies on Aging, and 246 Indian Tribal and Native Hawaiian Organizations to provide HCBS across the country (Administration for Community Living, 2015). Throughout its existence, however, OAA services have been characterized by relatively low funding and wide variations among agencies (Fox-Grage & Ujvari, 2014; Hudson, 2010).

In subsequent decades, U.S. public policy has shifted toward increasing older adults' access to HCBS. These efforts to rebalance public funding in a more equitable distribution between community and institutional care are motivated, in part, by a need to contain government costs and, in part, by a recognition that older adults and other individuals with disabilities often prefer to remain in their own home and community. An example of rebalancing is when the Social Security Act reauthorization of 1981 created 1915(c) waivers, through which states have the option to use Medicaid funding to provide recipients who qualify for nursing home care with a variety of HCBS, including adult day health services, case management, personal care services, and caregiver respite (Kapp, 2014). In this optional program, states have a great deal of flexibility in terms of who and where they serve. Medicaid HCBS became even more flexible in 2005 when the Deficit Reduction Act (DRA) permitted states to offer Medicaid-funded HCBS without having to obtain a waiver from the federal government, and allowed for less restrictive eligibility criteria for community care compared to institutional care.

A more targeted model that aims to help older adults age in place is the Program for All-Inclusive Care for the Elderly (PACE), developed by On Lok Senior Health Services in California in the 1970s. After a successful demonstration, PACE became a permanent Medicare program through the Balanced Budget Act of 1997 (Gross, Temkin-Greener, Kunitz, & Mukamel, 2004) and is now a Medicare Advantage program in which providers receive a fixed capitated payment to deliver a wide range of acute and long-term care services (Kane, Homyak, Bershadsky, & Flood, 2006). PACE programs take on the financial responsibility for providing participants with all needed services, even if the costs exceed the capitated rate (Hansen & Hewitt, 2012). PACE sites typically provide services in an adult day health setting and coordinate care through a multidisciplinary team of physicians, nurses, social workers, and physical therapists, among others (Hansen & Hewitt, 2012). Older adults can enroll in PACE if they meet the health and functioning requirements for nursing home placement and are either dually eligible for Medicare and Medicaid or are able to self-pay the portion covered by Medicaid (Mui, 2002). PACE programs serve frail older adults at risk for disability, disease, and other negative outcomes (Cramm, Twisk, & Nieboer, 2014). PACE has expanded across the country, but it remains a limited program with a relatively small number of older adults enrolled because few organizations offer PACE and few older adults without Medicaid coverage can afford their share of the expenses (Gross et al., 2004).

One of the key policies addressing the institutional bias of long-term services and supports was the 1999 Supreme Court decision in *Olmstead v. L.C.*, which defined unnecessary institutionalization as a civil rights issue in violation of the Americans with Disabilities Act of 1990. Specifically, the majority opinion in the case held that states should provide care in the least restrictive setting possible when (1) the services are appropriate, (2) the individual is not against community treatment, and (3) the community treatment can be reasonably accommodated. Furthermore, the Court's decision restricted the ability of states to argue that increased costs for community-based treatment would make the provision of such care unreasonable. Although this decision focused on the case of two women with mental disabilities, the *Olmstead* decision also applies to older adults with physical or cognitive disabilities (Tilly, 2016).

The *Olmstead* decision aligns with a shift in HCBS policy toward more consumer involvement and consumer direction. Older adults who depend on Medicaid to cover the costs of HCBS previously had very little control over these services. Participant-directed services give them the opportunity to select, supervise, and coordinate care and care providers. In Cash and Counseling, for example, older adults and those with disabilities served by Medicaid can receive a cash allowance or voucher to pay for HCBS, including in-home care, assistive devices, and home modifications, and hire their own paid caregivers, including family members, within some constraints (Carlson, Foster, Dale, & Brown, 2007). In states that offer this optional program, Medicaid beneficiaries have control over and responsibility for managing most aspects of their care (Kapp, 2014). Cash and Counseling started in 1996 as a demonstration, during which it was implemented and evaluated in three states (Arkansas, New Jersey, and Florida), with an additional twelve states participating in the replication phase. Cash and Counseling has been linked with a number of benefits for participants, including higher satisfaction with services, fewer unmet needs, and better quality of life than traditional agency-based care (Carlson et al., 2007). The demonstration phase ended in 2013, and some states continue to offer some form of Cash and Counseling.

Efforts to rebalance long-term care spending and to enhance consumer involvement have not only expanded options for HCBS but have reinforced the individual- and family-level responsibility that has characterized HCBS from the beginning. George W. Bush's Own Your Future campaign, for example, aligned with that administration's emphasis on creating an "ownership society" by encouraging older adults and their families to plan for their future care needs (Scharlach & Lehning, 2012). During this time, the federal government set up Aging and Disability Resource Centers (ADRCs) across the country to provide information on a variety of LTSS, with an emphasis on consumer-driven community-based options as an alternative to nursing home care (Elliott, 2013). A core service of ADRCs is Options Counseling, through which trained counselors help consumers and their families navigate LTSS and try to match services with individuals' needs and preferences (Elliott, 2013). ADRCs, Cash and Counseling, and similar publicly supported programs such as Money Follows the Person (which increases federal funding for home- and community-based services to help Medicaid beneficiaries move from institutional to community settings), reflect market-based principles such as competition, choice, and limited regulation (Hudson, 2010).

CURRENT HOME- AND COMMUNITY-BASED SERVICE POLICY

Continuing historic trends, three themes of current HCBS policy include (1) helping economically disadvantaged older adults cover the costs of services, (2) addressing the institutional bias of public payment mechanisms, and (3) supporting the preference of a majority of older Americans to age in place in their own home and community.

Medicare

Medicare is the largest source of public health insurance in the United States, covering almost 49 million people and approximately 98 percent of all adults over the age of 65 (Davis, Schoen, & Bandeali, 2015). However, Medicare plays a relatively minor role in HCBS policy, covering about one-fifth of all LTSS spending and only providing home health care for those who are homebound, under the care of a physician, and require intermittent or part-time care following an acute health problem such as an injury (Centers for Medicare and Medicaid Services, nd). Medicare does not cover round-the-clock support, or such HCBS as personal care or homemaker services. Many Americans, however, assume that Medicare will be available to meet their long-term HCBS needs. In one recent survey, nearly half of the respondents planned to use Medicare to cover community-based care (Robison et al., 2014).

Medicaid

It is much more likely that older adults who receive public funding for HCBS will access it through Medicaid rather than Medicare. Medicaid accounts for about 50 percent of all annual spending for LTSS, totaling

$117.3 billion in 2010 (National Health Policy Forum, 2013). Medicaid provides HCBS through three mechanisms: (1) a mandatory home health benefit, (2) optional 1915(c) waivers, and (3) an optional state plan personal care services benefit (Ng, Wong, & Harrington, 2014). In 2010, Medicaid spent $35.9 billion for 1915(c) waiver services, $12.5 billion for personal care, $4.8 billion for home health, and $1.4 billion on other types of HCBS (National Health Policy Forum, 2013). Institutional care continues to account for the majority of LTSS spending by Medicaid (Scharlach & Lehning, 2012). However, in recent decades Medicaid has been shifting funding away from nursing homes, covering HCBS for 3.3 million people in 2009 and increasing the proportion of LTSS spending for HCBS from 24 percent in 1997 to 47 percent in 2010 (National Health Policy Forum, 2013). Because Medicaid is the largest source of funding for LTSS in the United States, an increasing emphasis on HCBS may influence the availability and prioritization of HCBS in the public and private sectors.

One of the motivating factors behind rebalancing toward more HCBS is the need to constrain public long-term care spending. Medicaid has accounted for a growing proportion of state spending, particularly in recent years. According to Brand (2011), between 1999 and 2009, Medicaid spending increased at more than double the rate of state budgets. HCBS are less expensive per person than nursing homes; for example, in 2008 in California, annual cost for a nursing home was $32,406 compared to $9,129 for home- and community-based services (Fox-Grage & Walls, 2013). There is some concern among policy makers that greater availability of HCBS will increase the number of overall service recipients rather than simply provide a less-costly alternative for those who would otherwise be in a nursing home (Lehning & Austin, 2010). Although empirical support remains limited, there is evidence that spending more on Medicaid HCBS can reduce the number of people receiving care in a nursing home (Thomas, 2014) and decrease spending on LTSS overall (Kaye, 2012).

The push for more Medicaid support for HCBS also comes from a recognition that many older adults would prefer to maintain their independence and avoid institutional care. Reflecting this perspective, in 2014 the Centers for Medicare and Medicaid Services (CMS) made a regulatory change known as the Final Rule for Medicaid HCBS, which requires waiver services to be person centered and available in integrated community settings. First, the Final Rule mandates states to more consistently give recipients and their caregivers control over their HCBS plans in terms of the type, timing, and location of services, as well as who provides their care. A key aspect of this person-centered approach is giving consumers the information necessary to direct their care and identify their own preferences and goals. Second, it calls for HCBS to be offered in homelike, community-integrated environments. This has important implications for Medicaid HCBS offered in assisted living facilities, adult day health centers, or other settings if they are part of nursing homes, hospitals, or other institutions, and the rule change may curtail future construction of co-located services (Notarstefano, 2017). The outcomes of the Final Rule are currently unclear but may be problematic given that offering both HCBS and institutional services on the same site is sometimes necessary for providers to remain financially sustainable, particularly in rural areas (Notarstefano, 2017).

Despite progress toward rebalancing funding, many older adults still do not have access to Medicaid coverage for HCBS. First, Medicaid is a means-tested program for those who are poor, with most states setting income eligibility criteria at the federal poverty line or the even lower Supplemental Security Income (SSI) monthly payment (Ng, Stone, & Harrington, 2015). Middle-class older adults only qualify for Medicaid once they have exhausted their own personal resources. Through 1915(c) waivers, states can serve those whose income is up to 300 percent of SSI payments, but this is still quite low. Second, in contrast to institutional care, states are not required to provide waiver services to everyone who is eligible and can implement controls such as capping enrollment, targeting specific populations (such as older adults, individuals with intellectual and developmental disabilities, and individuals with behavioral health problems), and restricting enrollment to certain geographic areas (Elliott, 2013). A recent study of thirty-eight states found that 512,000 people were on HCBS waiting lists in 2011, which was 19 percent more than were on waiting lists in 2010 (National Health Policy Forum, 2013). Third, state HCBS waiver programs tend to focus more on other vulnerable populations than on older adults. As noted by Kaye (2012), Medicaid spends more on institutional care than HCBS for older adults in all but six states, whereas the opposite is true for HCBS for individuals with intellectual and development disabilities in many states. Compared to other waiver recipients, older adults have experienced a slower growth in the number of participants, programs, and financial outlays (Kitchener, Ng, & Harrington, 2007).

Older Americans Act

Adults age 60 and older can receive HCBS through programs funded by the Older Americans Act (OAA), including home-delivered meals, congregate meals, senior centers, health promotion, transportation, case management, and in-home assistance. The federal government distributes funds to State Units on Aging (SUAs) and Area Agencies on Aging (AAA) as well as to Indian Tribal and Native Hawaiian Organizations. This network, in turn, coordinates and funds local service providers to provide HCBS to approximately 11 million older adults and their family members each year (National Association of Area Agencies on Aging, 2016). Given the wide reach this legislation has on the aging network of HCBS, the OAA is discussed in greater detail in Chapter 3.

Affordable Care Act

The Patient Protection and Affordable Care Act of 2010 (ACA) aims to increase the number of Americans with access to health care. Arguably the most publicized provision of the ACA relevant to HCBS was the Community Living Assistance Services and Supports (CLASS) Act, which created a voluntary, federally administered, long-term care insurance program (Miller, 2012). Older adults who had paid into the program through payroll deductions during their working years would have received an average benefit of $75 per day to pay for long-term care services, including those provided by family members (National Council on Aging, 2010). However, because the CLASS Act was not financially solvent for the seventy-five years required by the law, Congress repealed it in 2013 (Archer, 2012).

The ACA does include other mechanisms to expand older adults' access to HCBS. The ACA increases funding for ADRCs to facilitate older adults' access to a single point of entry for HCBS, makes it easier for older adults to qualify for the Money Follows the Person demonstration, and extends protections against impoverishment for older adults when their spouse is receiving Medicaid HCBS (Miller, 2012). In addition, the State Balancing Incentive Program rewards states financially for making progress in shifting the proportion of Medicaid spending from institution-based to community-based LTSS (Miller, 2012). Finally, the law encourages greater coordination between Medicare and Medicaid through the federal Coordinated

Health Care Office, as well as the development, evaluation, and dissemination of promising models of care through the Center for Medicare and Medicaid Innovation (Miller, 2012).

FUTURE DIRECTIONS FOR HCBS POLICY

HCBS policy in the United States has a number of limitations in meeting the needs of older adults with physical or cognitive impairments. These limitations are due in large part to the fact that HCBS specifically and LTSS more broadly have never been a major focus of our country's policy agenda, with primary responsibility instead placed on older adults and their families (Hudson, 2010). This section presents some of the challenges to expanding and improving HCBS policy and concludes with some promising developments that offer a way forward.

The first challenge comes from the high costs of HCBS. In 2011 overall spending for LTSS from all public and private sources was nearly $211 billion, approximately one-third of which was for home- and community-based services (National Health Policy Forum, 2013). In 2016 the median monthly costs for common HCBS were $1,473 for adult day health, $3,861 for home health, and $3,813 for homemaker services (Genworth Financial, 2016). Such spending calculations do not take into account the economic value of informal caregiving, the bulk of payments for HCBS not provided by an agency, or other expenses such as food and housing (Scharlach & Lehning, 2012). Federal and state governments have struggled to constrain these costs at a time of growing need. Although HCBS are less expensive per person than institutional care, concerns remain that expanding access will increase overall costs by enlarging the number of service recipients (Kaye & Harrington, 2015). Research reporting that more than half a million people are on waiting lists for Medicaid waiver services, with an average waiting time of more than two years, highlights the inadequate funding currently allocated to HCBS (Ng & Harrington, 2012).

A second challenge is the limited involvement of the federal government in HCBS, which places burdens on state and local governments that lead to wide variations in access depending on where one lives. For example, the Medicaid waiver is an optional program that allows states to impose different functional and financial eligibility criteria for HCBS than institutional care and permits targeting specific areas and populations. This has resulted in disparities in Medicaid HCBS participation rates ranging from 3 per 1,000 population in Georgia to 15 per 1,000 in Washington, D.C. in 2007 (Ng, Harrington, & Howard, 2011), in spending ranging from $59 per capita in Nevada to $486 per capita in New York in 2009 (Eiken, Sredl, Burwell, & Gold, 2010), and in the proportion of LTSS spending on HCBS ranging from 27 percent in Mississippi and New Jersey to 78 percent in Oregon in 2012 (Eiken et al., 2014). OAA programs are designed to be flexible and reflect local needs, and a great deal of variation is found in the SUAs and AAAs across the country in terms of their administration, infrastructure, and resources (Browdie, 2008). The most recent federal action to address HCBS policy was the Commission on Long-Term Care created by the Americans Taxpayer Relief Act of 2012, but to date none of the policy recommendations in the commission's 2013 report have been addressed by any branch of the federal government (Kapp, 2014). Thus the federal government's role in HCBS continues to be limited.

A third challenge is the substantial level of unmet needs for assistance reported by older adults. For example, 58 percent of those enrolled in both Medicare and Medicaid, a population that often experiences health problems and disability, indicate they have unmet needs for care for activities of daily living (Komisar, Feder, & Kasper, 2005). One reason for unmet need is that some older adults do not know where to find information about the health and supportive services available in their community (Feldman, Oberlink, Simantov, & Gursen, 2004). This is not surprising given the complicated array of public HCBS offered through the programs discussed in this chapter as well as those provided by the U.S. Department of Veterans Affairs, the U.S. Department of Housing and Urban Development, and state and local governments, among others (Miller, Allen, & Mor, 2009). Because even those receiving HCBS report unmet needs, it appears that there are other significant gaps in care, including limited services available on nights and weekends, the absence of transportation assistance, and an inadequate supply of adult day health and respite services for caregivers (Robison et al., 2012).

A fourth challenge is the declining ability of families to provide the informal support that is necessary to keep many older adults in the community. More than 60 percent of informal caregivers are women, and the typical caregiver has been described as a woman in her forties providing assistance to her mother (National Alliance for Caregiving & AARP, 2015), but increased female participation in the workforce makes it more difficult for women to provide unpaid care. Lower birthrates combined with a rise in longevity mean fewer younger family members are available to care for multiple older relatives. Furthermore, as older adults live longer and potentially spend more years with a disability, spouses may be less able to care for their partner because of their own functional limitations. Due to these demographic and social changes, the caregiver support ratio, which compares those of caregiving age to those at a high-risk age for needing assistance, is projected to drop from 7.2 to 1 in 2010 to less than 3 to 1 by 2050 (Reinhard, Fenberg, Choula, & Houser, 2015).

A final challenge is the recruitment and retention of a qualified HCBS workforce across a range of skills and training levels. Home health aides and personal care aides are two of the fastest growing jobs in the United States (Seavey & Marquand, 2011), but HCBS agencies have difficulty finding qualified people to take these positions and even more difficulty keeping them. Indeed, the number of direct care workers is expected to increase by only 20 percent from 2010 to 2020, but the demand is projected to grow by 70 percent (Paraprofessional Healthcare Institute, 2013). Vacancy and turnover rates of paraprofessional direct care workers in HCBS are estimated at 25 to 50 percent in some states (Wright, 2005). One reason for this is that these jobs are characterized by low wages, few if any benefits, and high risk of injury (Bureau of Labor Statistics, 2015; Lipson & Regan, 2004). This is particularly problematic because a large proportion of the workforce is at risk for inequities in health and well-being; at least 80 percent of HCBS direct care workers are female, half belong to racial or ethnic minority groups, and one-quarter speak a language other than English in the home (Harris-Kojetin, Lipson, Fielding, Kiefer, & Stone, 2004; Montgomery, Holley, Deichert, & Kosloski, 2005). Professional health and long-term care providers are also in short supply. For example, in the United States there are slightly more than 7,000 geriatricians, which falls far below patient demand, and half of family medicine and 29 percent of internal medicine programs require less than twelve days of geriatric training (Institute of Medicine, 2012). Furthermore, only 4 percent of social workers and less than 1 percent of pharmacists, nurses, or physician assistants receive any training in geriatrics (Institute of Medicine, 2008).

These challenges are significant, but a number of actions can be taken to improve the quality of and access to HCBS in the future. The first is to increase funding at the federal, state, and local levels for HCBS. This includes expanding the number of Medicaid waivers to address waiting lists and unmet needs, supporting wider replication and implementation of promising pilots and demonstrations (such as Money Follows the Person), and providing more financial resources to the OAA's aging network. Second, to ensure more consistency in access across the country, the federal government could adjust Medicare to cover more long-term HCBS. Third, public policies should stop ignoring the needs of family caregivers. This requires more than just increasing funding for programs such as the National Family Caregiver Support Program (NFCSP). It requires using policy mechanisms to make programs not only more consumer driven but also more family driven, such as including a family caregiver assessment as part of the standard intake for Medicaid waiver services (Kelly, Wolfe, Gibson, & Feinberg, 2013). Fourth, government policies should improve older adults' access to quality care by addressing the workforce shortage among professional and paraprofessional providers. At the professional level, this could include expanding training opportunities, such as the Health Resources and Services Administration's Geriatrics Workforce Enhancement Program. For paraprofessionals, this could include strategies to improve wages, benefits, and working conditions, such as higher reimbursement rates for HCBS through Medicaid, Medicare, and other public funding sources. Finally, public policies, particularly at the federal level, should support the development and proliferation of promising practices that have come from the nonprofit and private sectors. These include aging-friendly community initiatives that are working to change the physical and social environment to better meet the needs of older adults, member-driven villages that aim to improve access to formal and informal supports, and naturally occurring retirement community supportive service programs that create cooperative partnerships to promote aging in place.

CHAPTER SUMMARY

- HCBS policy is driven by a residual approach in which public supports often are available only for those who have limited social, financial, or health resources.
- Medicare is the main public health insurance program for older adults, but Medicaid is the largest source of funding for HCBS.

- HCBS and the larger LTSS system depend on family caregivers to provide the majority of assistance, yet they receive very limited publicly funded support.
- Federal and state efforts to rebalance long-term care spending toward HCBS and away from institutional care are motivated by the need to limit costs as well as the desire of Americans to age in place in their homes and communities.
- Promising models for HCBS have emerged from both public and non-profit sectors, and these programs should continue to be evaluated and replicated.

DISCUSSION QUESTIONS AND EXERCISES

1. Review the statements in the Fact or Fiction? list near the beginning of the chapter. After reading this chapter, can you identify which are true and which are false?
2. What are the strengths of HCBS policy? What are some of the limitations? Think about your personal or professional experiences with the system of care in the United States.
3. Imagine that you have a client who needs daily personal care, home-delivered meals, and occasional transportation to medical appointments. How would you locate these services in your community?
4. The *Olmstead* decision requires states to provide care in the least restrictive setting possible. What are some barriers to moving older adults and others with disabilities back into a community setting?
5. HCBS policy is striving to become more consumer driven, but little guidance has been given for accomplishing this for older adults with cognitive impairments. How can services maximize participation for this population?
6. More than 34 million Americans are family caregivers, but public policies generally do not address their needs. What are some of the barriers to placing caregiver support on the policy agenda?

ADDITIONAL RESOURCES

AARP Public Policy Institute: http://www.aarp.org/ppi/

Altarum Institute's Center for Elder Care and Advanced Illness: http://altarum .org/research-centers/center-for-elder-care-and-advanced-illness

American Society on Aging's Policy and Advocacy: https://www.ncoa.org/public
-policy-action/
Community Catalyst's Center for Consumer Engagement in Health Innovation:
https://www.healthinnovation.org/
LeadingAge LTSS Center: http://www.leadingage.org/center-applied-research
National Council on Aging Public Policy & Action: https://www.ncoa.org/public
-policy-action/

REFERENCES

Administration for Community Living. (2015). *National aging network*. Retrieved
from https://aoa.acl.gov/AoA_Programs/OAA/Aging_Network/Index.aspx
Archer, P. M. (2012). Healthcare reform act's impact on older Americans. *Chart,
110*(4), 9–13.
Brand, R. (2011). Medicaid: The eight-hundred-pound gorilla. *State Legislatures,
37*(9), 14–19.
Browdie, R. (2008). The aging network and long-term care: Shared goals and different histories. *Generations, 32*(3), 77–80.
Bureau of Labor Statistics, U.S. Department of Labor. (2015). *Occupational employment statistics*. Retrieved from www.bls.gov
Carlson, B. L., Foster, L., Dale, S. B., & Brown, R. (2007). Effects of cash and
counseling on personal care and well-being. *Health Services Research, 42*(1),
467–487.
Centers for Medicare and Medicaid Services. (nd). *Home health services*. Retrieved
from: https://www.medicare.gov/coverage/home-health-services.html
Centers for Medicare and Medicaid Services. (2014). *Final Rule Medicaid HCBS*.
Retrieved from https://www.medicaid.gov/medicaid/hcbs/downloads/final
-rule-slides-01292014.pdf
Cramm, J. M., Twisk, J., & Nieboer, A. P. (2014). Self-management abilities and
frailty are important for healthy aging among community-dwelling older
people: A cross-sectional study. *BMC Geriatrics, 14*(1), 28.
Davis, K., Schoen, C., & Bandeali, F. (2015). *Medicare: 50 years of ensuring coverage and care*. New York: The Commonwealth Fund. Retrieved from http://
www.commonwealthfund.org/~/media/files/publications/fund-report/2015
/apr/1812_davis_medicare_50_years_coverage_care.pdf
Eiken, S., Sredl, K., Burwell, B., & Gold, L. (2010). *Medicaid long-term care expenditures in FY 2009*. Cambridge, MA: Thomson Reuters.

Eiken, S., Sredl, K., Gold, L., et al. (2014). *Medicaid expenditures for long-term services and supports in FY 2012.* Cambridge, MA: Truven Health Analytics.

Elliott, S. D. (2013). The historical, political, social, and individual factors that have influenced the development of Aging and Disability Resource Centers and Options Counseling. (Unpublished doctoral dissertation). Portland State University, Portland, Oregon.

Feldman, P. H., Oberlink, M. R., Simantov, E., & Gursen, M. D. (2004). *A tale of two older Americas: Community opportunities and challenges: AdvantAge initiative 2003 national survey of adults aged 65 and older.* New York, NY: Center for Home Care Policy and Research.

Fox-Grage, W., & Walls, J. (2013). State studies find home and community-based services to be cost effective. *Spotlight, 2.* AARP Public Policy Institute.

Fox-Grage, W., & Ujvari, K. (2014). *The Older Americans Act.* Washington, DC: AARP Public Policy Institute.

Genworth Financial. (2016). *Summary of 2016 findings.* Retrieved from https://www.genworth.com/dam/Americas/US/PDFs/Consumer/corporate/131168_050516.pdf

Gross, D. L., Temkin-Greener, H., Kunitz, S., & Mukamel, D. B. (2004). The growing pains of integrated health care for the elderly: Lessons from the expansion of PACE. *Milbank Quarterly, 82*(2), 257–282.

Hansen, J. C., & Hewitt, M. (2012). PACE provides a sense of belonging for elders. *Generations, 36*(1), 37–43.

Harris-Kojetin, L., Lipson, D., Fielding, J., Kiefer, K., & Stone, R. I. (2004). *Recent findings on frontline long-term care workers: A research synthesis 1999–2003.* Washington, DC: Institute for the Future of Aging Services.

Hudson, R. B. (2010). Analysis and advocacy in home- and community-based care: An approach in three parts. *Journal of Gerontological Social Work, 53*(1), 3–20.

Institute of Medicine (2008). *Retooling for an aging America: Building the health care workforce.* Retrieved from: http://www.nationalacademies.org/hmd/reports/2008/retooling-for-an-aging-america-building-the-health-care-workforce.aspx

Kane, R. L., Homyak, P., Bershadsky, B., & Flood, S. (2006). The effects of a variant of the Program for All-inclusive Care of the Elderly on hospital utilization and outcomes. *Journal of the American Geriatrics Society, 54*(2), 276–283.

Kapp, M. B. (2014). Home- and community-based long-term services and supports: Health reforms most enduring legacy? *Saint Louis University Journal of Health Law & Policy, 8*, 9–34.

Kassner, E. (2011). Home- and community-based long-term services and supports for older people. Washington, DC: AARP Public Policy Institute. Retrieved from http://assets.aarp.org/rgcenter/ppi/ltc/fs222-health.pdf

Kaye, H. S. (2012). Gradual rebalancing of Medicaid long-term services and supports saves money and serves more people, statistical model shows. *Health Affairs, 31*(6), 1195–1203.

Kaye, H. S., & Harrington, C. (2015). Long-term services and supports in the community: Toward a research agenda. *Disability and health journal, 8*(1), 3–8.

Kaye, H.S., Harrington, C., & LaPlante, M. P. (2010). Long-term care: Who gets it, who provides it, who pays, and how much? *Health Affairs, 29*(1), 11–21.

Kelly, K., Wolfe, N., Gibson, M. J., & Feinberg, L. (2013). *Listening to family caregivers: The need to include family caregiver assessment in Medicaid home- and community-based service waiver programs.* Washington DC: AARP Public Policy Institute.

Kemper, P., Komisar, H. L., & Alecxih, L. (2005). Long-term care over an uncertain future: What can current retirees expect? *Inquiry: A Journal of Medical Care Organization, Provision and Financing, 42*(4), 335–350.

Kitchener, M., Ng, T., & Harrington, C. (2007). Medicaid State Plan personal care services: Trends in programs and policies. *Journal of Aging & Social Policy, 19*(3), 9–26.

Komisar, H. L., Feder, J., & Kasper, J. D. (2005). Unmet long-term care needs: An analysis of Medicare-Medicaid dual eligible. *Inquiry, 42*(2), 171–182.

Lehning, A. J., & Austin, M. J. (2010). Long-term care in the United States: Policy themes and promising practices. *Journal of Gerontological Social Work, 53*(1), 43–63.

Lipson, D., & Regan, C. (2004). Health insurance coverage for direct care workers: Riding out the storm. Washington, DC: Better Jobs Better Care National Program Office.

Miller, E. A. (2012). The affordable care act and long-term care: Comprehensive reform or just tinkering around the edges? *Journal of Aging & Social Policy, 24*(2), 101–117. doi:10.1080/08959420.2012.659912

Miller, E. A., Allen, S. M., & Mor, V. (2009). Commentary: Navigating the labyrinth of long-term care: Shoring up informal caregiving in a home- and community-based world. *Journal of Aging & Social Policy, 21*, 1–16.

Montgomery, R. J., Holley, P. L., Deichert, J., & Kosloski, K. (2005). A profile of home care workers from the 2000 census: How it changes what we know. *The Gerontologist, 45*(5), 593–600.

Mui, A. C. (2002). The program of all-inclusive care for the elderly (PACE) an innovative long-term care model in the United States. *Journal of Aging & Social Policy, 13*(2–3), 53–67.

National Alliance for Caregiving and AARP. (2015). *Caregiving in the U.S.* Retrieved from http://www.caregiving.org/wp-content/uploads/2015/05/2015 _CaregivingintheUS_Final-Report-June-4_WEB.pdf

National Association of Area Agencies on Aging. (2016). *Policy priorities 2016: Fiscal year 2017 appropriations.* Retrieved from http://www.n4a.org/files/n4a _2016PolicyPriorities_FY2017Approps(1).pdf

National Council on Aging. (2010). Straight talk for seniors on health reform. Retrieved from http://www.ncoa.org/assets/files/pdf/130812-5-key-facts.pdf

National Health Policy Forum. (2013). *National spending for long-term services and supports, 2011.* Washington DC: The George Washington University.

Ng, T., & Harrington, C. (2012). *Medicaid home- and community-based service programs: 2009 data update* Report prepared for the Kaiser Commission on Medicaid & the Uninsured . Washington, DC: Kaiser Commission on Medicaid & the Uninsured.

Ng, T., Harrington, C., & Howard, J. (2011). *Medicaid home- and community-based service programs: data update.* Menlo Park, CA: Henry J. Kaiser Family Foundation.

Ng, T., Wong, A., & Harrington, C. (2014). State *Olmstead* litigation and the Afford- able Care Act. *Journal of Social Work in Disability & Rehabilitation, 13*, 97–109.

Ng, T., Stone, J., & Harrington, C. (2015). Medicaid home- and community-based services: How consumer access is restricted by state policies. *Journal of Aging & Social Policy, 27*, 21–46.

Notarstefano, P. (2017). *How will the HCBS settings rule impact new construc- tion of assisted living and adult day?* Retrieved from http://www.leadingage .org/members/how-will-hcbs-settings-rule-impact-new-construction-assisted -living-and-adult-day

Olmstead v. L.C., 527 U.S. 581 (1999).

Paraprofessional Healthcare Institute. (2013). *America's direct-care workforce.* Retrieved from: https://phinational.org/wp-content/uploads/legacy/phi-facts-3.pdf

Reinhard, S. C., Fenberg, L. F., Choula, R., & Houser, A. (2015). *Valuing the invaluable: 2015 update.* Washington, DC: AARP Public Policy Institute.

Robison, J., Shugrue, N., Fortinsky, R. H., & Gruman, C. (2014). Long-term sup- ports and services planning for the future: Implications from a statewide survey of baby boomers and older adults. *Gerontologist, 54*(2), 297–313.

Roosevelt, F. D. (1929). *Message to the New York state legislature.* Retrieved from https://www.ssa.gov/history/locations.html

Scharlach, A. E., & Lehning, A. J. (2012). Government's role in aging and long-term care. In A. O'Leary & J. Hacker (Eds.), *Shared Responsibility, Shared Risk.* New York: Oxford University Press.

Seavey, D., & Marquand, A. (2011). *Caring in America: A comprehensive analysis of the nation's fastest-growing jobs: Home health and personal care aides.* Bronx, NY: PHI.

Thomas, K., S. (2014). The relationship between Older Americans Act in-home services and low-care residents in nursing homes. *Journal of Aging & Health, 26*(2), 250–260. doi:10.1177/0898264313513611

Tilly, J. (2016). *Promoting community living for older adults who need long-term services and support.* Washington, DC: Center for Policy and Evaluation, Administration for Community Living.

Watson, S. D. (2009). From almshouses to nursing homes and community care: Lessons from Medicaid's history. *Georgia State University Law Review, 26,* 937–969.

Wright, B. (2005). *Direct care personnel in long-term care.* Washington, DC: AARP Public Policy Institute.

Yen, I. H., & Anderson, L. A. (2012). Built environment and mobility of older adults: Important policy and practice efforts. *Journal of the American Geriatrics Society, 60,* 951–965.

The Older Americans Act and the Aging Network

The Older Americans Act clearly affirms our nation's sense of responsibility toward the well-being of all of our older citizens. . . . Under this program every state and every community can now move toward a coordinated program of services and opportunities for our older citizens. We revere them; we extend them our affection; we respect them.

PRESIDENT LYNDON B. JOHNSON, 1965

LEARNING OBJECTIVES

In this chapter, you will:

- Gain an understanding of the history and evolution of the Older Americans Act.
- Determine some of the challenges associated with services and planning under the Older Americans Act.
- Learn the elements of the Andersen Health Behavioral Conceptual Model as it relates to home- and community-based services.
- Review existing and emerging evidence of the impact and effectiveness of Older Americans Act programs.
- Explore future directions for the aging network established through the Older Americans Act.

HAVING PROVIDED AN OVERVIEW OF the history and evolution of home- and community-based services (HCBS) in the United States in chapter 2, here we dive deeper into the landmark 1965 Older Americans Act (OAA), which established the national aging network, the backbone of HCBS. Medicare and Medicaid health insurance programs were added to the Social Security Act during this same year, and they provided health care insurance for older adults and low-income individuals with disabilities. The Medicaid program, in particular, has played a fundamental role in the growth and development of HCBS. The OAA was the first federal law to establish a network of comprehensive, organized, and coordinated services and planning to serve older Americans.

FACT OR FICTION?

Consider the following statements.

- The Older Americans Act established State Units on Aging and Area Agencies on Aging to serve all adults age 60 and older in the United States.
- The Older Americans Act provides the largest source of funding for home- and community-based services in the United States.
- The Older Americans Act includes Titles to fund Medicare and Medicaid.
- Funding for the Older Americans Act continues to grow as the number of older adults in the United States increases.
- Area Agencies on Aging are the regional planning and services agencies for older adults.

After reading this chapter, you will be able to affirm which statements are fact and which are fiction.

THE HISTORY AND CURRENT STATE OF THE OLDER AMERICANS ACT

The origin of the OAA can be traced to the first White House Conference on Aging (WHCoA) held in Washington, D.C. in 1961 (Colello & Napili, 2016). Thousands of individuals representing hundreds of organizations gathered to make policy recommendations for older Americans. This conference has been held almost every decade since 1961, the most recent being in 2015. These meetings continue to provide an avenue for policy planning.

Title II of the OAA set up the national infrastructure that still exists today to support the delivery of aging services. The 1965 law established the Administration on Aging (AoA), a federal office on aging responsible for implementing the OAA and supporting older adults so they can live independently in their homes and communities as long as possible. AoA is now part of the Department of Health and Human Services (DHHS), and in 2012 it became part of the Administration for Community Living (ACL). The AoA distributes federal funding to State Units on Aging (SUA) based on a funding formula. Each SUA then allocates funding to Area Agencies on Aging (AAAs), based on a within-state formula (Colello & Napili, 2016). Funding formulas are primarily dependent on the number of adults over the age of 60 living in the corresponding geographic area. Every state, the District of Columbia, and U.S. territory has an SUA that is responsible for developing and implementing a state plan that supports older adults and individuals with disabilities (figure 3.1). These state agencies have a variety of names such as state Departments, Offices, Commissions, and Bureaus. In 1973, the OAA was amended to establish regional planning and service areas and corresponding organizations called AAAs to support older adults locally (Administration on Aging, 2015). Every older adult living in the United States has access to the services provided by their local AAA.

The OAA consists of seven different Titles that support five categories of services for older adults and family caregivers: (1) accessing services,

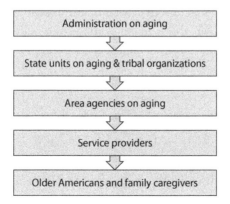

FIGURE 3.1 Aging Network.

(2) nutrition programs, (3) home- and community-based long-term services and supports, (4) disease prevention and health promotion, and (5) supporting the rights of vulnerable older adults (Niles-Yokum & Wagner, 2015). More than 70 percent of OAA funding goes toward Title III services, including nutrition, supportive services, family caregiving, and health promotion activities. These services support the purpose of Title III, which is to promote and develop a comprehensive and coordinated service delivery system by removing barriers to independent living for vulnerable older adults (Collello & Napili, 2016).

The OAA has been amended and reauthorized numerous times since its passage in 1965 and was most recently reauthorized in 2016. Of particular note to HCBS are the 2,000 amendments that added the National Family Caregiver Support Program to Title III (see chapter 2) and authorization of the Aging and Disability Resource Centers (ADRCs), which were added to Title II. ADRCs act as a single point of entry for information, referral, assessment, and care transition planning for older adults and individuals of all ages with disabilities. The focus of ADRCs is on HCBS and can be an "entity, network, or consortium" established by each individual state (Collello & Napili, 2016).

Annual funding for OAA has remained largely unchanged over the last decade, but the number of individuals aged 60 and over has increased and the cost of service delivery has risen (Fox-Grage & Ujvari, 2014). Though all individuals aged 60 and older are eligible to receive OAA services, AAAs must rely on other sources of funding to provide services, implement cost-sharing options, and target those individuals with greatest need, in particular, low-income minority persons, individuals with limited English proficiency, and older people living in rural communities. The law is clear that individuals should not be denied services due to the inability to pay (Fox-Grage & Ujvari, 2014).

MODEL OF CARE AND THE OLDER AMERICANS ACT

One of the most widely applied models of health care service utilization is the Andersen Health Behavioral model (Andersen & Newman, 1973). Andersen's model describes the utilization of health services as a function of societal determinants that affect that system. Both societal determinants and the health services system then affect individual determinants (figure 3.2).

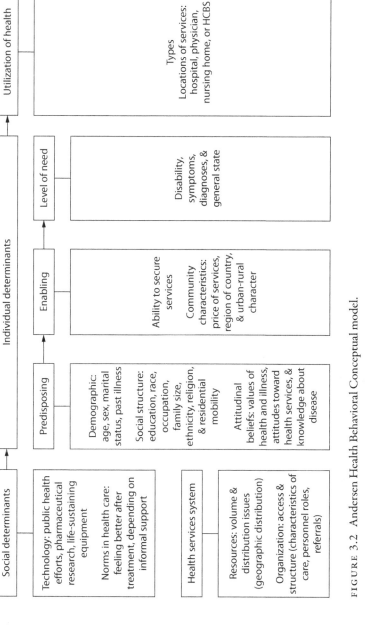

FIGURE 3.2 Andersen Health Behavioral Conceptual model.

Health utilization includes type or location of service, such as hospital, physician, nursing home, or HCBS. This model of care aligns closely with the goals of the OAA and has been used to study the utilization of many programs developed from this policy.

Societal determinants include technology and norms in health care. Technology encompasses many areas including public health efforts, pharmaceutical research, and life-sustaining equipment. Norms in health care are often reflected in formal legislation (Andersen & Newman, 1973).

A health services system such as HCBS is conceptualized by Andersen and Newman as comprised of two elements: resources and organization. *Resources* of the system are the labor and capital dedicated to care. Geographic distribution of these resources affects the provision of services. *Organization* includes access and structure. Access involves the means by which a person enters a care system and continues treatment. Structure is the internal organizational experience of the person within the care system, including the characteristics of care, personnel roles, and referrals.

Individual determinants of care utilization by individuals include predisposing, enabling, and subjective or objective level of need. The predisposing needs include demographic, social structural, and attitudinal belief variables. Age, sex, marital status, and past illness are key demographic variables. Social structure includes education, race, occupation, family size, ethnicity, religion, and residential mobility. Finally, beliefs include values concerning health and illness, attitudes toward health services, and knowledge about disease.

Enabling needs provide individuals with the ability to secure services. It allows a family to satisfy a health service need due to income, health insurance, and other accessibility issues. Community characteristics such as ratios of health care personnel and providers to population, price of services, region of country, and urban-rural character are important components of enabling needs. Assuming the presence of the other two components, illness or need level includes both an objective and a subjective account of need, including disability, symptoms, diagnoses, and general state.

The Andersen model has been adapted over time as it has been applied to the examination of HCBS by older adults. This model has been criticized for not recognizing issues of race/ethnicity, psychological health, and changes of these key factors over the life span. Andersen (1995) has worked with other scholars to adapt his original model (see Bradley et al., 2002; Miller & Weissert, 2000; Wallace, Levy-Storms, Kington, & Andersen, 1998; Wolinsky & Johnson, 1991). This model is a good place to begin understanding the issues related to the use of HCBS in general, including those provided through the OAA.

PRACTICE APPLICATIONS

The OAA was enacted in response to the limited availability of community services for older adults (Collello & Napili, 2016). Today, a complex array of federal and state programs fund HCBS at much higher levels, such as Medicaid (see chapter 2), but the OAA network continues to provide the organizational structure to support access to these services.

Although there is variability among AAAs, the staff is involved in assessment of need, determining service eligibility, assessing multiple service needs, authorizing or purchasing services, and monitoring the appropriateness and cost-effectiveness of services. One challenge to this service delivery model in practice is that AAA staff are unable to recommend particular service providers but instead share information about providers available in the community. Many AAAs have developed guides for families to use to assess the quality of care provided. Online reviews of service providers are available but have varying degrees of accuracy, often relying on self-reports from one or two consumers. Consumers often do not seek services from AAAs until faced with a crisis situation, if at all, and may not have the information, time, or experience needed to adequately determine which service provider offers the highest quality of services. Identifying potential funding sources for services such as Title III of OAA, private insurance, Medicaid, the Veteran's Administration, and private pay adds an additional challenge that AAA staff often work with consumers to determine. Publicly funded services may include a waitlist or a delay in enrollment due to limited resources.

AAAs play an important role in supporting access to services through information, referral, outreach, and care management. An overview of the key services provided by the OAA are shown in table 3.1. In addition, transportation services for medical appointments, social events, shopping, senior center activities, and congregate meal programs are provided through the OAA to increase access to health care, nutrition,

TABLE 3.1   Older American Act Services

SERVICE ACCESS	NUTRITION PROGRAMS	HCBS LONG-TERM SERVICES AND SUPPORTS	DISEASE PREVENTION AND HEALTH PROMOTION	VULNERABLE ELDER RIGHTS
• Information	• Home-delivered meals	• Home care	• Fitness	• Ombudsman program
• Referral	• Congregate meals	• Personal care	• Fall prevention	• Prevention of elder abuse, neglect, and exploitation
• Outreach	• Nutrition education/counsel	• Chores	• Chronic disease management	• Legal assistance
• Care management		• Adult day services		
• Transportation		• Caregiver support		

Source: Niles-Yokum & Wagner, 2015.

and social opportunities, often for the most vulnerable elders living at home (Robinson, Lucado, & Schur, 2012).

Community-based nutrition programs supported by the OAA serve vulnerable adults home-delivered meals and congregate meals and provide nutrition incentives programs and nutrition counseling and education. Nutritional services incentives programs vary, but the intent of the programs is to provide cash or food to supplement other nutritional services (Niles-Yokum & Wagner, 2015). Recipients of these nutrition services are more likely to be older, female, living alone, in rural areas, of poor or fair health, and to have difficulties with three or more activities of daily living when compared to the general U.S. population over the age of 60 (Kowlessar, Robinson, & Schur, 2015). The purpose of these programs is to reduce hunger, promote socialization, and support health and well-being, ultimately preventing or delaying institutionalization (Kowlessar et al., 2015).

HCBS include home care, personal care, chores, adult day services, and caregiver support. The majority of the appropriations from the OAA goes toward funding these services. For more in-depth exploration of home care, personal care, and chores, see chapter 6. Chapter 10 discusses adult day services, and chapter 5 focuses on family caregiving. A smaller amount of OAA funding goes toward evidence-based fitness, fall prevention, and chronic disease management education programming.

Finally, ombudsman programs and prevention of elder abuse, neglect, and exploitation are supported through Title VII (Niles-Yokum & Wagner, 2015). Ombudsman support and services advocate and resolve conflicts between residents and the staff and owners of nursing homes, board and care homes, and assisted living facilities. Long-term care ombudsman offices are located in each state, and locally paid and volunteer ombudsmen can be found throughout the United States. Services are available at no cost to consumers. At this time, OAA funds may not pay for ombudsman services in HCBS. However, twelve states and the District of Columbia have expanded ombudsman services to include HCBS through state law and appropriations. In addition to these services, AAAs frequently provide health promotion and disease prevention programs, insurance counseling, case management, respite care, and assessment for care planning (National Association of Area Agencies on Aging & Miami University Scripps Gerontology Center, 2014). Despite outreach efforts, many older adults and caregivers seeking HCBS are not aware of AAAs.

The OAA is credited with establishing the aging network, but funding for services has been minimal relative to demand. AAAs rely on multiple sources of funding to keep their doors open, including state general revenue, local funding, and Medicaid waiver programs. AAAs have engaged in a number of initiatives funded from multiple sources that focus on HCBS, including nursing home diversion and transition programs, Medicaid managed care, and integrated systems of care that combine physical, behavioral, long-term, and acute care options (National Association of Area Agencies on Aging & Miami University Scripps Gerontology Center, 2014). AAAs should be the first stop for individuals with disabilities and their caregivers needing support and services. To find the AAA that serves a particular area visit the Elder Care Locator at www.eldercare.gov. The Elder Care Locator is a public service provided by the AoA to assist older adults and their families in accessing elder care services in local communities.

CASE STUDY

Martha is an 82-year-old who lives alone in a senior apartment building in Detroit, Michigan. Martha's husband, Richard, died three years ago from congestive heart failure. Martha has macular degeneration and, despite treatment, her vision has worsened and she no longer feels comfortable driving. Martha's neighbor, Ray, has offered to drive her to the Eye Institute, but Martha does not want to rely on Ray for transportation. Since Richard died, Ray stops by Martha's apartment frequently and sometimes stays for hours. Martha suspects that Ray might be interested in a romantic relationship with her, and Martha is not interested but doesn't want to hurt Ray's feelings.

Martha listens to public radio and on Saturday for the first time heard *The Senior Solutions* radio program. During the show, the host provided the telephone number for the Detroit Area Agency on Aging. She decided to give them a call. After answering a few questions, the person on the phone recommended she contact the American Red Cross to schedule transportation to the Eye Institute. Martha had to pay a small co-pay, but she was so relieved to have transportation arranged for her appointments.

Consider the following statements and questions in relation to this case:

1. Martha heard about the Detroit Area Agency on Aging through a radio program. What other ways might she learn about the Area Agency on Aging?
2. If you are the assessor at the Detroit Area Agency on Aging, what types of questions might you ask Martha?
3. Why might Martha not be able to use public transportation such as a bus to get to her medical appointments?
4. Are there any other OAA services from which Martha might benefit?

Perspectives from the Field

An Interview with Pam Matura, BSW, MHS
Executive Director, Area Agency on Aging 7
Rio Grande, Ohio

What is your professional background and training?

I have a bachelor's degree in Social Work and a master's degree in Health Sciences with a Certificate of Gerontology. I am a Certified Rehabilitation Counselor and a Licensed Professional Counselor.

What is your role at the AAA?

As CEO, I direct a team of approximately 180 staff, comprised mostly of social workers and registered nurses. We are an independent, nonprofit organization that provides information and assistance, screening and assessment, and case management for Medicaid-waiver services and a variety of Older Americans Act programs and state-funded initiatives.

What successes and challenges have you faced working with an AAA?

Funding for programs other than Medicaid for low-income, disabled persons has not kept pace with the growing needs. We face challenges with new competitors, dwindling resources, turf battles, and increased assumption of risk in contract negotiations; as a result, we are undergoing rapid transformation in honing our business acumen.

What advice would you give someone interested in working for an AAA?

I would tell any perspective employee of the AAA to know you will be working, first and foremost, to keep someone at home and living as independently as possible. You will manage care plan costs with an increasingly per-member per-month methodology. Documentation of these efforts will ensure compliance and qualitative outcomes. Twenty-seven years later, I am still happy I get to come here to work every day.

RESEARCH AND EVIDENCE

The aging network and OAA programs are part of a complex system of services and programs for older adults, family caregivers, and individuals with disabilities. It can be a challenge to identify specific program outcomes that tie exclusively back to the OAA. As we explore evidence of the effectiveness of OAA, first we must consider the reach and scope of the services provided. Are older adults in need receiving help? A 2015 report by the U.S. Government Accountability Office (GAO) suggests that the answer to this question is "no," which seems congruent with the lack of increases in OAA funding despite the growth in the number of people with disabilities. The GAO estimated that 83 percent of low-income food insecure older adults do not receive meals, and 83 percent of low-income older adults who have difficulties with two or more activities of daily living do not receive meals. The GAO indicated that a number of SUAs and AAAs noted that the need for home-delivered meals, in particular, is greater than they can fund. Two-thirds of older adults who have difficulties with one or more activities of daily living do not receive home-based care. Finally, transportation services are underutilized. The GAO estimated that 8.5 million older people are at risk for needing transportation services, but only 32,000 individuals received escorted transportation services in 2012. An additional 24.5 million unassisted rides, such as on the bus, were provided, but it is unclear how many people were served by these transportation services.

The Lewin Group (2013) was charged by the AoA with considering global outcomes of the Title III OAA programs. They recommended examining (1) HCBS use, (2) health care use, (3) nursing home admission/community tenure, and (4) cost savings. To explore these four global outcomes, the Lewin Group recommended a seven-year retrospective study examining existing data from federal sources coupled with a prospective study in which data regarding specific variables of interest are collected from older adults in nursing homes and compared to those utilizing HCBS and those not using either service. This study has not yet been commissioned.

To identify the recommended global outcomes and study design, the Lewin Group conducted a literature review focused on predisposing variables, enabling variables, and need variables and their associations to the four identified global outcome measures. Predisposing variables associated with HCBS use included were age, gender, race/ethnicity, education level, geographic location (metropolitan/nonmetropolitan), living alone, marital status, informal caregiver availability, and having children. Previous studies have found that older women are more likely to utilize HCBS compared to younger people and men. Although race/ethnicity, education level, and geographic location appear to be predictors of HCBS use, findings from previous studies have been mixed in terms of whether these variables are associated with higher or lower use of HCBS. Additional studies are needed to examine the direction of the relationship by type of services used, level of need, program eligibility criteria, and availability of service providers.

Living alone has been found to be associated with using transportation and congregate meal services. Being married to an older adult without dementia appears to be a protective factor against institutionalization, whereas the opposite appears to be true for individuals married to an older adult with dementia as their risk of institutionalization increases. It remains unclear whether having informal caregiver support increases or reduces HCBS use. Having an information caregiver appears to be associated with the use of adult day services (Anderson, Dabelko-Schoeny, & Johnson, 2013; Dabelko & Balaswamy, 2000), but the impact on other HCBS is unclear. Finally, having children reduces the likelihood of institutionalization, which supports the notion of the important role informal caregivers play with HCBS.

The Lewin Group identified three enabling variables that are associated with HCBS use: income, payment method, and level of state HCBS spending. In terms of income and payment method, they cite Borrayo, Salmon, Polivka, and Dunlop's (2004) study, which found that Medicaid-eligible individuals 60 years and older living in Florida with available caregivers were more likely to use HCBS; and Casado, van Vulpen, and Davis (2011), who through a national sample found affordability of services as well as a lack of awareness, reluctance, and availability predicted unmet HCBS needs. Finally, in examining the level of state HCBS spending, the Lewin Group cite several studies indicating that the higher the state's funding for HCBS, the lower the risk for nursing home admissions. Most studies examine HCBS based on the Medicaid population, the poor and functionally disabled, not on the broader population served by the OAA.

Need variables associated with HCBS identified by the Lewin Group include unmet needs, poor health, cognitive status/Alzheimer's, comorbidities/chronic conditions, and functional limitations (ADLs/IADLs). Need for HCBS, as measured by functional limitations or overall poorer health, is associated with higher HCBS use. Poor health associated with nutritional risk was a significant influence on the use of congregate meals by African Americans in an urban community (Weddle, Wilson, Berkshire, & Heuberger, 2012). Individuals with cognitive impairment have consistently been found at higher risk of institutionalization compared to HCBS users.

Finally, functional limitations have been one of the most studied and strongest predictors of HCBS use.

A review of the current evidence suggests OAA is underfunded and does not reach all of the older adults in need. In addition, a number of predisposing, enabling, and need factors are associated with HCBS use. Most research that supports these factors are studies of the Medicaid population; few delineate OAA services from other sources of HCBS. The complexities of OAA and the corresponding aging network makes identifying which OAA programs are having positive outcomes for whom a challenge.

An Expert Weighs In

Robert Applebaum, PhD, MSW
Director of the Ohio Long-Term Care Research Project
Professor, Department of Sociology & Gerontology
Miami University
Miami, Ohio

For those of us who spent the early parts of our careers critiquing the long-term care system for its institutional bias, the fact that today the United States spends as much on HCBS as on nursing home care is truly remarkable. This growth, which means that individuals with severe disabilities have a much better chance of receiving assistance in their setting of choice, is an important milestone of progress. However, the fact that we now spend more than $50 billion on Medicaid HCBS means that what was once a small piece of the expenditure pie is now receiving a lot of interest and attention. These system changes have sparked the need for additional research. First, it is critical to understand how to efficiently and effectively offer this array of services. Recent efforts to better manage HCBS have received considerable attention. A number of states, with encouragement from the Centers for Medicare and Medicaid Services, are testing either Medicare and Medicaid integrated care programs or Medicaid managed long-term programs. The theory behind these efforts is that the managed care delivery system, usually proprietary, can more efficiently deliver the benefit. It is critical that empirically based studies evaluate the optimum way to deliver these long-term services programs. To date, the evaluation research is lagging behind the policy decisions in this arena. Improved studies will be critical as we double the number of older people likely to experience disability between now and 2050.

FUTURE OF THE OLDER AMERICANS ACT

If the past is a predictor of the future, it is likely that the OAA will remain underfunded and lack the reach required to provide services for elders in need. The current political climate and the challenges in documenting the direct impact of a complex system make increasing funding a challenge (Fox-Grage & Ujvari, 2014). HCBS users will need to continue to rely on other sources of funding to meet their needs such as Medicaid and the Veteran's Administration. The AAAs will likely continue to serve as planning and service organizations on the local level, but they will need to continue to diversify their role as they take on nursing home diversion and transition programs, Medicaid managed care, and integrated systems of care that combine physical, behavioral, long-term, and acute care options (National Association of Area Agencies on Aging & Miami University Scripps Gerontology Center, 2014).

CHAPTER SUMMARY

- OAA established the Administration on Aging, State Units on Aging, and Area Agencies on Aging.
- The service areas covered by OAA include accessing services, nutrition programs, home- and community-based services, disease prevention, health promotion, and rights of vulnerable older adults.
- The majority of OAA funding (70 percent) goes toward Title III nutrition, supportive services, family caregiving, and health promotion activities.
- Annual funding for the OAA has remained unchanged over the last decade even though the number of older adults has increased and the cost of care has risen.
- The Anderson health behavior model is one of the most commonly applied conceptual models used when examining health care utilization, including HCBS.
- All regions of the United States are served by AAAs who have staff that assess need, determine service eligibility, service needs, authorize services, and monitor cost-effectiveness of services.

- Despite the availability of AAAs, many individuals and families do not know about them.
- Attempts have been made to determine the influence of the OAA and other HCBS programs to determine HCBS use, health care use, nursing home admission/community tenure, and cost savings.
- HCBS are provided through a complex network of service providers and funding sources, and many of them have much higher appropriations than the OAA.

DISCUSSION QUESTIONS AND EXERCISES

1. Review the statements in the Fact or Fiction? list near the beginning of the chapter. After reading this chapter, can you identify which are true and which are false?
2. Imagine you are a case manager at an Area Agency on Aging. What kind of questions might you need to ask an older adult who called to request assistance with meals?
3. What groups are primarily served by Older Americans Act services?
4. Design a study that could examine the effectiveness of Older Americans Act services.
5. The Older Americans Act funding has not kept up with the demand for services. Imagine that you are speaking with your congressional representative. What talking points would you share about the Older Americans Act?

ADDITIONAL RESOURCES

Elder Care Locator: www.eldercare.gov
National Association of Area Agencies on Aging: https://www.n4a.org
National Association of States United for Aging and Disabilities: http://www
.nasuad.org/
National Council on Aging: https://www.ncoa.org/

REFERENCES

Administration on Aging. (2015). *Historical evolution of programs for older Americans.* Retrieved from https://aoa.acl.gov/AoA_Programs/OAA/resources/History .aspx

Andersen, R. M. (1995). Revisiting the behavioral model and access to medical care: Does it matter? *Journal of Health and Social Behavior, 36*(1), 1–10.

Andersen, R., & Newman, J. F. (1973). Societal and individual determinants of medical care utilization in the United States. *The Milbank Memorial Fund Quarterly, 51*(1).

Anderson, K. A., Dabelko-Schoeny, H., & Johnson, T. D. (2013). The state of adult day services: Findings and implications from the MetLife National Study of Adult Day Services. *Journal of Applied Gerontology, 32*, 729–748.

Borrayo, E. A., Salmon, J. R., Polivka, L., & Dunlop, B. D. (2004). Who is being serviced? Program eligibility and home- and community-based services use. *Journal of Applied Gerontology, 23*, 120–140.

Bradley, E. H., McGraw, S. A., Curry, L., Buckser, A., King, K. L., Kasl, S. V., & Andersen, R. (2002). Expanding the Andersen model: The role of psychological factors in long-term care use. *Health Services Research, 36*, 1221–1242.

Casado, B. L., van Vulpen, K. S., & Davis, S. L. (2011). Unmet needs for home and community-based services among frail older Americans and their caregivers. *Journal of Aging and Health, 23*(3), 529–553.

Colello, K. J., & Napili, A. (2016). *Older Americans Act: Background and overview.* Congressional Research Service. Prepared for Members and Committees of Congress. Retrieved from https://fas.org/sgp/crs/misc/R43414.pdf

Dabelko, H. I., & Balaswamy, S. (2000). Use of adult day services and home health care services by older adults: A comparative analysis. *Home Health Care Services Quarterly, 3*, 65–79.

Fox-Grage, W., & Ujvari, K. (2014). *Insights on the issues: The Older Americans Act.* AARP Public Policy Institute. Retrieved from http://www.aarp.org/content /dam/aarp/research/public_policy_institute/health/2014/the-older-americans -act-AARP-ppi-health.pdf

Johnson, L. B. (1965). *Remarks at the signing of the Older Americans Act.* Retrieved from http://www.presidency.ucsb.edu/ws/?pid=27079

Kowlessar, H., Robinson, K., & Schur, C. (2015). *Older Americans benefit from Older Americans Act nutrition programs.* Research Brief No. 8. Department of Health and Human Services, Administration on Aging. Retrieved from https:// aoa.acl.gov/Program_Results/docs/2015/AoA-Research-Brief-8-2015.pdf

Lewin Group. (2013). *Exploratory study of the global outcomes of the Older Americans Act programs and services.* Prepared for Department of Health and Human Services, Administration on Aging. Retrieved from https://aoa.acl.gov/Program _Results/docs/GlobalOutcomesFinalReport_March2013.pdf

Miller, E. A., & Weissert, W. G. (2000). Predicting elderly people's risk for nursing home placement, hospitalization, functional impairment, and mortality: A synthesis. *Medical Care Research and Review, 57,* 259–297.

National Association of Area Agencies on Aging & Miami University Scripps Gerontology Center. (2014). *Trends and new directions: Area Agencies on Aging survey, 2014.* Retrieved from http://www.n4a.org/files/AAA%202014 %20Survey.pdf

Niles-Yokum, K., & Wagner, D. L. (2015). *The aging networks: A guide to programs and services* (8th ed.) New York: Springer.

Robinson, K., Lucado, J., & Schur, C. (2012). *Use of transportation services among OAA Title III program participants.* Research Brief No. 6. Department of Health and Human Services, Administration on Aging. Retrieved from https://aoa .acl.gov/Program_Results/docs/2012/AoA_6th_xation_Brief_Oct_2012.pdf

U.S. Government Accountability Office. (2015). *Older Americans Act: Updated information on unmet need for services.* Prepared for the Subcommittee on Primary Health and Retirement Security, Committee on Health, Education, Labor, and Pensions, United States Senate. Retrieved from http://www.gao .gov/assets/680/670738.pdf

Wallace, S. P., Levy-Storms, L., Kington, R. S., & Andersen, R. M. (1998). The persistence of race and ethnicity in the use of long-term care. *Journal of Gerontology: Psychological and Social Sciences, 53*(2), S104-S120.

Weddle, D., Wilson, F. L., Berkshire, S. D., & Heuberger, R. (2012). Evaluating nutrition risk factors and other determinants of use of urban congregate meal program by older African Americans. *Journal of Nutrition in Gerontology and Geriatrics, 31*(1), 38–58.

Wolinsky, F. D., & Johnson, R. J. (1991). The use of health services by older adults. *Journal of Gerontology, 46*(6), S345–S357.

Multidisciplinary and Interdisciplinary Practice Across Home- and Community-Based Service Settings

Given this complexity of information and interpersonal connections, it is not only difficult for one clinician to provide care in isolation but also potentially harmful. Now, more than ever, there is an obligation to strive for perfection in the science and practice of inter-professional team-based health care.

MITCHELL ET AL., 2012, p. 2

LEARNING OBJECTIVES

In this chapter, you will:

- Gain an understanding of the history and evolution of interprofessional and interdisciplinary education and practice.
- Explore the principles of good interdisciplinary teamwork and person-centered care.
- Identify the common skills and care practices used by interprofessional teams providing home- and community-based services.
- Review the existing and emerging research on the impact and effectiveness of interprofessional education and practice.
- Explore future directions for collaborative interprofessional educational practice in home- and community-based services.

THE OLDER AMERICANS ACT ESTABLISHED the aging network in the United States and has been described as one of the most important U.S. laws supporting community-based living for older adults. In this chapter, we look at home- and community-based services (HCBS) that are provided by a wide range of professionals, including doctors, nurses, social workers, and a variety of therapists in the rehabilitation sciences. In addition, many service recipients obtain support from direct care staff such as home health aides and personal care assistants. HCBS staff must work together in multidisciplinary or interdisciplinary teams to provide high-quality care to older adults and their caregivers. The terms *multidisciplinary* and *interdisciplinary* are often used interchangeably, but when participating in activities such as care planning, case conferencing, and care coordination, they mean very different things. *Multidisciplinary teams* draw on the expertise, knowledge, and skills of each member, but each practitioner maintains a unique professional perspective or approach to care. *Interdisciplinary teams* analyze and synthesize information and develop a new coordinated way of care delivery (Choi & Pak, 2006). *Interprofessional* and *multiprofessional* are similar in meaning but refer only to professional team members; nonprofessional and paraprofessional staff, such as nursing assistants and aides, are excluded. Although care is delivered by practitioners representing different disciplines, some universal skills and care processes are relevant across disciplines and HCBS settings, including program enrollment, assessment, care planning, case management, crisis intervention, and care transitions. Each care provider plays a different role and provides unique knowledge, skills, and expertise to these care processes.

FACT OR FICTION?

Consider the following statements.

- Interprofessional teams are the same thing as multidisciplinary teams.
- Interprofessional education affects the quality of interprofessional practice.
- Working collaboratively as a team in home- and community-based services is the same as working in an institutional setting.
- Good communication strategies and structures are key to effective collaborative practice.
- Institutions of higher education are structured to support interprofessional education opportunities.

After reading this chapter, you will be able to affirm which statements are fact and which are fiction.

HISTORY AND CURRENT STATE OF INTERPROFESSIONAL EDUCATION AND PRACTICE

The development and implementation of Medicare and Medicaid legislation in the mid-1960s and early 1970s identified "the need for comprehensive care" and required interdisciplinary collaboration between physicians, nurses, and allied health professionals for older adults and individuals living in poverty and utilizing health care. Despite this requirement, interprofessional teams were not widely employed (Brandt, 2015). In 1972, the Institute of Medicine issued a report, *Educating for the Health Team*, in which they considered these questions:

- Why educate teams?
- Who should be so educated?
- How should students be educated (classroom emphasis)?
- How should students and professionals be educated (clinical emphasis)?
- What are the requirements for educating health care delivery teams?
- What are the obstacles?

This report resulted in some confusion and a lack of agreement among medical professionals about who should be included on interdisciplinary teams. Some felt interdisciplinary meant collaboration within the medical profession, meaning surgeons, primary care doctors, and pediatricians working together, and others saw the value in cross-disciplinary teams including nurses, therapists, dietitians, and social workers. The importance of cross-disciplinary teams has been more widely recognized today, but the challenges of working in interdisciplinary teams, as described in the 1972 report, largely remain, including an emphasis on professional hierarchy rather than interdependence and limited opportunities in higher education for students to learn about the roles and contributions of each profession. In addition, organization and administrative obstacles are in place in higher education that limit strategies such as team teaching and shared clinical and field practicum opportunities. The budgeting models in many institutions for higher education and in health insurance payment and reimbursement plans create competition between departments and professionals instead of incentives for collaboration.

The term *interprofessional teamwork* was first coined in 1975, and the 1980s and 1990s were a time of growth in the health and social services delivery systems, and in HCBS in particular. However, interprofessional education and practice were often viewed as "add-ons," and little research was conducted to examine team-based education, outcomes, or impacts on health care delivery. The Institute of Medicine tried again to influence education practices of health sciences with their 2003 report, *Health Professions Education: Bridge to Quality*, which identified five core competencies for all health professionals: (1) delivering patient-centered care, (2) working as part of interdisciplinary teams, (3) practicing evidence-based medicine, (4) focusing on quality improvement, and (5) utilizing information technology. The report did result in some curricular changes in Colleges of Medicine, Nursing, Social Work, and Rehabilitation Sciences in the United States through accrediting agency requirements related to practice competencies affecting interprofessional communication and practice.

The Patient Protection and Affordability Care Act (ACA) in 2010 explicitly called for new models of interprofessional education and practice focused on teamwork, quality improvement, and competence while holding practitioners more accountable for patient populations, payment reform, and care coordination (Brandt, 2015). Finally, the National Center for Interprofessional Practice and Education (NCIPE), established in 2012 to support evaluation, research, data, and evidence, ignited the field of interprofessional practice and education. NCIPE acts as a clearinghouse for educational resources, research, and professional networks of individuals studying and practicing interprofessional approaches. Although there is a recognized need for interprofessional approaches in health and social services, there is a lack of agreement about what this means and which professions should be involved. Multiple policy efforts have been implemented to encourage the development and evaluation of practicing in interdisciplinary teams.

OVERVIEW OF PRACTITIONERS INVOLVED IN HCBS

A wide range of practitioners with various levels of formal education and practicum experiences provide health and social services in HCBS, including medical doctors, nurses (nurse practitioners, registered nurses, licensed practical nurses), social workers, physical therapists, occupational therapists, speech and hearing pathologists, nursing assistants/ aides, pharmacists, and other health care providers such as podiatrists and optometrists. These professionals work in partnership with family and friends to support the health and well-being of older adults while engaged in HCBS. The role practitioners play for service users varies significantly depending on the HCBS setting. In general, health care providers such as physicians and nurse practitioners make referrals to HCBS and diagnose and treat common conditions faced by those served by HCBS. Registered nurses often assess, manage, and deliver the day-to-day health care of individuals in HCBS. Licensed practical nurses provide basic medical care through medication administration, monitoring vital signs, and managing medical equipment, often under the supervision of registered nurses. Nursing assistants or aides provide support with activities of daily living such as dressing, eating, and bathing. Others may suggest that nursing assistants and aides are not providing medical services, but we intentionally include assistants and aides under medical providers because we believe their services are important in supporting the physical functioning of individuals receiving HCBS. Social workers often are involved with assessments and case management activities as well as providing support for family caregivers. Finally, therapists of various disciplines offer the same occupational, physical, speech, and hearing therapies that they would typically deliver in an office setting in homes and community-based settings.

Nonmedical providers such as transportation providers and housekeepers play important roles in HCBS as well. These nonmedical providers often spend more unstructured time with older adults than do professionals, and they have the opportunity to build high levels of trust resulting in the potential for these individuals to be an important, yet often untapped resource for health professionals.

FRAMEWORKS OF CARE FOR INTERDISCIPLINARY TEAMWORK

Nancarrow et al. (2013) identified ten principles of good interdisciplinary teamwork based on a systematic literature review and a series of qualitative interviews with care teams.

TEN PRINCIPLES OF GOOD INTERDISCIPLINARY TEAM WORK

1. Recognized and competent leadership and management
2. Strong communication skills and systems
3. Opportunities for personal rewards, training, and development
4. Appropriate resources, procedures (to uphold vision), and structures (meetings and so forth)
5. Appropriate skill mix and full complement of staff
6. Team culture of trust and valuing contributions
7. Individual knowledge, experience, skills, self-awareness, and reflective practice
8. Clarity of vision and clear set of values
9. Focus on patient-centered care, quality, and outcomes
10. Respecting and understanding roles

First, effective interdisciplinary teams identify a leader who provides clear direction while also listening to input and providing supervision to team members. Who the leader of the team is depends on the HCBS setting and the care being provided. For example, a registered nurse is often the leader of a hospice care team in the community, a physician is the team leader with a physician house call program, and a social worker often leads a team investigating a case of elder abuse in the community. Second, high performing teams have well-developed communication strategies that facilitate collaborative decision making. Technology has provided opportunities for more efficient communication with team members, but questions remain as to whether technology supports effective decision making. Many teams continue to meet routinely in person to discuss cases, but virtual attendance via conference calling or video conferencing may grow in popularity. Third, a successful team values professional development through training, recognition, and prospects for career growth. Health care delivery is continually changing at a rapid speed. High-functioning teams ensure members have the skills and tools they need to provide high-quality care. Recognition for good work and opportunities for advancement are particularly important when teams consist of both professional and nonprofessional members. All sectors of long-term care continue to face significant turnover and shortages of direct care workers. Advancement and recognition efforts could make a positive impact on this issue. Fourth, interdisciplinary teams with sufficient and appropriate staffing mixed with identified roles and structural resources, such as identified care processes, provide high-quality services. Fifth, the disciplines represented on the team are needed and have complementary competencies. Sixth, good interdisciplinary teams have a culture in which individual expertise and opinions are valued and reaching consensus for action is supported. Seventh, individual reflective practice is critical for a successful interdisciplinary team in which practitioners "know what they know and know what they don't know." Eighth, shared values and a clear vision for patient care leads to (ninth) quality care outcomes that are patient-centered, recorded, and continually evolving. Finally, sharing and respecting roles and responsibilities within the team support both collaborative and autonomous practice efforts. Ideally these characteristics lead to patient-centered care, a system of care and practice that is gaining an increasing amount of attention from policy makers and program developers.

> Patient centeredness refers to health care that establishes a partnership among practitioners, patients, and their families (when appropriate) to ensure that decisions respect patient's wants, needs and preferences and that patients have the education and support they need to make decisions and participate in their own care. (Institute of Medicine, 2001)

Sometimes referred to a "person-centered" or "family-centered care," implementation of this measure of quality of care is still in development. Person-centered care suggests a broader picture of an individual that goes beyond his or her health care status. Family-centered care suggests an equal role for family members in making care decisions. The Institute of Medicine's definition is ambiguous in terms of the role of families and patient-centered care and assumes patients have the physical and cognitive abilities to make informed decisions. What happens when patients and clients do not agree on the treatment plan? What does patient-centered care look like when caring for an individual with dementia? Despite the vagueness of the concept and a lack of clear guidelines for implementation, patient-centered care has been mandated in HCBS as part of the ACA since 2010 and is being used for marketing and promotion by many care providers. The "devil is in the details" as HCBS strive to provide person-centered care.

In 2015, the American Geriatrics Society convened an interprofessional panel with assistance from the SCAN Foundation and the Keck School of Medicine with the University of Southern California to address the ambiguous elements of person-centered care and to provide a consistent definition to improve service delivery and research in this area. The panel included experts in gerontology, medicine, social work, nursing, policy and finance, law, long-term care delivery, and public health. The panel created the following refined definition:

> "Person-centered care" means that individuals' values and preferences are elicited and, once expressed, guide all aspects of their health care, supporting their realistic health and life goals. Person-centered care is achieved through a dynamic relationship among individuals, others who are important to them, and all relevant providers. This collaboration informs decision-making to the extent that the individual desires. (American Geriatrics Society Expert Panel on Person-Centered Care, 2016)

Some unique features of HCBS make implementation of person-centered care more of a challenge than care in institutional settings such as in hospitals and nursing homes (Ruggiano & Edvardsson, 2013). Individuals receiving HCBS are often engaged with multiple service providers that include both medical (such as nursing) and nonmedical (such as housekeeping) personnel. Because care is being delivered in the home, the opportunity for face-to-face interaction with interprofessional teams is limited. An additional challenge is posed by the financing structure that includes both short-term funding for rehabilitation by Medicare and long-term funding for Medicaid waiver programs. Other challenges are posed by the significant variability in level of regulation across industries: for example, the home health industry is much more regulated than other sectors such as adult day services. Also, older adults receiving in-home services may lack access to information for a variety of reasons, making it difficult for them to be informed consumers and play an active role in the decision-making process.

CASE STUDY

Mr. Garcia is a 75-year-old, widowed Mexican American recently discharged to return home from the hospital after a minor stroke. He does not have any physical limitations due to the stroke, but he is experiencing some mild to moderate memory impairment. He has poor vision, arthritis, high blood pressure, and difficulties hearing.

(CONTINUED)

Mr. Garcia lives alone in a ground floor apartment in a housing complex located in a suburban area. His daughter and her family live in the same suburb.

As a home health care nurse, you visit Mr. Garcia to provide follow-up care. You knock of the door, and Mr. Garcia calls for you to come in. You notice a clear plastic bag of prescription bottles with pills that have spilled inside the bag. You also notice some dirty plates and stacks of newspapers on the coffee table. You ask Mr. Garcia how he is doing, and he tells you he is doing just fine. Mr. Garcia's daughter interrupts him to tell you that her father called her last night to say that someone was trying to get into his apartment. His daughter reports that there was no evidence of a break-in. Mr. Garcia keeps a gun in the drawer of his nightstand to protect himself. Mr. Garcia's daughter wants him to move in with her. Mr. Garcia states that he is fine and that he wants to stay in the apartment.

As a member of an interprofessional team, think about the following statements and questions in relation to this case:

1. What are your concerns about this situation?
2. With Mr. Garcia's permission, what other individuals might you consult as you consider next steps? How would you communicate with these other individuals?
3. What additional information do you need to collect to better understand this situation? Are you the appropriate member of the team to conduct this assessment?
4. Mr. Garcia and his daughter seem to disagree about what the best living situation is for him. What is your role in this situation? What is the role of your team members?

PRACTICE APPLICATIONS

Across all HCBS settings, multidisciplinary teams engage in common skills and care processes. These include program enrollment, assessment, care planning, case management (service scheduling, monitoring, information, and referral), crisis intervention, and care transitions. Significant variability in *program enrollment* is found across care settings. This variability includes referral sources, eligibility requirements, the person enrolling individuals, and the type and nature of the information gathered as part of program enrollment. For example, enrollment in a hospice program begins with a physician referral and is available only for individuals who have a terminal illness with a predicted six or fewer months to live. A nurse or social worker may initiate enrollment in home health care by initiating and completing an electronic medical record. A much less formal enrollment process can be found in "village" communities, neighborhoods in which older adults have organized and developed a system of paid and volunteer care providers to meet their needs. Enrollment often includes gathering basic demographic information, contact information, financial status, and insurance coverage, if applicable.

After enrollment individuals and sometimes families will engage in an *assessment process* to identify the needs and desires of the individual and families receiving services. In some settings, this process occurs at program enrollment; at other times, this process is initiated soon after program enrollment and continues on a routine basis while the individual is receiving care. Assessments vary by setting but typically include diagnosis, current medications, functional status (including activities of daily living such as ability to eat, dress, bath, toilet, transfer, and ambulate independently), instrumental activities of daily living (such as the ability to do housework, prepare meals, and manage money), and cognitive assessments (including mental health status). The specific nature of the assessment varies depending on the setting and the reason the individual is receiving services as well as on what is required for insurance reimbursement. In HCBS settings, questions about access to transportation, safe and accessible housing, and healthy nutritional food may be explored. Licensed professionals such as doctors, nurses, social workers, and therapists typically conduct assessments. In HCBS, these assessments often are conducted by an interprofessional team, either individually or collaboratively.

The information collected as part of the assessment process should drive the care planning goals. Unfortunately, because of gaps in services in our health and social care systems, care plans include only those services available to the individual due to eligibility criteria and service availability. There may not be available interventions for some identified needs. The care plan includes specific interventions and the frequency of those interventions that will be put in place to support individual needs. *Care planning* typically includes multiple team members and consists of a written or electronic document identifying what services the individual will receive. Funders of HCBS often require care plans to be reviewed periodically and whenever there is a change in the status of the individual receiving services. Because multiple service providers often are supporting individuals living in the community with health and social service needs, case management is a common care process. *Case management* and care coordination includes activities such as scheduling services, monitoring care being provided, and providing information and referrals. In HCBS, case management activities typically are conducted by nurses or social workers. These same individuals are often involved in supporting individuals and their families during care transitions, such as a move to a nursing home or a discharge from a hospital.

Care transitions occur frequently within HCBS and from in-patient care settings such as hospitals and nursing homes to HCBS. Care transitions can transpire when level of care needs change, and care is delivered at different locations (Golden & Shier, 2013). Multiple practitioners from multiple disciplines often are involved in partnership with one another, and with older adults and caregivers, in coordinating care transitions. Poor care transitions can result in negative health care outcomes, costly hospital readmissions, and even death. Challenges to successful care transitions include inadequate communication between care providers and older adults and caregivers, lack of accountability for poor transition, fragmented patient data, and older adults and families taking on more complex health care self-management responsibilities (Golden & Shier, 2013). Increasingly, we are learning more about what elements need to be in place to support successful care transitions, many of the elements are similar to the principles of good interdisciplinary team work identified by Nancarrow et al. (2013) and listed earlier in this chapter. These elements include working in partnership, communication, patient-centered care, adequate time and resources, and respecting and understanding roles and responsibilities (Enderlin et al., 2013; Schoenborn, Arabaje, Eubank, Maynor, & Carrese, 2013).

As the result of the Affordable Care Act of 2013, the Centers for Medicare and Medicaid specified financial penalties for hospitals with readmissions after thirty days of discharge for patients with specific heart conditions, pneumonia, and hip and knee replacements. This financial penalty has increased the urgency in identifying transition care models that work. AcademyHealth (2017), a nonprofit organization dedicated to health services research, created a roadmap of the evidence related to effective transition care models that have been tested since 2011. These models have been developed by and include a number of disciplines including nursing, social work, and medicine.

Perspectives from the Field

An interview with Melinda McGuire, BA, MSW
Social Worker, Ohio Health Hospice
Columbus, Ohio

What is your professional background and training?

I worked as a social worker and contracts relation manager in an adult day center before I started my position at Hospice. In addition to my MSW, I have a graduate Interdisciplinary Specialization in Aging.

What is your role when working on an interprofessional team?

I provide emotional support to patients and family members and provide information on available community resources. I assess physical, mental, and emotional needs and relay these needs to the team members. I also provide emotional and listening support to my colleagues.

What would your average day look like working with your team members?

I start my mornings contacting each nurse and chaplain on the team to discuss daily schedules and assess visit needs. I visit three to four patients each day; if I notice a need that should be addressed by another member of my team, I contact that member to provide an update on the patient. I attend weekly care planning meetings with nurses, chaplains, doctors, pharmacists, and clinical managers to discuss patients' plan of care and new needs.

What are the benefits of working in teams?

Working with an interdisciplinary team enables us to take a systems approach to each patient. Instead of just prescribing a pill to alleviate pain or symptoms such as shortness of breath or anxiety, we can offer nonpharmacological approaches such as guided meditation or deep breathing exercises. Communication is the key to a successful interprofessional team.

RESEARCH AND EVIDENCE

Despite an increasing emphasis on interprofessional education in higher education, research on the efficacy of interprofessional teams in practice is limited (Ravet, 2012). The World Health Organization (WHO) reports that interprofessional education and collaborative practice can improve health systems and health outcomes, and best practice models of interprofessional education have been identified (Bridges, Davidson, Odegard, Maki, & Tomkowiak, 2011). These models support students in their understanding of their own professional identity while providing an opportunity for students to learn about the professional roles of others. Successful interprofessional models depend on commitment from departments and colleges, calendar and scheduling agreements, curricular mapping, training of facilitators and faculty, a shared sense of community, adequate space, technology, and community relationships for practice application (Bridges et al., 2011).

WHO (2010) notes the potential of interprofessional education and collaborative practice to mitigate the shortage of health care workers and address issues of fragmented care. Existing research on primary and acute care settings suggests collaborative practice can improve access to and coordination of health services, appropriate use of specialists, outcomes for individuals with chronic diseases, and patient care and safety. Additional studies suggest collaborative practice can decrease patient complications, length of stay in a hospital, tension and conflict among caregivers, staff turnover, hospital admissions, clinical errors, and mortality rates (WHO, 2010). Terminally and chronically ill patients who receive home care from interdisciplinary teams are more satisfied with their care, have fewer clinic visits and symptoms, and report improved overall health (WHO, 2010). A systematic review of the most rigorous research designs by the Cochrane Collaboration suggests positive outcomes of interprofessional education and practice in the areas of diabetes care, emergency department culture and patient satisfaction, collaborative team behavior and reduction of clinical error rates in emergency departments, collaborative team behavior in operating rooms, management of care delivered in domestic violence cases, and mental health competencies related to patient care (Reeves, Perrier, Goldman, Freeth, & Zwarenstein, 2013).

The benefits of well-integrated collaborative care models are supported for improving the processes of care and reducing hospital or nursing care in primary and acute care environments, but the effectiveness and cost savings that can occur through interprofessional teams working with older adults living in the community is less clear. Potential areas of influence on the effectiveness of health care include individual health, physical functioning, quality of life, resource use, and caregiver burden (Trivedi et al., 2013). Consistent documentation of the benefit of collaborative practice on individual and caregiver outcomes may be limited because of the variability of care models, including case management, collaboration, and integrated models of care. To more clearly identify the benefits of the key components of interprofessional education that are effective in improving health care outcomes in HCBS, future studies must (1) examine the difference between interprofessional interventions and single profession interventions, (2) use mixed methods including qualitative approaches with experimental designs, and (3) include cost-benefit analyses (Reeves et al., 2013). It is difficult to measure impact when the nature of the intervention is not consistent and the financial implications are not examined. Is it possible to provide person-centered care with a standard model of care? This question and others raise the challenge of measuring influence in HBCS and the "ideal" versus the "real" of delivering interdisciplinary team-based care.

An Expert Weighs In

Cynthia Dougherty, PhD
Director Office of Geriatrics and Interprofessional Aging Studies
College of Medicine, The Ohio State University
Columbus, Ohio

The care of older adults has long included multidisciplinary and interdisciplinary teams; however, the research regarding this care and its outcomes, particularly with regard to HCBS, is scarce. With the population shift and the declining numbers of family caregivers, the demand for HCBS will increase. This will improve the ability of researchers and practitioners to work together to show evidence of the benefits of interdisciplinary teams in HCBS across various settings. It is imperative that these partnerships develop to help researchers answer a variety of questions and disseminate information about what works to further advance best practices. In addition, there is a need to research the impact of interprofessional education, commonly referred to as IPE, on the delivery of health and social services to older adults. If the belief is that interprofessional teams have a positive impact on care, and if the evidence supports that, then learning what makes these teams successful (for example, Does IPE do this?) is an appropriate line of inquiry. Furthermore, to determine what mechanisms of IPE positively influence interdisciplinary teamwork, and what mechanism of interdisciplinary teams positively influence health and social care outcomes, more research needs to be done in the area of measurement as it relates to these phenomena and areas of practice. Patients, participants, and providers can share anecdotal stories of success related to the work of interdisciplinary teams, but as students, practitioners, and researchers, we must make a concerted effort to share this information in a more systematic way through rigorous research practices.

FUTURE OF INTERPROFESSIONAL AND MULTIDISCIPLINARY PRACTICE IN HCBS SETTINGS

Demands for cost-effective high-quality health care delivered in the community will continue to grow as the number of older adults needing care increases. With improved understanding of the potential impact interprofessional collaborative practice might play in supporting better patient outcomes and smoother care transitions, policy makers and entities that fund health services will continue to pay more attention to this approach to care. The World Health Organization (2010) outlined actions and desired outcomes to advance collaborative practice (see box). Some of these recommendations include creating environments that encouraged interprofessional engagement and cooperation, allowing and scheduling time for interprofessional teamwork, and creating policies, procedures, and structures that encourage shared decision making and collaborative service delivery.

As our understanding of what educational experiences lead to more effective team-based delivery of health and social services, interprofessional or multidisciplinary practice in HCBS settings will continue to evolve. Institutions of higher education will need to identify which curricular and experiential training opportunities make the most difference on health outcomes for patients.

ACTIONS AND DESIRED OUTCOMES TO ADVANCE COLLABORATIVE PRACTICE

ACTIONS	DESIRED OUTCOMES
1. Structure processes that promote shared decision making, regular communication, and community involvement.	• A model of collaborative practice that recognizes the principles of shared decision making and best practice in communication across professional boundaries.
2. Design a built environment that promotes, fosters, and extends interprofessional collaborative practice both within and across service agencies.	• Improved communication channels. • Improved satisfaction among health workers.
3. Develop personnel policies that recognize and support collaborative practice and offer fair and equitable remuneration models.	• Improved workplace health and well-being for workers. • Improved working environment. • Improved interaction between management and staff.
4. Develop a delivery model that allows adequate time and space for staff to focus on interprofessional collaboration and delivery of care.	• Greater cohesion and communications between health workers. • A sustained commitment to embedding interprofessional collaboration in the workplace.
5. Develop governance models that establish teamwork and shared responsibility for health care service delivery between team members as the normative practice.	• Updated governance model, job descriptions, vision, mission, and purpose.

Source: WHO, 2010.

CHAPTER SUMMARY

- Multidisciplinary teams use the knowledge, skills, and expertise of each member caring for the same individual. Interdisciplinary or interprofessional teams synthesize knowledge, skills, and expertise to deliver a new model of care.
- Awareness of the potential benefits of interprofessional teams began in the 1960s when Medicare and Medicaid policy called for comprehensive patient care.

- Communication policies and procedures and mutual trust are critical to successful interdisciplinary teamwork.
- Common skills and practices across disciplines are used in HCBS including intake, assessment, care planning, case management, crisis intervention, and care transitions.
- Access to and quality of interprofessional education affects the effectiveness and efficacy of collaborative practice.
- Evidence suggests that interprofessional practice can have a positive impact on health outcomes.
- Continual refinement of the elements of interprofessional education and collaborative practice that make a difference in health outcomes are needed.
- HCBS include many professionals and will continue to include team-based care in the future.

DISCUSSION QUESTIONS AND EXERCISES

1. Review the statements in the Fact or Fiction? list near the beginning of the chapter. After reading this chapter, can you identify which are true and which are false?
2. Imagine you are a member of an interdisciplinary team that provides care for seniors living in affordable housing. Describe who might be on your team and what role each person might play?
3. Describe some challenges that might arise when working on an inter-professional team caring for an individual with disabilities living at home.
4. Imagine you are writing a proposal to a dean in health or social sciences to develop interprofessional education opportunities for students at your university. What would the curriculum include? What would the experiential or applied learning activities look like?
5. The evidence that interprofessional teams have a positive outcome on the health of service users is mixed. Design a study that could further build our understanding of the potential benefits of providing collaborative care.
6. Imagine that you are a member of an interdisciplinary team that provides hospice care for patients living in the community. One of your team members has repeatedly disregarded your recommendations for the care plan. Describe what you might do in this situation.

ADDITIONAL RESOURCES

AcademyHealth: http://www.academyhealth.org/

Agency for Healthcare Research and Quality: https://www.ahrq.gov/

National Center for Interprofessional Practice and Education: https://nexusipe
.org/

World Health Organization: http://www.who.int/en/

REFERENCES

AcademyHealth (2017). Evidence roadmap: Transitional care models to prevent hospital readmissions. Retrieved from http://www.academyhealth.org/files /AH_Evidence%20Roadmap%20Transitional%20Care%20Models %20FINAL.pdf

American Geriatrics Society Expert Panel on Person-Centered Care. (2016). Person-centered care: A definition and essential elements. *Journal of the American Geriatrics Society, 64*(1), 15–18.

Brandt, B. F. (2015). Interprofessional education and collaborative practice: Welcome to the "new" forty-year-old field. *The Advisor, 34*(1), 9–17.

Bridges, D. R., Davidson, R. A., Odegard, P. S., Maki, I. V., & Tomkowiak, J. (2011). Interprofessional collaboration: Three best practice models of interprofessional education. *Medical Education Online, 16*(1). doi: 10.3402/meo.v16i0.6035

Choi, B. C., & Pak, A. W. (2006). Multidisciplinary, interdisciplinary and trans-disciplinary in health research, services, education and policy: Definitions, objectives and evidence of effectiveness. *Clinical and Investigative Medicine, 29*(6), 351–364.

Enderlin, C. A., McLeskey, N., Rooker, J. L., Steinhauser, C., D'Avolio, D., Gusewelle, R., & Ennen, K. A. (2013). Review of current conceptual models and frameworks to guide transitions of care in older adults. *Geriatric Nursing, 34,* 47–52.

Golden, R., & Shier, G. (2013). What does "care transitions" really mean? *Generations, 36*(4), 6–12.

Institute of Medicine. (1972). *Educating for the health team.* Washington, DC: National Academy of Sciences.

Institute of Medicine. (2001). *Envisioning the national health care quality report.* Washington, DC: National Academies Press.

Institute of Medicine. (2003). *Health professions education: Bridge to quality.* Washington, DC: National Academies Press.

Mitchell, P., Wynia, M., Golden, R, McNellis, B., Okun, S, Webb, C. E., Rohrbach, V., & Von Kohorn, I. (2012). *Core principles & values of effective team-based health care.* Washington, DC: Institute of Medicine.

Nancarrow, S. A., Book, A., Ariss, S., Smith, T., Enderby, P., & Roots, A. (2013). Ten principles of good interdisciplinary team work, *Human Resources for Health, 11*(19).

Ravet, J. (2012). From interprofessional education to interprofessional practice: Exploring the implementation gap. *Professional Development in Education, 38,* 49–64.

Reeves, S., Perrier, L., Goldman, J., Freeth, D., & Zwarenstein, M. (2013). Interprofessional education: Effects on professional practice and healthcare outcomes (update) (Review). *Cochrane Database of Systematic Reviews, 3,* 1–16.

Ruggiano, N., & Edvardsson, D. (2013). Person-centeredness in home- and community-based long-term care: Current challenges and new directions. *Social Work in Health Care, 52,* 846–861.

Schoenborn, N. L., Arbaje, A. I., Eubank, K. J., Maynor, K., & Carrese, J. A. (2013). Clinician roles and responsibilities during care transitions of older adults. *Journal of the American Geriatrics Society, 61,* 231–236.

Trivedi, D., Goodman, C., Gage, H., Baron, N., Schiebl, F., Lliffe, S., . . . Drennan, V. (2013). The effectiveness of inter-professional working for older people living in the community: A systematic review. *Health and Social Care in the Community, 21*(2), 113–128.

World Health Organization. (2010). *Framework for action on interprofessional education and collaborative practice.* Retrieved from http://apps.who.int/iris/bitstream/10665/70185/1/WHO_HRH_HPN_10.3_eng.pdf

5

Family Caregiving

It is hard to envision a world without caregiving. It would have to be a world without caring.

GAUGLER & KANE, 2015, p. 375

WE HAVE DISCUSSED INTERDISCIPLINARY TEAMS and practice skills necessary for the delivery of home- and community-based services (HCBS). Despite the services and supports provided by practitioners representing different disciplines, however, family members or friends provide the majority of the care for noninstitutionalized older adults. In fact, almost 40 million Americans provided on average 24.4 hours a week of unpaid care for disabled adults in 2014. The most frequently provided support was assistance with activities of daily living (ADLs) such as eating, bathing, grooming, and getting in and out of bed or a chair (AARP Public Policy Institute & National Alliance for Caregiving, 2015). As Gaugler and Kane (2015) note, caregivers are giving care to our world. The estimated economic value of this uncompensated care was $470 billion in 2013 (AARP Public Policy Institute & National Alliance for Caregiving, 2015). *Informal caregivers* or *family caregivers* are individuals who provide various levels of physical and emotional assistance to adults with functional or cognitive limitations. Family caregivers are typically not paid for the work they do and often do not identify themselves as caregivers. When you speak to family caregivers, many will tell you that they are just doing what is expected of a spouse or adult child of an individual who needs some help. Family caregivers provide critical support for older adults living independently or in community-based settings. Often the difference between being able to receive care in a community setting instead of an institution is the availability and capability of a family caregiver.

FACT OR FICTION?

Consider the following statements.

- Most care provided for older adults in their homes is delivered by home health care providers.
- Little has changed over the last couple of decades with regard to family caregiving.
- Family caregivers of individuals with dementia often experience high levels of stress.
- The National Family Caregiver Support Program (NFCSP) supports caregivers regardless of their ability to pay.
- Research has demonstrated that there are few differences between spousal and adult children caregivers of individuals receiving HCBS.

After reading this chapter, you will be able to affirm which statements are fact and which are fiction.

HISTORY AND CURRENT STATE OF FAMILY CAREGIVING

Family members, primarily women, have been taking care of individuals with disabilities for decades. Changing demographic, economic, and social factors have influenced the context of family caregivers today. Advances in public health practices and medical science have enabled many individuals to live longer, but this increase in life expectancy sometimes has been accompanied by chronic illnesses and disabilities (Ortman, Velkoff, & Hogan, 2014). The fastest growing population cohort are people 80 years and older, and it is this group that most likely will need caregivers. Many diseases, such as Alzheimer's disease, are more prevalent in later years; as more people live longer, the number of people who experience this and other debilitating diseases increases (Alzheimer's Association, 2016).

Although many individuals are living longer, significant disparities in life expectancies are present depending on race and gender. For example, the life expectancy for males born in 2014 is 76.4 years and for females 81.2 years. Black males are at an even greater disadvantage with a predicted life expectancy of 72 years compared to 76.5 years for white males. When poverty is included in these measures, the discrepancies are even greater (Arias, 2016).

Economic and social factors have accompanied these demographic factors in changing the face of family caregiving. The number of women participating in the workforce continues to increase, providing challenges to the traditional female-dominated family caregiving models of the past. Today, 40 percent of family caregivers are men (AARP Public Policy Institute & National Alliance for Caregiving, 2015). Women and men are more geographically mobile today, resulting in adult children living in different cities, states, and even countries than their aging parents (Shultz & Eden, 2016). People are choosing to have no children or to have fewer children, and are waiting until they are older to have children. Finally, more people are divorced or never married than ever before, reducing the availability of spousal caregivers (Shultz & Eden, 2016). The shrinking size of families in the United States has meant there are fewer adult children and spouses to care for the growing number of older adults (Johnson, Toohey, & Wiener, 2007).

HCBS providers rely on family caregivers. Unlike institutional settings such as nursing homes, paid care providers are not always present and available, leaving family members to provide care and services when needed. There is significant variability in the intensity, duration, and nature of the care provided by family members. Care recipients may become impaired suddenly because of a critical event such as a stroke, whereas for others care needs increase gradually over time due to progressive illnesses such as cancer or Parkinson's disease. Caregiving tasks range from providing emotional support to transportation to administering medication and providing baths. Shultz and Eden (2016) identify six domains of family caregiver activities and tasks: (1) household tasks; (2) self-care, supervision, and mobility; (3) emotional and social support; (4) health and medical care; (5) advocacy and care coordination; and (5) surrogacy. Household tasks and self-care, supervision, and mobility include assistance with activities of daily living (ADLs) such as bathing, grooming, dressing, feeding, toileting, and transferring; instrumental activities of daily living (IADLs) include paying bills, preparing meals, doing laundry, and grocery shopping. Emotional and social support and health and medical care include companionship, treatment compliance, and wound care. Family caregivers often are involved in advocacy and care coordination by arranging appointments and communicating with care providers. Finally, surrogacy activities include items such as support with financial and legal matters as well as advanced planning and treatment decisions. With such a diverse range of activities with various levels of intensity and duration, it is important not to make assumptions about a family caregiver's experiences.

THEORIES OF CARE

One of the most widely applied theoretical models related to the challenges and outcomes of family caregiving is the stress process model (SPM), which provides a framework for examining the context, stressors, and outcomes of family caregiving (Pearlin, Mullan, Semple, & Skaff, 1990). Specifically, the SPM identifies how conditions, experiences, and activities give rise to or mediate experiences of family caregivers (figure 5.1). Originally, this model was developed as a framework for caregivers of individuals with Alzheimer's disease, but it has since been applied to many different caregiving populations.

The SPM includes four domains: background and context, stressors, mediators of stress, and outcomes of stress. Stressors are further divided

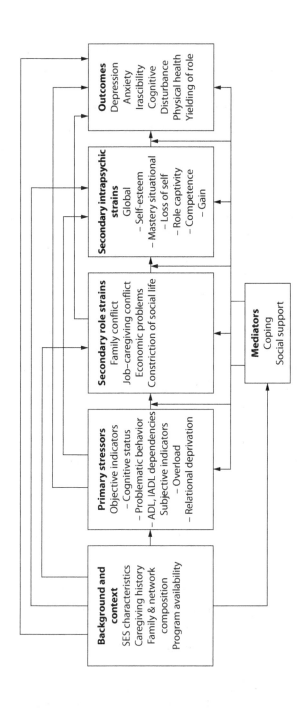

FIGURE 5.1 Pearlin's Stress Process model.

into primary stressors and secondary role and intrapsychic strains. Primary stressors are thought to lead to secondary stressors. The background and context domain includes key demographic characteristics of caregivers such as age, gender, ethnicity, and socioeconomic characteristics. Caregiving history, such as length of time involved with caring, influence caregiver stress, mediators, and outcomes. The SPM suggests that contextual factors, including access to and use of familial and formal programmatic supports such as HCBS, influence the caregiving experience.

Primary and secondary stressors are defined as situations, experiences, and events that influence physical and psychological states of the caregiver. Primary stressors are the direct result of the needs of the care receiver and the nature of the caregiving experience. Objective indicators of primary stressors include the cognitive status, problematic behaviors, and functional limitations of the care receiver. Subjective indicators reflect how the caregiver is experiencing stress, such as feeling overwhelmed with various roles and the absence of a mutually beneficial relationship between the caregiver and care receiver. These primary stressors result in secondary role and intrapsychic strains. These secondary stressors can result from primary stressors. Examples of secondary stressors are role strain from balancing employment, family obligations, and caregiving responsibilities. Individual coping behaviors and social supports can mediate the outcomes of caregiver stress according to the SPM. Outcomes identified by the SPM are considered interrelated and include emotional distress, such as depression, anxiety, irascibility (anger easily), cognitive disturbance, and physical health and well-being. For a full description of the SPM, see Pearlin et al. (1990).

The SPM has been modified and adapted over time by a number of researchers. Of particular note, Lawton, Kleban, Moss, Rovine, and Glicksman (1989) suggest that the objective treatment of burden and stress in the SPM should be replaced by a subjective analysis of burden or stress referred to as a "caregiver appraisal" of the associated factors related to caregiving. These factors may or may not be perceived as stressful by different caregivers. For example, one family caregiver might perceive a decline in cognitive status of a care recipient more or less challenging than changes in physical abilities. All family caregivers do not appraise stressors or strains in the same way. Another example of adapting the SPM comes from Aranda and Knight (1997), who argue that the influence of ethnicity and culture should be given more emphasis in the SPM.

In particular, they found important differences related to the appraisal of stress events, perception and use of social support, and coping skills among Latino families.

The SPM largely assumes that the caregiving experience is burdensome, resulting in negative outcomes for the caregiver. Some scholars have suggested alternative models from the stress coping perspective. Carbonneau, Caron, and Desrosiers (2010) proposed a conceptual framework illustrating the positive aspects of caregiving based on existing evidence that includes three domains of caregiving: (1) quality of caregiver/care receiver daily relationship, (2) caregiver's feeling of accomplishment, and (3) meaning of the caregiver's role in daily life. The positive aspects of caregiving are determined by the caregiver's sense of self-efficacy and engagement in enrichment events in daily life resulting in positive outcomes such as the caregiver's well-being and ability to continue providing care.

PRACTICE APPLICATIONS

Family caregivers often put the care recipient's needs first and neglect their own health and well-being. Thinking of family caregivers as recipients of services is not only a challenge for care providers, it is difficult for caregivers themselves. To encourage self-care by family caregivers, a number of organizations have adapted the "Caregiver's Bill of Rights," first published in 1986 by Jo Horne in the AARP book, *CareGiving: Helping an Aging Loved One.* The intent of this statement of rights is for caregivers, care recipients, and the public to recognize what family caregivers are entitled to while in the role of a caregiver.

Assessment

Family caregivers are critical partners with providers of HCBS, but the staff involved in providing care through HCBS often collects little information about family caregivers. HCBS providers may ask the name and contact information for the primary caregiver, but it is rare for staff to employ formal assessment tools regarding the caregiver, such as measures of caregiving burden, health, or the ability to continuing caring. An available, engaged, and capable family caregiver is an important predictor of the ability of an individual with functional limitations to remain in the community, yet our HCBS providers often fail to formally assess family caregivers or connect them to services.

DOMAINS OF CAREGIVER ASSESSMENT

1. Background on the caregiver and the caregiving situation
2. Caregiver's perception of health and functional status of the care recipient
3. Caregiver's values and preferences with respect to everyday living and care provision
4. Health and well-being of the caregiver
5. Consequences of caregiving on the caregiver
6. Care-provision requirements (skills, abilities, knowledge)
7. Resources to support the caregiver

Source: Family Caregiver Alliance, 2012.

The Family Caregiver Alliance (2012) has compiled a list of seven key domains that should be included in the assessment of family caregivers (see box). First, *care providers should consider the background of the caregiver and the caregiving situation.* In addition to basic demographic information such as gender, age, and relationship to care recipient, other important information includes what led to the caregiving situation, how long care has been provided, and the nature of the care being delivered. Key questions such as these should be asked: What tasks involve the caregiver? How frequently? Is the caregiver employed? What kind of social supports does the caregiver have?

Second, *the caregiver's perception of the health and functional status of the care recipient* should be assessed. Consideration should be given to the following questions: Has there been a sudden or gradual change in the care receiver's health? What impact has that change had on the care recipient's ability to complete ADLs? What is the level of assistance needed? Does the care receiver have psychosocial needs? Third, the *caregiver's values and preferences with respect to everyday living and care provision* should be assessed. Explore tasks such as financial management, housekeeping, and personal care that the caregiver may want to provide. Is the caregiver willing to give care, and is the care receiver willing to accept care?

Fourth, a caregiver assessment should be gathering information about the *health and well-being of the caregiver.* Measures of emotional and physical health and quality of life should be employed. Understanding the current state of well-being of the family caregiver will allow the assessor to examine the ability of the family caregiver to provide the needed care. Fifth, gather closely related information about the *consequences of caregiving*. What does the caregiver view as the biggest challenges in providing care? What are the greatest rewards? Sixth, if care has already been provided or will be provided in a new way, it is critical to assess the *skills, abilities, and knowledge of the caregiver to provide the care that is needed*. The information gathered around this domain reflects the caregiver's confidence and competence in providing the needed care. Some required tasks may be familiar to caregivers, such as grocery shopping or housekeeping, but the caregiver may need to learn how to change a dressing on a wound or how to pay bills for the care receiver. Finally, information collected during the assessments provides a guide for the *potential resources a caregiver might need*. Based on the information collected, what services are available to support the caregiver? Providing potential resources should go beyond simply handing the family caregiver a list of local support groups. What assistance might the caregiver need to access the support?

Finding opportunities to assess family caregivers of individuals receiving HCBS can be a challenge. Gathering information from the caregiver might happen over the course of a series of phone calls, standing at the front door of his or her home, or sitting in the lobby at an adult day program. Finding a private, quiet office for a comprehensive caregiver assessment during one sitting often is not a realistic goal.

Interventions

Intervention strategies recommended for family caregivers should be based on the information collected during the assessment. Too often practitioners offer family caregivers information about programs available in the local community without careful consideration of the needs identified in the assessment process. Interventions for family caregivers fall into two general categories: (1) interventions that provide psychosocial and educational support for family caregivers, and (2) interventions that reduce the amount or intensity of care provided by the family caregiver through respite or environmental modifications. Common interventions that support psychosocial and education or training needs of family caregivers can be delivered individually through private counseling or training or through a support group. Private counseling may focus on issues such as stress management, depression/anxiety, and role captivity. Individuals may receive education and training from medical personnel on how to operate adaptive equipment, safely transferring a care recipient, or changing a dressing on a wound. Education about a disease, positive coping strategies, and available community resources may be provided. Individual level support may be provided in person at a care setting, in someone's home, or in a professional's office. Increasingly, individuals are receiving education and psychosocial support through online resources such as the AARP Caregiver Information Center and the Family Caregiver Alliance's National Center on Caregiving. Group support is frequently offered through disease-specific support groups, agency-based trainings such as from the area Agency on Aging office, or through programming offered by a HCBS provider. Support groups offer an avenue for peer-to-peer education and support that provides unique benefits.

Interventions to reduce the number of hours of care provided by the caregiver include respite programs and environmental modifications. Respite programs offer a break from caregiving either by having someone come to the home so the caregiver can spend time away or by placing the care receiver temporarily in another setting such as a nursing home, assisted living venue, or an adult day services program. Environmental modifications that can reduce the care provided by family caregivers may include items such as mechanical lifts, a shower bench, or wheelchair accessible kitchen countertops.

CASE STUDY

Luis Madera, age 85, is a retired car mechanic who lives in Lancaster, Ohio, in a farm house that his family purchased when they moved to the United States from Puerto Rico. His wife died twelve years ago. Luis's daughter, Maria, who is 65 and also a widow, lives with him. Maria's daughter, Alondra, attends Ohio University in Athens and drives to Lancaster to help Luis and Maria with their care a couple of times a week.

Luis suffered a stroke, uses a walker, and has difficulties swallowing. In addition, Luis has dental problems and difficulty chewing. He has lost a significant amount of weight and often refuses to eat. Maria assists him in and out of bed daily. Maria uses a cane to walk because of polio she had as a child. Alondra believes that Luis should get a feeding tube inserted into his stomach so that he can receive nutrition to regain his strength. Maria has mixed feelings about the feeding tube, but she wants Luis to gain some strength because she is fearful of her ability to care for him in this weakened state.

(CONTINUED)

> Alondra has called you, a staff person with the National Family Caregiver Support Program with the Buckeye Hills Area Agency on Aging, to ask you what she should do.
>
> 1. What are the conditions, experiences, and activities that might influence Maria's or Alondra's ability to continue providing care for Luis?
> 2. What questions might you invite Alondra to consider as she and Maria continue to provide support for Luis?
> 3. What are some programs and supports that you might suggest Alondra investigate?
> 4. What home- and community-based services exist that might support Maria and Alondra?

The nature, cost and availability of interventions that provide psychosocial and educational support for family caregivers and interventions that reduce the amount or intensity of care provided by the family caregiver vary tremendously from individual to individual and from community to community. Private counseling may or may not be covered by private health care insurance or offered at a reduced fee. Support groups are typically provided at no additional cost to caregivers, as are basic level training from medical personnel about health care that needs to be delivered at home by a family caregiver.

The National Family Caregiver Support Program (NFCSP) is the largest U.S. program for family caregivers in terms of the amount of funding and the number of caregivers served. This program, adopted in 2000 as part of the Older Americans Act (see chapter 3), requires State Units on Aging to partner with regional Area Agencies on Aging and local providers in an attempt to standardize the access, availability, and nature of support for family caregivers. NFCSP provides information and assistance accessing services, individual counseling, education, caregiver training, support groups, respite services, and limited supplemental services for all caregivers across the United States. NFCSP was allocated $145.5 million in 2015 and delivered more than 1.3 million caregiver services, such as counseling, respite, and information referral. In 2015, 115,585 family caregivers received counseling, training, or attended a support group, and more than 64,000 caregivers received respite services through the NFCSP (Shultz & Eden, 2016). It is clear that this program has a limited reach, for there are more than 40 million family caregivers in the United States today.

Perspectives from the Field

An interview with Patty Callahan LISW-S, CIRS-AD
Caregiver Advocate, Central Ohio Area Agency on Aging (COAAA)
Columbus, Ohio

What is your professional background and training?

I have a BSW and an MSW with a focus on geriatrics and medical social work.

What is your role in family caregiving?

I have managed the National Family Caregiver Support Program for the Central Ohio Area Agency on Aging since it was implemented in 2001. I work with the partner agencies in eight counties to align those programs with state and federal policy. I also collaborate with other COAAA staff on developing resources and provide consultation, supportive counseling, and education to caregivers.

What challenges have you faced in working with family caregivers?

Scarce resources throughout the care continuum frequently leave us without the tools to support caregivers in caring for their loved ones. Ideally, every caregiver—not just the person receiving care—would have access to a case manager.

What advice would you give to someone interested in working with family caregivers?

Caregivers have very little time to acquire the knowledge they need to navigate complex, overwhelmed systems of care. An important way to support them is to have a solid working knowledge of HCBS, Medicare, Medicaid, veteran's benefits, community resources, housing options, public benefits, mental health services, community providers, and the health care system. We can't be experts on everything, but a strong knowledge base enables us to help caregivers understand their options at each crossroad.

DIVERSITY IN FAMILY CAREGIVING—A FOCUS ON WOMEN

Despite recent growth in the percentage of men in caregiving roles, family caregiving continues to be a gendered experience with women bearing much of the burden. In fact, two-thirds of family caregivers are women, and women spend 50 percent more time than men in caregiving activities. The typical female caregiver is 49 years old, married, and employed (Family Caregiver Alliance, 2017). Midlife is also a time when many women are raising teenage children or just beginning to move into their grandmother role. These women often are referred to as the "sandwich generation"—caring for children at the same as they are caring for their aging parents. Sandwich caregivers, in particular, are pulled in many directions and are forced to juggle time and to stretch resources. (For more on the sandwich generation, see Parker and Patten, 2013.)

Caregiving can have positive characteristics, such as personal growth and fulfilling family promises; however, caregiving also can have deleterious impacts on physical, emotional, social, and financial well-being. The Family Caregiver Alliance (2003) provides a compendium of statistics on women's role in family caregiving and the impact this has on their lives. Among these statistics are the following: 33 percent of women caregivers had to decrease their work hours; 29 percent had to pass up promotions; 20 percent had to switch to part-time work; and 16 percent were forced to quit working to provide care. The average cost in terms of lost wages and retirement benefits for women caregivers was estimated at more than $324,000. Not surprisingly, women caregivers also reported that their social networks and activities tend to decline due to caregiving responsibilities. One study found that women who cared for a disabled spouse or an aging parent were 6 times and 2 times, respectively, more likely to suffer symptoms of depression or anxiety than their non-caregiving peers (Cannuscio, Jones, Kawachi, Colditz, Berkman & Rimm, 2002). Finally, 25 percent of women caregivers reported that they had health problems as a result of caregiving (Family Caregiver Alliance, 2003). Practitioners should be aware of the gendered experience of caregiving and be particularly attentive to the needs faced by women in the caregiving role.

RESEARCH AND EVIDENCE

The physical, psychological, social, and financial impact of caregiving varies widely and is based on a number of factors, including caregiver and care recipient characteristics and the amount, duration, and nature of the care provided by the caregiver. Those caring for individuals with dementia are reported to be some of the most stressed and experience the highest levels of negative impacts (Kim, Chang, Rose, & Kim, 2011). Elevated levels of stress hormones associated with poor immune system functioning, wound healing, and cardiovascular disease have been found in family caregivers (Kiecolt-Glaser, McGuire, Robles, & Glaser, 2002). Other reported physical impacts of providing care include increases in frailty, medication use, hospitalization, and mortality. Higher levels of emotional distress, depression, anxiety, and social isolation also have been documented in family caregivers (Shultz & Eden, 2016). Family caregivers experience more financial stresses due to care expenses and a reduction in time spent in paid employment. Family caregivers spend an average of 20 percent of their annual income on family caregiving expenses, and the burden is greatest for Hispanic/Latino and African American caregivers who spend 44 percent and 34 percent, respectively, compared to 14 percent by white caregivers. Caregivers report working fewer hours, tapping into savings, and reducing overall savings because of caregiving responsibilities (Rainville, Skufca, & Mehegan, 2016).

Although not as widely examined, increased attention is being paid to examining the positive impact of caregiving (Shultz & Eden, 2016). Some studies suggest that caregiving activities can build confidence and skills, provide a sense of purpose and meaning, and enhance relationships Also, family caregivers of individuals receiving HCBS can benefit from interventions such as education, individual and group support, and respite services. In particular, researchers have documented how various interventions have led to changes in dementia caregiver's knowledge, burden, self-efficacy, mental health (anxiety/depression), confidence, skills, and time to institutional placement as well as reductions in hospital readmissions and emergency room visits.

Many HCBS providers do not have a strong record of supporting family caregivers. There are two notable exceptions: adult day services (ADS) and hospice. The work of Zarit, Kim, Femia, Almeida, and Klein (2014) suggests that the respite ADS provides can reduce daily stress and increase positive affect of family caregivers of people with dementia. ADS programs with enhanced caregiver support, such as the ADS Plus program, appear to improve the quality of life of family caregivers through reduced levels of depression, enhanced well-being, and more confidence by the caregiver in managing challenging behaviors of the care recipient (Gitlin, Reever, Dennis, Mathieu, & Hauck, 2006). Hospice provides respite and support for family caregivers during the end of life process (see chapter 11). When compared to similar elderly spousal caregivers, those receiving hospice support had a lower mortality rate after becoming widowed, and women caregivers experienced the greatest reduction in mortality rate (Christakis & Iwashyna, 2003).

An Expert Weighs In

Caroline Rosenthal Gelman, PhD
Associate Dean for Academic & Faculty Affairs (Acting)
Silberman School of Social Work, Hunter College
New York, New York

Improvements in health care mean that more people are living longer, albeit with multiple complex chronic conditions, requiring that medical and nursing tasks be provided by untrained, poorly supported, family caregivers. Changes in family structure, unprecedented growth of minority populations, increasing numbers of women in the workforce, and financial pressures experienced in the context of an uncertain national picture for health insurance and long-term services and supports underscore the need for research in two main areas for family caregiving:

1. Understanding the experiences and needs of increasingly diverse family caregivers in ever-more complicated contexts; and
2. Developing, implementing, and evaluating interventions and policies to address these identified and expressed needs.

There is great variation in the experience of family caregivers, often shaped by characteristics such as race, ethnicity, socioeconomic status, and immigration status. It is critical for us to understand these varied, complex experiences to plan, implement, and evaluate relevant interventions and policies that successfully address these manifold needs. This is a critical area for future research in family caregiving, and questions remain. What interventions can be developed to provide culturally relevant and accessible information to family caregivers about different diseases? How will we provide person-centered respite and emotional support to facilitate and extend caregivers' capacity to provide care at home, which is both what most older adults and their families prefer and a tremendous public health imperative? How can technology be harnessed to assist in these endeavors? What policies can back such efforts and to what likely effect?

THE FUTURE OF FAMILY CAREGIVING

Caring for family members with physical and cognitive limitations will likely continue to create physical, psychological, social, and financial challenges for individuals, families, and society. The number of individuals available to provide care continues to decrease, and the number of individuals who need care continues to increase. HCBS are in a strong position to be leaders in providing needed education, psychosocial support, and respite services to enable family caregivers to continue in their helping roles. Opportunities exist for the private sector and large U.S. employers to create new workplace programs that keep their employees who are caregivers healthy and productive. In addition, new market opportunities exist that could reduce the burden of caregivers, such as MedCottages or "granny pods," which provide mobile, module, care dwellings placed on the property of caregivers. Despite these opportunities, the realities of the rising cost of health care and long-term care services and supports for individuals with disabilities may result in more family caregivers struggling to maintain their own mental, physical, and financial well-being. The future of family caregiving will likely be driven by cost-containment measures and creative program development and planning.

CHAPTER SUMMARY

- Family members or friends, not organizations, provide the majority of care for older adults.
- Changing demographic, economic, and social factors have influenced the context of family caregivers today.
- One of the most widely applied theoretical models related to the challenges and outcomes of family caregiving is the stress process model.
- Often putting the care recipient's needs first, family caregivers neglect their own health and well-being, which puts them at a higher risk for a number of mental and physical health challenges.

- Even though family caregivers are critical partners with providers of HCBS, the staff involved in providing care through HCBS often collects little information about family caregivers.
- Existing evidence suggests that family caregivers of individuals receiving HCBS can benefit from interventions such as education, individual and group support, and respite services.

DISCUSSION QUESTIONS AND EXERCISES

1. Review the statements in the Fact or Fiction? list near the beginning of the chapter. After reading this chapter, can you identify which are true and which are false?
2. Imagine you are a member of an interdisciplinary team at a hospital. What kind of questions might you ask the family caregiver about his or her ability to continue in that role?
3. Can you describe some situations in which an individual might be in a good position to be a family caregiver?
4. Describe the evidence regarding interventions for family caregivers that seem to work. Can you design a new program based on the stress process model that you think might result in positive outcomes for family caregivers?
5. There is limited funding for programs to support family caregivers directly. Most of our medical and social service systems are set up to provide care for the patient, client, or consumer. Imagine you are speaking with a member of Congress. What talking points would you share with him or her about the need for programs to support family caregivers?

ADDITIONAL RESOURCES

AARP Caregiver Information Center: http://www.aarp.org/home-family/caregiving/
Family Caregiver Alliance, National Center on Caregiving: http://www.caregiving.org/
Rosalynn Carter Institute for Caregiving: http://www.rosalynncarter.org/about_us/

REFERENCES

AARP Public Policy Institute & National Alliance for Caregiving. (2015). *Valuing the Invaluable: 2015 Update. Insight on the Issues.* Retrieved from http://www .aarp.org/content/dam/aarp/ppi/2015/valuing-the-invaluable-2015-update -new.pdf

Alzheimer's Association. (2016). *Risk factors*. Retrieved from http://www.alz.org /alzheimers_disease_causes_risk_factors.asp#age

Aranda, M. P., & Knight, B. G. (1997). The influence of ethnicity and culture on the caregiver stress and coping process: A sociocultural review and analysis. *The Gerontologist, 37*(3), 342–352.

Arias, E. (2016). *Changes in life expectancy by race and Hispanic origin in the United States, 2013–2014*. Data Brief No. 244. Centers for Disease Control, National Center for Health Statistics. Retrieved from http://www.cdc.gov/nchs/products /databriefs/db244.htm

Cannuscio, C. C., Jones, C., Kawachi, I., Colditz, G. A., Berkman, L., & Rimm, E. (2002). Reverberations of family illness: A longitudinal assessmet of informal caregiving and mental health status in the nurses' health study. *American Journal of Public Health, 92*(8), 1305–1311.

Carbonneau, H., Caron, C., & Desrosier, J. (2010). Development of a conceptual framework of positive aspects of caregiving in dementia. *Dementia, 9*(3), 327–353.

Christakis, N. A., & Iwashyna, T. J. (2003). The health impact of health care on families: A matched cohort study of hospice use by decedent and mortality outcomes in surviving, widowed spouses. *Social Science & Medicine, 57*(3), 465–475.

Family Caregiver Alliance. (2003). Women and caregiving: Facts and figures [updated 2015]. Retrieved from https://www.caregiver.org/women-and-caregiving -facts-and-figures

Family Caregiver Alliance. (2012). *Selected caregiver assessment measures: A resource inventory for practitioners* (2nd ed.). Retrieved from https://www.caregiver.org /selected-caregiver-assessment-measures-resource-inventory-practitioners-2012

Family Caregiver Alliance. (2017). Caregiver statistics: Demographics. Retrieved from https://www.caregiver.org/caregiver-statistics-demographics

Gaugler, J. E., & Kane, R. L. (2015). A perfect storm? The future of family caregiving. In *Family caregiving in the new normal* (pp. 357–380). Waltham, MA: Academic Press.

Gitlin, L. N., Reever, K., Dennis, M. P., Mathieu, E., & Hauck, W. W. (2006). Enhancing quality of life of families who use adult day services: Short- and long-term effects of the adult Day Services Plus program. *Gerontologist, 46*(5), 630–639.

Horne, J. (1986). Caregiver's bill of rights. In J. Horne (Ed.), *CareGiving: Helping an aging loved one*. Washington, D.C.: AARP Books. Retrieved from https:// www.caregiver.org/caregiver's-bill-rights

Johnson, R. W., Toohey, D., & Wiener, J. M. (2007). *Meeting the long-term care needs of the baby boomers: How changing families will affect paid helpers and institutions.* Retrieved from http://www.urban.org/sites/default/files/alfresco/publication-pdfs/311451-Meeting-the-Long-Term-Care-Needs-of-the-Baby-Boomers.PDF

Kiecolt-Glaser, J. K., McGuire, L., Robles, T. F., & Glaser, R. (2002). Psychoneuroimmunology and psychosomatic medicine: Back to the future. *Psychosomatic Medicine, 64,* 15–28.

Kim, H., Chang, M., Rose, K., & Kim, S. (2011). Predictors of caregiver burden in caregivers of individuals with dementia. *Journal of Advanced Nursing 68*(4), 846–855.

Lawton, M. P., Kleban, M. H., Moss, M., Rovine, M., & Glicksman, A. (1989). Measuring caregiving appraisal. *Journal of Gerontology: Psychological Sciences, 44*(3), 61–71.

Ortman, J. M, Velkoff, V. A., & Hogan, H. (2014). *An aging nation: The older populations in the United States.* Retrieved from https://www.census.gov/prod/2014pubs/p25-1140.pdf

Parker, K., & Patten, E. (2013). *The sandwich generation: Rising financial burdens for middle-aged Americans.* Pew Research Center. Retrieved from http://www.pewsocialtrends.org/2013/01/30/the-sandwich-generation/

Pearlin, L. I., Mullan, J. T., Semple, S .J., & Skaff, M. M. (1990). Caregiving and the stress process: An overview of concepts and their measures. *The Gerontologist, 30*(5), 583–594.

Rainville, C., Skufca, L., & Mehegan, L. (2016). *Family caregiving and out-of-pocket costs: 2016 report.* AARP Research. Retrieved from http://www.aarp.org/content/dam/aarp/research/surveys_statistics/ltc/2016/family-caregiving-cost-survey-res-ltc.pdf

Schulz, R., & Eden, J. (Eds.). (2016). *Families caring for an aging America.* National Academies of Sciences, Engineering, and Medicine, Committee on Family Caregiving for Older Adults. Washington, DC: National Academies Press.

Zarit, S. H., Kim, K., Femia, E. E., Almeida, D. M., & Klein, L. C. (2014). The effects of adult day services on family caregivers' daily stress, affect, and health: Outcomes from the Daily Stress and Health (DaSH) study. *The Gerontologist, 54*(4), 570–579.

Home Health Care

Home is where we belong. It is our experience, recollections, imagination, and aspirations. Home provides the physical and social context of life experience, burrows itself into the material reality of memories, and provides an axial core for our imagination.

CHAUDHURY & ROWLES, 2005, p. 3

LEARNING OBJECTIVES

In this chapter, you will:

- Learn about the evolution of home health care services.
- Gain an understanding of the services that are provided by home health care agencies and the older adults who receive these services.
- Examine eligibility requirements for home health care services.
- Learn about the funding mechanisms for home health care services and the cost of this care platform.
- Explore existing research on the effectiveness of home health care services for older adults.
- Look toward the future of home health care services and how this form of care can evolve to meet the desires and needs of the growing older adult population.

WE HAVE DISCUSSED THE COMPLEXITIES of delivering care in teams and the multifaceted nature of family caregiving. Much of this caregiving takes place in the *home*—a complex concept that encompasses the physical, emotional, social, communal, and spiritual domains of life. Any number of adages speak to the importance of home: Home is where the heart is. Home sweet home. There's no place like home. These sayings are permanent fixtures in our vernacular and are found in needlepoint and cross-stitching hung on our walls. Most people know what it feels like to be home and view their home as a place of comfort, security, familiarity, social engagement, and refuge. For older adults, who may have lived in their homes, apartments, and communities for many years, home can take on a special significance. Home is also a powerful symbol of independence for older adults, and we hold onto it closely and value it dearly. Given the significance of home, it is no wonder that older adults (and their family members) overwhelming prefer to receive their health care services in the home rather than in an institutional setting such as a hospital or nursing home. Fortunately, home health care has advanced in capacity and complexity to facilitate care at home for most older adults. *Home health care* is "the provision of healthcare services to people of any age at home or in other non-institutional setting" (Dieckmann, 2017, p. 9) Home health care has two key goals: "(1) direct provision of health services to those at home, and (2) the education and assistance of both patient and family toward the goals of health and independence from formal care systems" (Dieckmann, 2017, p. 10). "Home health care encompasses a wide range of health and social services. These services are delivered at home to recovering, disabled, chronically or terminally ill persons in need of medical, nursing, social, or therapeutic treatment and/or assistance with the essential activities of daily living" (National Association for Home Care & Hospice, 2017). This chapter describes how home health care has become the primary modality for delivering home- and community-based services for older adults in the United States and describes some of the challenges for this model of care.

FACT OR FICTION?

Consider the following statements.

- Home health care has a long history in the United States, beginning with the benevolent societies of the 1800s.

- Home health care services are limited to nursing services delivered by nursing assistants and health aides.
- Home health care services are primarily paid out of pocket by older adults and their families; Medicare and Medicaid only cover nursing home care.
- Home health care accounts for only a small percentage of overall health care spending in the United States.
- Research has yet to clearly demonstrate that certain types of home health care can be effective in reducing rehospitalization and containing costs of care.
- Home health care is expected to grow in the future as we become more capable of caring for complex conditions in home- and community-based settings.

After reading this chapter, you will be able to affirm which statements are fact and which are fiction.

HISTORY OF HOME HEALTH CARE IN THE UNITED STATES

As with other sectors of home- and community-based services (HCBS), the history of home health care has been driven by organizational strategies for delivering services, by social movements, and by patterns of funding (Harris, 2017). Home health care traces its roots back to the early 1800s when laypeople from "benevolent societies" went out in the field to care for the ill and for newborns and mothers. With the development of formal nursing education programs in the United States in the mid- to late-1800s, home health care took shape in the form of visiting nurse programs. These visiting nurses cared not only for the poor but also for the wealthy as private duty nurses. Visiting nursing programs blossomed during the Progressive Era (1905–1915) as the medical community learned more about the relationship between hygiene and communicable disease and began to employ infant mortality prevention measures (Hughes & Desai, 2016). These early home health programs were run by "voluntary agencies" often associated with charitable organizations. Other public health programs also provided home health services and were funding by local municipalities.

The Great Depression of the 1930s was marked by reductions in spending on home health programs by both government and voluntary agencies. Fortunately, several landmark policies and programs emerged during this time that buoyed the home health care industry, most notably portions of the Social Security Act, which opened federal funding to voluntary agencies. Public health nursing and visiting nursing programs continued to evolve in the 1940s as nursing education matured and the country wrestled with World War II. The next landmark in the history of home health came with initiation of Medicare and Medicaid in 1965. Medicare is a health insurance program for contributing individuals, and Medicaid is a health insurance program primarily for lower-income older adults and individuals with disabilities. "Adequate funding for home health care through Medicare and Medicaid was a welcome financial infusion for voluntary organizations, resulting in increased breadth of and among services provided" (Harris, 2017, p. 7). Originally a complementary service, home health care became a mandatory Medicaid benefit in 1967and was widely available by 1981when states could apply for Medicaid waiver programs. These waiver programs released funds for HCBS for lower-income older adults that would otherwise be used to pay for nursing home care (Hughes & Desai, 2016). Policies and economic and political trends continue to shape the industry, but home health care remains an essential component of our care approach for older adults (see chapter 13 for a description of these policies).

PRACTICE APPLICATION

The National Study of Long-Term Care Providers (NSLTCP) estimated that 12,400 home health care providers served approximately 5.3 million patients a year in 2014 (Harris-Kojetin et al., 2016). The study stated that home health agencies vary in size or capacity with 42 percent serving 1–100 patients, 27 percent serving 101–300 patients, and 31 percent serving 301 or more patients each year. The vast majority of home health providers are private, for-profit agencies (80 percent), and a much smaller number are either nonprofit (15 percent) or government operated (5 percent). The majority of home health agencies are free-standing entities and not part of a hospital system. Given the importance of government funding, almost all agencies are Medicare certified (99 percent) or Medicaid certified (78 percent). This simply means that they are eligible to receive reimbursement from these sources; however, it should be noted that many agencies accept private pay and insurance programs as well. To be Medicare and Medicaid certified, home health care agencies must adhere to certain conditions of participation regarding staffing, quality standards, billing, and reporting. This can be a tedious, costly, and time-consuming affair, but most home health care agencies choose to undergo the certification process.

So precisely what services are offered in home health care? Home health agencies have evolved from the visiting nurse programs of old to providers offering an array of increasingly complex services. Figure 6.1 illustrates the primary services offered in home health care, including skilled and basic nursing, therapeutic services such as physical therapy, occupational therapy and speech therapy, social work services, mental health screenings, pharmacy, and hospice care. Specific services, often coordinated, managed, or delivered by nurses, can include wound care, infusion therapies, injections, pain management, psychosocial assessments, case management, parental and enteral nutrition therapies, and safety monitoring. Patient and family education is an important thread that runs through all of these services with the goal being increased independence.

Staffing is largely dictated by the services offered by each home health agency and by reimbursement policies. Just over 53 percent of agencies employ full-time registered nurses, 19 percent employ full-time licensed practical or vocational nurses, 26 percent employ full-time aides, and 2 to 3 percent employ full-time social workers; however, most agencies employ these professionals at least on a part-time basis.

Home health agencies serve clients with a wide range of abilities, needs, living and family situations, and sociodemographics. Almost 83 percent of home health care patients are age 65 and older, and most are women (62 percent). The vast majority are non-Hispanic white (75 percent) with

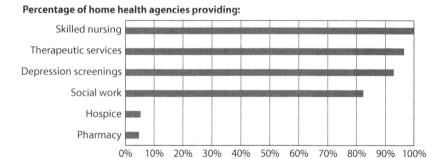

FIGURE 6.1 Services offered in home health care.
Source: Harris-Kojetin et al., 2016.

Percentage of home health care patients diagnosed with:

FIGURE 6.2   Health Conditions of home health care patients.

Source: Jones, Harris-Kojetin, & Valverde, 2012.

the remainder categorized as non-Hispanic black (14 percent), Hispanic (8 percent), and "other" (3 percent). Patients are referred to home health care by existing and former patients, hospital discharge planners, primary care practitioners (physicians, nurse practitioners), and hospices. Many older adults are referred to home health care following an acute event, such as a hospitalization, a surgery, or an emergency department visit. Data from 2007 revealed that the three most common diagnoses of home health care patients were hypertension (48 percent), heart disease (39 percent), and diabetes (32 percent; Jones, Harris-Kojetin, & Valverde, 2012; see figure 6.2 for more detailed information). In 2014, surveyors found that 45 percent of home health care patients had diabetes, 38 percent had depression, and 31 percent had some form of dementia (Harris-Kojetin et al., 2016). These differences may be related to changing disease rates and to different study methodologies; however, it is clear that home health care is providing services to patients with significant care needs and complex diagnoses. Many older adult home health care patients have multiple health conditions and require the services of an interprofessional team of care providers.

Perspectives from the Field

The National Association for Homecare and Hospice website includes a series of short stories from nurses working in home health care agencies across the United States. These stories document the lived experiences of home health care nurses and the impact nurses and patients can have on each other. A nurse in Arizona, for example, tells the story of caring for a 98-year-old home care patient with end-stage dementia. "Despite her cognitive problems and impaired speech, Margaret continued to teach indelible lessons well into her last days. She taught me that dementia can never silence a person's heart and soul, though it steals their power of speech." May, an 80-year-old home care patient speaks about her relationship with her home care nurse. "Janean is special in my life. I can depend on her. She's not only a nurse, she's like a friend." Take a moment now to read some of their stories at http://www.nahc.org/consumer-information /home-care-nurses-tell-their-stories-2015/.

ELIGIBILITY, COST, AND FUNDING FOR HOME HEALTH CARE

The two primary payer sources for home health care for older adults are Medicare and Medicaid. Home health care agencies must be Medicare or Medicaid certified to receive government reimbursement. Medicare Parts A and B covers home health care services for "homebound" individuals under the care of a physician who are certified by that physician to need intermittent skilled nursing care (not continuous or twenty-four-hour care) and therapeutic services. These therapeutic services are only available if one or more of the following conditions is met:

- Your condition must be expected to improve in a reasonable and generally predictable period of time.
- You need a skilled therapist to safely and effectively make a maintenance program for your condition.
- Or you need a skilled therapist to safely and effectively do maintenance therapy for your condition. (Medicare.gov, 2015)

The physician must certify that the older adult is "homebound," meaning that the older adult is primarily limited to the home except for short outings or for additional services, such as adult day care. It is important to remember that not all older adults are covered by Medicare Parts A and B. Medicare is an insurance program that older adults must pay into during their working careers. Medicare coverage for home health care is also time limited, and skilled nursing care is covered only if needed on an intermittent basis (less than seven days each week or less than eight hours each day). Coverage typically extends for twenty-one days or less and commonly follows discharge from an acute care setting such as a hospital. Exemptions to these stringent time limits are granted in certain situations (Agency for Health Care Administration, 2014).

Medicaid covers home health care services for low-income qualified older adults through state home- and community-based waiver programs. To be eligible for the Medicaid waiver program in the state of Florida, for example, older adults (defined as age 65 and older) must have an annual total income below $15,800 for a one-person household or an annual income of $21,307 for a two-person household. Older adults who qualify for Social Security Disability Insurance automatically qualify for Medicaid in Florida. The eligibility requirements for home health care for these older adults generally parallel the requirements previously discussed for Medicare. One key provision is that the home health services provided through the Medicaid waiver program cannot duplicate another provider's service. This is particularly relevant for those older adults who qualify for both Medicare and Medicaid—referred to as "dual eligible" (Agency for Health Care Administration, 2014). Medicaid benefits and eligibility criteria vary from state to state and change over time, particularly in states with waiver programs (Medicaid.gov, 2015). Contrary to Medicare-covered home health care, Medicaid-covered home health care is generally not as stringent in terms of time limits. Home health care can be ongoing and may be referred to as "custodial care." The goal of custodial care is to prevent or delay institutionalization and, in turn, save costs.

As with other health care programs, the cost and funding for home health care for older adults fluctuate with demand, reimbursement rates, and location. In 2016, the estimated national median rate for homemaker and home health aide services was approximately $20 per hour, an increase of 2.6 percent from 2015 and a five-year annual growth rate of 2.1 percent (Genworth Financial, 2016). These rates vary by location, as do the rates for other home health services. In Arizona, for example, the hourly rate for registered nursing services in the home range from approximately $36 to $62 depending on the activity involved. The hourly rate for physical therapists, occupational therapists, and speech pathologists was set at approximately $111 (Arizona Health Care Containment System, 2017). In Ohio, the hourly rate for registered nursing services was set at approximately $45, and the hourly rate for therapists was set at approximately $70

(Ohio Department of Medicaid, 2016). Note that these services are often billed and reimbursed in fifteen-minute blocks.

According to the latest spending estimates from the Centers for Medicare and Medicaid Services (CMS, 2016), government reimbursement to home health care agencies totaled $88.8 billion in 2015. Costs in the home health care sector increased by over 4 percent in 2014 and by over 6 percent in 2015. Medicare and Medicaid accounted for 76 percent of the spending ($67.5 billion) on home health care in 2015. Private health insurance and out-of-pocket spending accounted for the remainder of the annual cost ($21.3 billion). Although these dollar figures are large, it should be noted that home health care spending accounted for only 3 percent of the overall health care expenditures in 2015. For reference, hospital spending accounted for the largest percentage, an estimated 32 percent, or $1 trillion, of overall health care expenditures. Although home health care can be expensive, the costs are dwarfed by hospital expenditures. Home health care can play an important role in preventing hospitalization (and rehospitalization) and potentially reduce the cost of caring for older adults.

DIVERSITY IN HOME HEALTH CARE—A FOCUS ON MINORITY HEALTH

The Centers for Disease Prevention and Control (2017) states, "minority health determines the health of the nation," and reducing health disparities is a primary objective in health care. Disparities in health care for racial and ethnic minority older adults are fairly common across settings, and home health care is no different. These disparities exist on both the care recipient and care provider sides of home health care. In a recent national study of home health care, researchers found that non-white patients had lower scores that white patients in perceived quality of care and perceived quality of communications with care providers. "With regard to findings for specific minority groups, Asian, non-Hispanic patients reported the poorest experience with home health care of any minority groups" (Smith et al., 2015, p. 15). The researchers speculated that these differences could be related to differences in the expectations of patients, a lack of cultural competence in providers, and concordance or discordance between the race of care recipients and care providers. Access to quality home health care and culturally appropriate evidence-based interventions also contribute to health disparities for older adults of racial and ethnic minorities (Correa de Araujo, 2016).

Discordance on race and ethnicity (particularly in terms of language) has been linked with lower levels of job satisfaction of home health aides as well (Weng & Landes, 2016). In another study, black home health aides reported significantly higher levels of perceived racial discrimination on the job (Lee, Muslin, & McInerney, 2016). The research on disparities in home health is limited, but existing studies suggest that cultural competence training and person-centered care that incorporates the preferences of patients may hold promise in reducing disparities in experiences and perceptions. Recent initiatives, such as the Geriatric Workforce Enhancement Programs, are aware of the need for cultural competence in this sector and are developing and implementing training programs that help to reduce health disparities and racial discrimination in HCBS.

CASE STUDY

Nadif, a 78-year-old man, lives alone in Minneapolis, Minnesota. He retired twelve years ago from his work as a hotel clerk and collects a small income from savings and Social Security. Nadif was widowed ten years ago after his wife died of lung cancer. He has four adult daughters, two of whom live across town. Nadif immigrated to the United States in the 1980s from Somalia. He still holds his homeland close to his heart but is proud of his American citizenship. Nadif is a devout Muslim, attends mosque services regularly, and practices the customs of his Somali heritage. He is well-connected and has many friends in the Somali community in Minneapolis, the largest and oldest Somali population in the country.

Nadif has struggled with a degenerative condition in his joints caused by years of being on his feet in the hotel. Nadif's ability to take care of household chores, to walk, and to bathe and dress have progressively declined. He walks precariously and is at high risk of falls. Nadif has not been able to regularly attend services at his mosque, something that bothers him considerably. Nadif's daughters try to help, but he is reluctant to receive assistance, particularly in terms of bathing and dressing. Nadif's daughters are struggling to help their father while respecting his dignity, culture, and faith. Nadif's financial situation is unknown as he refuses to discuss money with his daughters. They contact you at the Area Agency on Aging for help.

1. What are the main factors involved in Nadif's situation that you must consider?
2. If you are not from the Somali community, how would you go about learning more about this culture?

(CONTINUED)

3. We tend to think that older adults prefer to have family members as their caregivers. Why is this not always the case?
4. What online resources are available to help inform and educate Nadif and his family members? (See the Family Caregiver Alliance for some ideas.)
5. What are some of your concerns if Nadif requires care beyond what can be provided by home health care services?

RESEARCH AND EVIDENCE

As we have seen and will see with other sectors of HCBS, gauging the effectiveness of home health care is not a simple matter. First, we need to identify quality measures to define effectiveness in this case. CMS (2017a) categorizes two types of quality measures: (1) outcome measures and (2) process measures. Outcome measures include the following:

- Improvement measures
  - Patients' general health and functional ability (for example, ADLs, mobility).
- Measures of potentially avoidable events
  - Occurrences that have a negative impact on patients and could potentially be prevented, such as falls.
- Utilization of care measures
  - Acute care hospitalization.
  - Rehospitalization within the first thirty days of home health.
  - Emergency department use with hospitalization.
  - Emergency department use without hospitalization.

Process measures refer to "the rate of home health agency use of specific evidence-based processes of care" (CMS, 2017a). Process measures include:

- Timeliness of home care admissions.
- Rate of immunization.
- Use of screening and risk assessment tools for falls, pain, depression, and pressure ulcers.
- Diagnosis specific measures, such as diabetes management and care planning for depression.

The latest data reported by CMS (2017b) indicates that certified home health agencies are highly effective in meeting these quality standards. For example:

- 92.9 percent of agencies initiated care in a timely manner.
- 96.8 percent educated family caregivers.
- 99.3 percent assessed for fall risk and 98.0 percent assessed for depression.
- 69.0 percent of patients improved in mobility.
- 72.6 percent of patients improved in their ability to bathe themselves.
- 90.3 percent of patients with wounds had improved healing.
- 16.3 percent of patients were readmitted to the hospital.
- 12.5 percent of patients required emergency department visits.

CMS (2017c) also collects patient satisfaction data and found the following:

- 88.5 percent of patients reported that the home health team provided care in a professional way.
- 85.0 percent of patients reported that the home health team communicated with them well.
- 84.0 percent of patients rated their home health agency as a 9 or a 10 on a scale from 0 (lowest) to 10 (highest).
- 78.0 percent of patients reported that they would recommend their home health agency to friends and family.

These data are nuanced and certainly warrant some interpretation. It appears that certified home health agencies are highly successful from a process standpoint (that is, initiating care and educating caregivers) and that patients seem quite satisfied with home health care services. There are varying degrees of success in terms of outcome measures, however, and it is challenging to compare these rates. For example, is a 12.5 percent rate of emergency department visits a sign of effectiveness, or does this illustrate a deficiency in home health care? Another issue is the fact that home health care is being called upon to provide care for increasingly more complex and acute conditions. This increases the risk of adverse events and health care utilization. We may see upward trends in the future, but this may not be an indicator of declining quality in home health care services.

Systematic reviews reveal mixed evidence in terms of differences in quality of care and outcomes based on the location of care, and researchers have called for additional studies before reaching conclusions about the effectiveness of home health care (Boland et al., 2017). Certain approaches and interventions in home health care have been effective, such as a depression management intervention (Bruce et al., 2015), a social work–based transitional care intervention (Boutwell, Johnson, & Watkins, 2016), and a technology-supported care transition support program for patients with heart failure and chronic obstructive pulmonary disease (Ritchie et al., 2016). These and other interventions have been shown to have potential benefits for home health care patients and their families and demonstrate the fact that the home setting can be an appropriate and effective location for care. Finally, we must consider the cost effectiveness of home health care. One area amenable to cost analyses is post acute care following hospitalization. This care can be provided in the home, in a facility (such as a nursing home or post acute care facility), or even in an adult day center. Researchers have found that referring patients to home health care following hospitalization is more cost effective than referring patients to in-patient post acute care in terms of both cost of care and rates of rehospitalization (Crowley et al., 2016; Sacks et al., 2016). Expanding the capacities and utilization of home health care may be one way to reduce the growing costs of post acute care (Mechanic, 2014).

An Expert Weighs In

Teresa Lee, JD, MPH
Past Executive Director, Alliance for Home Health Quality and Innovation
Arlington, Virginia

For many types of patients, home health care is the least restrictive and least costly alternative for post acute care, allowing patients to receive skilled nursing and therapy where they generally prefer to be—at home. In addition, Medicare home health care is often used for patients who reside in and are referred from the community. These patients meet the eligibility requirements of the Medicare home health benefit; they need intermittent skilled nursing or therapy services, meet the definition of homebound, and have a physician-established plan of care. One can think of these patients as "pre-acute" or "non-post-acute" patients who we seek to care for in the community to prevent any hospitalization or institutional care.

The government's efforts to ensure program integrity have led to heightened administrative requirements that present real-world barriers to delivering higher-quality and cost-effective health care to seniors. Further, physicians are not incentivized to coordinate care with home health agencies to serve their patients. Hospitals are increasingly seeing home health agencies as partners in addressing readmissions and controlling care in bundled payment episodes, but the challenge of dealing with a fragmented health care delivery system still plagues home health care.

The home health agency of the future should have four key characteristics: be patient and person centered, seamlessly connected and coordinated, of high quality, and technology enabled. This envisioned future for home health is challenged by key issues in the current environment, including financing and regulatory issues, and the need to shore up quality measurement approaches, workforce, operational capabilities, and the infrastructure for long-term care.

THE FUTURE OF HOME HEALTH CARE

"Home health care stands to be a 'big winner' with a substantial increase in utilization as a result of payment and delivery reforms" (Landers et al., 2016). This was one of the primary findings from the 2015 Institute of Medicine (IOM) and National Research Council (NRC) workshop on "The Future of Home Health Care." The leaders who attended this workshop indicated that home health care will continue to grow based on the following conditions (IOM & NRC, 2015; Landers et al., 2016):

- Home is preferred by patients and families as the location to receive care.
- Home health care has a lower-cost setting than post acute care.
- There is a trend toward more personalized and consumer-driven health care.
- Payment and reimbursement reforms will increasingly favor the use of home health care services.
- As technology advances, the capacity of home health care to serve complex needs will expand.
- Innovative models will continue to be developed that increase the effectiveness and cost-effectiveness of home health care.

Landers and colleagues suggested a model for home health care in the future (see figure 6.3). In this model, home health care sits at the hub of

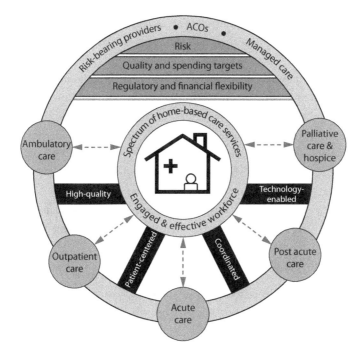

FIGURE 6.3 Model of the future of home health care.
Source: Avalere Health.

a wheel of services, including acute care, post acute care, outpatient care, ambulatory care such as physician office visits, and palliative care and hospice. Home health care is connected to these services through high-quality, coordinated, technology-enabled, and patient-centered care. If this model holds true in the future, the desires of patients and families will be met and the cost of caring for a growing older adult population will be less daunting—two lofty goals of shared importance.

CHAPTER SUMMARY

- Home health care has a long history in the United States, beginning in the 1800s with benevolent societies and public health nursing.
- Home health care services are delivered by a variety of health care professionals and include skilled nursing, basic nursing care and support, therapeutic services, case management services, pharmacy services, and education and support for older adults and their family caregivers.

- Medicare and Medicaid fund approximately three-quarters of home health care services. Private insurance and out-of-pocket payments cover the remainder.
- Home health care can help older adults remain in their homes and can delay or even prevent relocation from the home setting. Although research is not conclusive, certain home health care services and interventions effectively prevent adverse situations such as falls and reduce health care utilization such as hospitalizations.
- Patients and family members are generally quite satisfied with the services they receive through home health care agencies.
- The future of home health care is promising as we continue to find novel and cost-effective ways to care for older adults in their own homes.

DISCUSSION QUESTIONS AND EXERCISES

1. Review the statements in the Fact or Fiction? list near the beginning of the chapter. After reading this chapter, can you identify which are true and which are false?
2. Home health care services are interprofessional and are often delivered by coordinated teams. How might a team address the needs of the family in the case study for this chapter?
3. A number of policy issues related to the home health care industry are outlined on the National Association of Home Care & Hospice website. Please follow this link to learn more about these issues: http://www.nahc.org/advocacy-policy/.
4. Calculate the annual costs of home health care for a patient who needs home health aide services for ten hours per week and registered nursing care for two hours per week. Would this level of care be affordable for most older adults without the support of Medicare and Medicaid?
5. Using the Medicare Home Health Compare tool available at https://www.medicare.gov/homehealthcompare/search.html, locate and compare the certified home health care agencies in your area. Review the detailed survey results in terms of quality of patient care and patient satisfaction.

ADDITIONAL RESOURCES

Home Health Compare: https://www.medicare.gov/homehealthcompare/About/What-Is-HHC.html

Medicaid Home Health Care Services: https://www.medicaid.gov/medicaid
/index.html

Medicare Home Health Care Services: https://www.medicare.gov/coverage
/home-health-services.html

National Association for Home Care & Hospice: http://www.nahc.org

REFERENCES

Agency for Health Care Administration. (2014). *Home health services coverage and limitations handbook*. Retrieved from www.Home%20Health%20Services%20Coverage%20and%20Limitations%20Handbook_Adoption%20.pdf

Arizona Health Care Containment System. (2017). *FFS home and community-based services rates*. Retrieved from https://www.azahcccs.gov/PlansProviders/Downloads/FFSrates/HCBS/FSHCBSFinalRates20170101.pdf

Boland, L., Legare, F., Perez, M. M. B., Menear, M., Garvelink, M. M., McIsaac, D. I., . . . Stacey, D. (2017). Impact of home care versus alternative locations of care on elder health outcomes: An overview of systematic reviews. *BMC Geriatrics*. doi: 10.1186/s12877-016-0395-y

Boutwell, A. E., Johnson, M. B., & Watkins, R. (2016). Analysis of a social work-based model of transitional care to reduce hospital readmissions: Preliminary data. *Journal of the American Geriatrics Society, 64*(5), 1104–1107.

Bruce, M. L., Raue, P. J., Reilly, C. F., Greenberg, R. L., Myers, B. S., Banerjee, S., . . . Leon, A. C. (2015). Clinical effectiveness of integrating depression care management into Medicare home health: The depression CAREPATH randomized trial. *JAMA Internal Medicine, 175*(1), 55–64.

Centers for Disease Prevention and Control. (2017). *Health disparities*. Retrieved from https://www.cdc.gov/aging/disparities/

Centers for Medicare & Medicaid Services. (2016). *National health expenditures 2015 highlights*. Retrieved from https://www.cms.gov/Research-Statistics-Data-and-Systems/Statistics-Trends-and-Reports/NationalHealthExpendData/Downloads/highlights.pdf

Centers for Medicare & Medicaid Services. (2017a). *Quality measures*. Retrieved from https://www.cms.gov/Medicare/Quality-Initiatives-Patient-Assessment-Instruments/HomeHealthQualityInits/HHQIQualityMeasures.html

Centers for Medicare & Medicaid Services. (2017b). *Home health care—national data*. Retrieved from https://data.medicare.gov/Home-Health-Compare/Home-Health-Care-National-Data/97z8-de96

Centers for Medicare & Medicaid Services. (2017c). *Home health care—Patient survey.* Retrieved from https://data.medicare.gov/Home-Health-Compare /Home-Health-Care-Patient-survey-HHCAHPS-National-D/vxub-6swi

Chaudhury, H., & Rowles, G. D. (2005). Between the shores of recollection and imagination: Self aging, and home. In H. Chaudhury & G. D. Rowles (Eds.), *Home and identity in later life: International perspectives* (pp. 3–20). New York, NY: Springer.

Correa de Araujo, R. (2016). Health disparities: Access and utilization. In L. Cummings-Vaughn & D. M. Cruz-Oliver (Eds.), *Ethnogeriatrics: Healthcare needs of a diverse population* (pp. 89–114). New York, NY: Springer.

Crowley, C. Stuck, A. R., Martinez, T., Wittgrove, A. C., Zeng, F., Brennan, J. J., . . . Castillo, E. M. (2016). Survey and chart review to estimate Medicare cost savings for home health as an alternative to hospital admission following emergency department treatment. *Journal of Emergency Medicine, 51*(6), 643–647.

Dieckmann, J. L. (2017). Home health care: A historical perspective and overview. In M. D. Harris (Ed.), *Handbook of home health care administration* (pp. 9–26). Burlington, MA: Jones & Bartlett Learning.

Genworth Financial. (2016). *Genworth cost of care survey 2016.* Retrieved from https://www.genworth.com/dam/Americas/US/PDFs/Consumer/corporate /131168_050516.pdf

Harris, M. D. (2017). Early development of home health. In M.D. Harris (Ed.), *Handbook of home health care administration* (pp. 1–8). Burlington, MA: Jones & Bartlett Learning.

Harris-Kojetin, L., Sengupta, M., Park-Lee, E., Valverde, R., Caffrey, C., Rome, V., & Lendon, J. (2016). Long-term care providers and services users in the United States: Data from the National Study of Long-Term Care Providers, 2013–2014. *Vital Health Statistics, 3*(38). Retrieved from https://www.cdc.gov/nchs/data /series/sr_03/sr03_038.pdf

Hughes, S. L., & Desai, P. (2016). Home health care. In G. B. Rowles & P. B. Teaster (Eds.), *Long-term care in an aging society: Theory and practice* (pp. 115–147). New York, NY: Springer.

Institute of Medicine & National Research Council. (2015). *The future of home health care: Workshop summary.* Washington, DC: National Academies Press.

Jones, A. L., Harris-Kojetin, L., & Valverde, R. (2012). *Characteristics and use of home health care by men and women aged 65 and older.* Retrieved from https:// www.cdc.gov/nchs/data/nhsr/nhsr052.pdf

Landers, S., Madigan, E., Leff, B., Rosati, R. J., McCann, B. A., Hornbake, R., . . . Breese, E. (2016). The future of home health care: A strategic framework for optimizing value. *Home Health Care Management & Practice, 28*(4), 262–278.

Lee, D., Muslin, I., & McInerney, M. (2016). Perceived racial discrimination among home health aides: Evidence from a national survey. *Journal of Health and Human Services Administration, 38*(4), 414–437.

Mechanic, R. (2014). Post-acute care—the next frontier for controlling Medicare spending. *New England Journal of Medicine, 370,* 692–694.

Medicaid.gov. (2015). *State Medicaid & CHIP profiles.* Retrieved from https://www.medicaid.gov/medicaid/by-state/by-state.html

Medicare.gov. (2015). *Your Medicare coverage: Home health services.* Retrieved from https://www.medicare.gov/coverage/home-health-services.html

National Association of Home Care & Hospice. (2017). *What is home care?* Retrieved from http://www.nahc.org/faq/#110

Ohio Department of Medicaid. (2016). *Home health rates.* Retrieved from http://www.medicaid.ohio.gov/Portals/0/Providers/FeeScheduleRates/HomeHealth/HHS-20160101.pdf

Ritchie, C. S., Houston, T. K., Richman, J. S., Sobko, H. J., Berner, E. S., Taylor, B. B., . . . Locher, J. L. (2016). The E-Coach technology-assisted care transition system: A pragmatic randomized trial. *Translational Behavioral Medicine, 6*(3), 428–437.

Sacks, G. D., Lawson, E. H., Dawes, A. J., Weiss, R. E., Russell, M., Brook, R. H., . . . Ko, C. Y. (2016). Variation in hospital use of postacute care after surgery and the association with care quality. *Medical Care, 54*(2), 172–179.

Smith, L. M., Anderson, W. L., Kenyon, A., Kinyara, E., With, S. K., Teichman, L., . . . Goldstein, E. (2015). Racial and ethnic disparities in patients' experiences with skilled home health care services. *Medical Care Research and Review, 72*(6), 756–774.

Weng, S. S., & Landes, S. D. (2016). Culture and language discordance in the workplace: Evidence from the National Home Health Aide Survey. *Gerontologist.* doi:10.1093/geront/gnw110

7

The Village Concept and Naturally Occurring Retirement Communities

Perhaps the most heartening thing is the extent to which seniors are taking matters into their own hands. In many parts of the country, they are not waiting for government or professionals to act. . . . We have much to learn from these efforts as the older generation harnesses its lifetime of skills, knowledge, and experience, and transforms its communities into good places in which to grow old.

VLADECK, 2005, p. 121

LEARNING OBJECTIVES

In this chapter, you will:

- Gain an understanding of the features of a naturally occurring retirement community (NORC) and the Village model.
- Explore the services provided in NORCs and Villages.
- Identify ways in which a needs assessment can be utilized to plan and implement services and supports in NORCs.
- Review the existing and emerging research on NORCs and Villages.
- Explore future directions for aging in place in NORCs and Villages.

HOME HEALTH CARE SERVICES PLAY an important role in helping older adults remain in their homes and in their communities. Ninety percent of adults over age 65 want to age in place (Farber et al., 2011). *Aging in place* is the ability of a person to remain living in his or her home (sometimes with the use of supportive services) in spite of age or health-related changes that may make it challenging to do so (Fields & Dabelko-Schoeny, 2015). The desire to age in place has spurred a movement toward "age-friendly communities." Characteristics of age-friendly communities include age-appropriate housing, navigable and available transportation options, opportunities for socialization and social inclusion, access to employment and volunteer opportunities, and available and affordable support and health care services (World Health Organization, 2007). Traditional HCBS help older adults age in place, but some models of cooperative community care have emerged organically from older adults themselves. Groups of older adults have taken proactive steps in designing care programs rather than accepting the sometimes limited and limiting options available in their communities. In this chapter, we discuss two types of community-based models within the aging service network that help older adults age in place: naturally occurring retirement communities and the Village concept.

Naturally occurring retirement communities (NORCs) are communities such as housing developments, apartment complexes, or neighborhoods that were not originally built for older adults but where large numbers of older adults have either continued to live over time (aged in place) or to which older adults have relocated (Hunt & Gunter-Hunt, 1985). NORCs are not planned retirement communities; rather, they have emerged "naturally" as places with high concentrations of older adults. Typically, NORCs appear in geographical regions densely populated with older adults. However, NORCs are not limited to metropolitan areas and also may be found in some rural areas. Many suburban areas are beginning to see the advent of NORCs as well. As NORCs are not intentionally designed for older residents, they may not have the health and supportive social services older adults may need to age in place.

The *Village model* shares similarities with NORCs; however, Villages are founded and led by older adults. The Village is a membership-driven grassroots community run by volunteers as well as paid staff who help coordinate access to affordable and vetted services for older adults living in the community (Village to Village Network, n.d.). The aim of a Village is to help older adults remain in their own home for as long as possible with the support of staff and volunteer services such as transportation, companionship, housekeeping, handyman, yard care, assistance with technology, and advocacy for health care needs (Graham, Scharlach, & Wolf, 2014).

Consider the following statements.

- NORCs and Villages are cost-reduction initiatives introduced by the Centers for Medicare and Medicaid Services.
- NORCs and Villages identify promoting older adults' access to service as their most important goal, followed by reducing social isolation.
- The Village model depends heavily on involvement from the consumer, and health care professionals largely play a "contractual" role.
- Villages rely on membership dues rather than government funding, grants, or service fees.
- NORCs and Villages are limited to urban areas due to the enhanced sense of community and neighborhood in these areas.

After reading this chapter, you will be able to affirm which statements are fact and which are fiction.

HISTORY AND CURRENT STATES OF NORCS AND VILLAGES

The population of individuals age 65 and over is projected to be 83.7 million by 2050 (Ortman, Velkoff, & Hogan 2014). In many cities and rural areas across the United States, large numbers of older adults want to age in place in the homes where they have lived for many years. Large numbers of older adults are aging in place in concentrated neighborhoods, apartment buildings, or housing complexes called naturally occurring retirement communities (NORCs), a term coined in 1985 by Michael Hunt at the University of Wisconsin. NORCs are typically housing complexes or neighborhoods that were not initially designed for older people but that became de facto retirement communities over time as large numbers of residents became older adults. A geographic area is generally defined as a NORC if more than 50 percent of the residents are at least 60 years old; however, some studies report proportions as low as 25 percent and a minimum age of 50 years old (Hunt, Arch, & Ross, 1990; Ivery & Akstein-Kahan, 2010; Ormond, Black, Tilly, & Thomas, 2004).

The NORC model was first identified in 1986 at a cooperative of apartments located in New York City (Altman, 2005). Since that time, approximately 100 NORC programs have been developed in the United States, and roughly half are located in New York (Greenfield, Scharlach, Lehning, Davitt, & Graham, 2013). There are two types of NORCs: vertical and horizontal. Vertical NORCs (also known as housing-based NORCs) are located within a single age-integrated apartment building, housing complex, or an area in which several apartment buildings are grouped together. Horizontal NORCs (also known as neighborhood-based NORCs) are typically one- to two-story family homes in a geographically defined area of the community (Scharlach & Lehning, 2016). Both types of NORCs evolved as a result of the aging in place of existing older adults and relocation of older adults to these areas because of the NORCs location and features.

NORCs were not intentionally designed for older adults, and they typically do not have services that support individuals who want to age in place. Some NORCs are "healthier" than others because of the existing physical and social environment. Masotti, Fick, Johnson-Masotti, and MacLeod (2006) have identified some key characteristics of a healthy NORC:

- A vibrant senior community with large numbers of individuals being physically and socially active.
- Sidewalks and walking paths are well-lit, clean, and accessible.
- Basic needs and amenities are within walking distance.
- Adequate public transportation.
- Perceived as safe and free from crime.
- Opportunities exist to participate in formal and informal social and physical activities.
- Presence of community activities and participation is encouraged.
- Regular, unplanned, social interaction for residents occurs.
- Local government involvement and participation by older adults.
- Local governments have policies that are friendly toward older adults.
- Private sector markets respond to the needs of older persons.

NORCs and the Village model share many similar features, including an emphasis on aging in place in a particular geographical location, the coordination of support systems for older adults, enhancing older adults' civic engagement, and increasing the availability, accessibility, and affordability of existing services (Greenfield, Scharlach, Lehning, & Davitt, 2012).

However, the Village model is distinct from NORCs in that they are typically initiated and managed by the older adults that live there. Villages rely on membership dues rather than government funding, grants, or service fees (McWhinney-Morse, 2009). The Village model dates back to 2001 with the founding of Beacon Hill Village in Boston, Massachusetts, by a group of older adults who wanted to age in place. The Beacon Hill Village organized a grassroots membership with a focus on three key areas: community building through shared social activities, information and services for members, and health care and wellness (McWhinney-Morse, 2009). Since development of the Village model, at least 200 Villages have opened, and more than 150 are in development (Village to Village Network, n.d.)

As a part of the Village model, services and programs are prescreened for residents, and members gain access to affordable or discounted services through these vetted providers for an annual fee. Membership dues are approximately $429 per year on average and provide members with access to social and emotional support, educational and recreational activities, transportation, health care advocacy, shopping, technological assistance, and home maintenance and repair (Greenfield et al., 2013). Many Villages offer discounted memberships or scholarships to help low-income residents (Lehning, Davitt, Scharlach, & Greenfield, 2014). Studies suggest that Village members may benefit from reduced isolation, expanded access to supports and services for aging in place, and increased well-being (Graham et al., 2014).

Typically, the Village model is dependent on involvement by the consumer, and these older adults tend to be more functionally independent, more economically secure, and have more socioeconomic resources than residents in NORCs. In contrast to NORC residents, Village consumers tend to oversee the operations of the Village, provide supportive peer services, and finance the Village organization (Greenfield et al., 2013). However, funding is one of the most common challenges to the sustainability of Villages because membership dues may not provide enough financial support for the organization (Lehning, Scharlach, Wolf, Davitt, & Wiseman, 2015). The Village model has seven core characteristics (Scharlach & Lehning, 2016):

- Grassroots (developed by the consumers).
- Membership-driven (members are leaders).

- Self-governing (independent, not for profit).
- Self-supporting (dues and donations).
- Service provision (by paid staff or volunteers).
- Service coordination (prescreened, discounted providers).
- Holistic approach (services to meet needs of members).

MODELS OF CARE IN NORCS AND VILLAGES

Older adults who wish to age in place face many challenges. The NORC-Supportive Services Program (NORC-SSP) was developed because residents in NORCs were found to be aging in place without services or supports that they may need. The United Jewish Appeal Federation of New York was instrumental in developing the first NORC-SSP for older adults in age-integrated, multiunit, housing developments (Altman, 2005). The NORC-SSP is designed as a community-level intervention that allows older residents living in a NORC to access a variety of health and social services on-site or provided nearby to assist with aging in place (Bedney, Goldberg, & Josephson, 2010). The NORC-SSP recognizes that medical care (diagnosis, treatment), community care (resources, support), and self-care (lifestyle choices, empowerment) are all fundamental components for aging in place (Kyriacou & Vladeck, 2011; see figure 7.1).

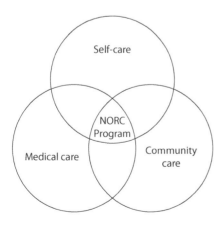

FIGURE 7.1

Components of a NORC-SSP.

Source: Adapted from Kyriacou & Vladeck, 2011.

Service providers that collaborate with a NORC-SSP typically offer case management and social work services, health care management, health care prevention programs, education, social and recreational activities, and volunteer opportunities (Greenfield, Scharlach, Lehning, & Davitt, 2012). Service coordinators may provide counseling; service referrals; collaborate with building managers, local organizations, and businesses; recruit volunteers; raise awareness about the NORC-SSP; and lead efforts to meet the needs of residents (Bedney et al., 2010). Service coordinators also may monitor residents and watch for signs of physical, emotional, or cognitive decline.

DEFINING ELEMENTS OF A NORC-SSP

- Coordinated health services, social services, and activities on-site including:
  - social work
  - case management
  - education
  - recreation
  - volunteerism
- Partnerships that unite housing entities with:
  - residents
  - health/social service providers
  - government organizations
  - philanthropic organizations
- Promotion of independence and healthy aging by:
  - engaging older adults before a crisis
  - responding to the changing needs of older adults over time
- Provision of older adults with vital roles such as:
  - development/operation of the program
  - governance
  - volunteer opportunities
- Fill gaps in existing services that may be insufficient or inadequate including:
  - Medicare
  - Medicaid
  - Older Americans Act

Source: Bedney, Goldberg, & Josephson, 2010.

NORC-SSPs receive funding from a variety of sources including government agencies, housing partners, philanthropic organizations, corporations, and residents (Greenfield, Scharlach, Graham, Davitt, & Lehning, 2012). Both private and nonprofit organizations with professional staff typically provide the leadership in NORC programs and oversee the services of the program (Greenfield et al., 2013). However, NORC residents are considered essential to the NORC-SSP's development, governance, and volunteer service provision (Greenfield & Fedor, 2015). An important feature of the NORC model is that it aims to strengthen older adults' relationships with the community and creates opportunities for older adults to help one another (Greenfield, 2014). The foundational principles of the NORC-SSP model are empowerment and community building (Enguidanos, Pynoos, Denton, Alexman, & Diepenbrock, 2010). Older adults are viewed as contributors to their own well-being and the well-being of others through mutual assistance and neighbors helping neighbors (Bookman, 2008).

Similar to NORC-SPPs, the Village model offers services and support to help older adults remain independent for as long as possible and age and place. The Village to Village (VtV) Network was formed in 2010 as a national organization to help maximize the growth, impact, and sustainability of Villages (Village to Village Network, n.d.). The VtV Network offers technical assistance, facilitates the sharing of resources, and helps to organize national and regional meetings. The VtV Network is "the largest and fastest growing of all of the age-friendly development networks" (Grantmakers in Aging, 2013, p. 16).

In 2012, more than one-third of all Villages were directly or indirectly involved in efforts to make their communities more age friendly (Scharlach, Davitt, Lehning, Greenfield, & Graham, 2014).The eight domains of age-friendly communities are outdoor spaces and buildings, transportation, housing, social participation, respect and social inclusion, civic participation and employment, communication and information, and community and health services (WHO, 2007). In one national study, 85.5 percent of Villages provided assistance in many of these domains:

- Social participation (social, cultural, or recreational gatherings were offered by 93 percent of Villages).
- Civic participation (volunteer opportunities were offered by 86 percent of Villages).

- Community support services (friendly visitors were offered by 87 percent of Villages; financial services by 58 percent; legal services by 55 percent; and care management by 77 percent).
- Health services (health/medical services were offered by 48 percent of Villages; home health care or personal care by 80 percent of Villages).
- Communication and information (central phone number or email for information assistance was offered by 99 percent of Villages).
- Transportation (transportation assistance was offered by 99 percent of Villages).
- Housing (home repair/maintenance was offered by 97 percent of Villages and house cleaning/housekeeping by 81 percent). (Scharlach et al., 2014)

However, questions remain as to whether the efforts of the Village truly enhance the age-friendliness of communities. The Village model may play an important role in the future of aging-friendly initiatives both nationally and internationally.

CASE STUDY

Elise Johnson, age 75, is a retired teacher who lives in a northern suburb of Charlotte, North Carolina. Her husband passed away approximately five years ago, and she has been living alone since his death. Her three children live in various cities throughout North Carolina, but none live nearby. Mrs. Johnson has lived in the same home and neighborhood for nearly fifty years. Many of her neighbors did the same and have also remained in their homes through the years.

Recently, Mrs. Johnson has been finding it difficult to manage her household tasks including cleaning, grocery shopping, and cooking. She has stopped driving at night. Her adult children have expressed concerns that she lives alone and have encouraged her to consider moving to a retirement community. Mrs. Johnson is strongly against moving to a retirement community because of her ties to her neighbors and their neighborhood. At a recent supper club with her neighbors, Mrs. Johnson learned about the Village model. The next day, Mrs. Johnson calls you, a staff person at the greater Charlotte Area Agency on Aging, to ask about creating a Village for older adults in her neighborhood.

Consider these questions in relation to this case:

1. What types of services and supports does Mrs. Johnson currently need or anticipate needing in order to age in place?

(CONTINUED)

2. What home- and community-based services exist that might support Mrs. Johnson and her neighbors in their pursuit of aging in place?

3. What type of social support network is in place within Mrs. Johnson's neighborhood (such as transportation assistance, community engagement activities, or grocery store/errands volunteers)?

4. What key partnerships with health and other social service providers does Mrs. Johnson need to consider for the creation of a successful Village model?

PRACTICE APPLICATION

Bringing services and supports to NORCs is an important part of enabling older adults to age in place. However, a comprehensive assessment should be conducted to identify the specific needs of the community, the NORC, and residents. A needs assessment can help determine gaps in services, locate missing links between services and the community, and identify the accessibility and availability of services. A needs assessment might include focus groups or a survey of residents as well as an assessment of the residents' needs from the perspective of service providers. Focus group sessions with older adults may include questions such as these:

- What are the needs of older adults in this community?
- What features of this community make it a place where you want to age in place?
- What help do you need to access services and supports?
- If you could create a service to meet a need in this community, what would it be?

A needs assessment survey is used to collect data from older residents about their perceived need for services and supports in the NORC. Various methods can be used to distribute the survey, such as through the mail or through existing service providers, and efforts should be made to reach diverse groups of older adults. The survey should elicit information about the health, wellness, and needs of older adults in the NORC, including their need for supportive services and the supportive services that they currently use. A variety of other information should be gathered from older residents including their physical and social activities, activities of interest, and barriers to participating in activities such as transportation access and availability.

The involvement of service providers is integral to implementing supports for older adults in NORCs. Interviews and focus groups with service providers to identify the needs of older adults as well as the perceived barriers to service use may be included in the needs assessment. Services providers including health and social service agencies, medical facilities, personal care services, fire/police departments, senior advocacy groups, and public and private transportation services may all provide valuable information for the needs assessment. Questions for service providers may include these issues:

- What do you perceive as service gaps for older adults in this community?
- What do you perceive as barriers to service provision for older adults in this community?
- What level of awareness do you think older adults have about services and supports in this community?
- If you could provide one new service that older adults in this community need, what would it be?

A comparison of the three parts of the needs assessment (resident focus groups, resident surveys, and provider interviews) will indicate consistencies as well as differences in the identified needs of older adults who want to age in place. The information collected as part of the needs assessment should inform the planning, implementation, and evaluation of services and supports for NORC residents.

Perspectives from the Field

Interview with Joanna Stolove, LCSW
Assistant Director, Morningside Retirement and Health Services, Inc.
New York, New York

What is your professional background and training?

I have a master's degree in social work and completed postgraduate work in psychoanalytic psychotherapy. The majority of my career has been spent as a clinical social worker.

What does your average day look like working in a NORC?

Case management work varies from supportive counseling to addressing more complex needs, such as maintaining residents with advanced dementia in their homes. Complicated cases can involve acting as a liaison with the family and home health aides, providing daily money management, seeking outside opportunities for engagement, and monitoring medical care with the assistance of our nurse. Administrative tasks include managing and updating the agency website, editing social media, and managing our email outreach.

What successes and challenges have you faced in working in NORCs?

The community has to be invested in the NORC for it to be successful. Morningside Retirement and Health Services was founded in 1966 on two principles: self-help for older adults and neighbors helping neighbors. One of the challenges we are currently facing is the changing demographics of the community.

What do you see as the future of NORCs?

As our family structures continue to change, older adults may need to rely more and more on their community. This is a cost-effective program that allows older adults to remain in their community with an emphasis on their quality of life.

What advice would you give to someone who is interested in working in a NORC?

I would suggest having an interest in community-based work. NORC-based work also requires flexibility because your role will vary depending on the circumstances.

DIVERSITY IN NORCS AND VILLAGES—A FOCUS ON LGBT OLDER ADULTS

Lesbian, gay, bisexual, and transgender (LGBT) older adults have unique needs and face challenges and barriers that are often distinct from those of the general population. Emlet (2016) found that LGBT older adults have higher rates of health risk behaviors (such as smoking and drinking), higher rates of mental health issues, greater limitations in activities of daily living (ADLs), and higher rates of disability in comparison to their heterosexual older adult counterparts. Some of these disparities are the direct result of a lack of access to health care services, especially services that are culturally appropriate. LGBT older adults also are more likely to be economically disadvantaged due to institutional and societal discrimination such as hiring practices and marriage laws. Poverty can have corrosive effects on well-being and health (for a succinct review, see Emlet, 2016). Health and social services need to be tailored to the needs and preferences of this population.

Services and Advocacy for LGBT Elders (SAGE) is a NORC that serves LGBT older people of color in Harlem, New York. Most of the individuals in the SAGE Harlem NORC are African American and Latino. The goals of the SAGE Harlem NORC include increasing awareness of the needs of LGBT older adults, making services and supports more available to LGBT older adults, and providing culturally competent services for LGBT older adults in Harlem. The SAGE Harlem NORC is a "safe space" for LGBT older adults that provides opportunities for participation and socialization, offers social services, facilitates educational opportunities, and raises the visibility of unique issues facing LGBT older adults.

RESEARCH AND EVIDENCE

Although Village and NORC models have been well described in the literature, more research is needed to analyze the approach and implementation of these programs. A retrospective survey of 282 Village members from five Village sites in California examined the impact of Village membership on a number of issues: (1) social engagement, (2) perceived service and health care access, (3) perceived health and well-being, and (4) self-efficacy and maintaining independence (Graham et al., 2014). The researchers found that Village membership had the strongest impact on providing social engagement, facilitating access to services, and enhancing members' confidence in their ability to age in place. Fewer positive impacts were found among Village members who were in poorer health, which calls into question the effectiveness of the Village model for older adults who are frail and in need of higher levels of health-related care services. In a longitudinal study, Village members reported greater confidence and perceptions of support and were more likely to feel confident about aging in place after one year of membership (Graham, Scharlach, & Kurtovich, 2016). However, the researchers indicated that Villages focus more on meeting the social than the health care needs of older adults, which may become an issue in the future for members who begin to experience health-related declines. Other researchers point out that lack of a uniform definition of the Village model makes it difficult to collect empirical evidence related to outcomes of Village membership (Lehning, Scharlach, & Davitt, 2017) and suggest that more research is needed to establish the efficacy of this model for aging in place.

In a small study of fifty-eight older adults, those who received support with health and social work services, transportation services, and activities through the NORC-SSP felt less socially isolated and less depressed than those who did not participate in the program (Cohen-Mansfield, Dakheel-Ali, & Frank, 2010). Another study suggests that residents in vertical NORC-SSPs receive a greater number of services and report greater satisfaction with the program than residents in horizontal, neighborhood NORCs (Enguidanos et al., 2010).

More research is needed regarding outcomes for older adults in both NORC and Village settings. Moreover, current research suggests that both NORC and the NORC-SSP are in need of public investment, conceptual frameworks, metrics, and infrastructure to demonstrate the efficacy of these settings (Scharlach, Lehning, Davitt, Greenfield, & Graham, 2017; Vladeck & Altman, 2015). Finally, Greenfield and colleagues (2013) surveyed sixty-two NORCs and sixty-nine Villages to measure the benefits and services offered by these programs, types of services provided, types of service environment, how services are provided, characteristics of program beneficiaries, and sources of funding. Here is a summary of the study findings:

- Most NORCs and Villages identify promoting older adults' access to services as their most important goal, followed by reducing social isolation.
- NORCS are more likely to provide assistance with home delivered or congregate meals, whereas Villages are more likely to provide assistance with transportation, technology assistance, and home maintenance and repair.

- NORCs are more likely than Villages to offer health care, health promotion activities, and social services.
- NORC programs are most likely to be located in apartment buildings or neighborhoods, whereas Villages are more likely to encompass larger catchment areas.
- NORC programs are more likely to be in communities with low to middle socioeconomic status; older adults in Villages are more likely to have middle to high or high socioeconomic status.
- NORC programs are more likely to serve adults aged 85 and older, and Villages are more likely to serve adults aged 65 to 74.
- NORC programs have a greater percentage of impoverished, economically insecure individuals who need help with household tasks.
- NORC programs have more paid staff than Villages.
- A greater numbers of services in Villages are being provided by older member as volunteers.
- Membership dues comprise a larger portion of the budgets of Villages, whereas government grants and contracts comprise the largest portion of the budget for NORC programs.

An Expert Weighs In

Emily A. Greenfield, PhD
Associate Professor, School of Social Work
Affiliate of the Institute for Health, Health Care Policy, & Aging Research
Rutgers, The State University of New Jersey

NORC programs and Villages—models that emerged most prominently across the United States in the early 2000s—exemplify innovation in supportive services for older adults. Both models, for example, explicitly seek to integrate individual service delivery within broader community-change efforts. Both models strategically aim to integrate formal and informal sources of care for older adults in need. And both models focus on offering a range of supports across a continuum of prevention and intervention. Despite the broad appeal of the models for reasons such as these, NORC programs and Villages are more the exception than the rule when it comes to aging services available within any given community. Therefore, a critical direction for research is to understand the diverse community, organizational, and societal contexts that influence the start-up and maintenance of NORC programs and Villages. For example, are there key indicators to identify which communities have the best likelihood of long-term operations? What is the place of more rigorous evidence regarding the impact of NORC programs and Villages on individual outcomes to encourage greater investments in these models? How can leaders leverage nationwide innovations, especially within health care, to support the expansion of NORC programs and Villages? How might the program models themselves evolve in response to shifting political, financial, and social landscapes for health and social services? Such research offers the potential to strengthen NORC programs and Villages, but it also encourages more robust research, policy, and practice on aging services in general.

FUTURE OF NORCS AND VILLAGES

Age in place is of growing concern for older adults who choose to continue to live in their familiar homes and neighborhoods but who will eventually require supports and services to meet their physical, psychological, and social needs. The current system of supports and services for older adults is often fragmented and uncoordinated, resulting in substantial unmet needs for this population (Harrington, Ny, Kaye, & Newcomer, 2009). As communities begin to focus on how to make cities more livable for older adults, there is a greater need to include home- and community-based services in these initiatives. NORCs and Villages have emerged as promising community models for promoting age-friendly communities and supporting aging in place as they strive to enhance the social connectivity, independence, and well-being of older adults. The future of NORCs and Villages will likely depend on the ongoing efforts of both older adults and service providers to create accessible, sustainable, cost-effective programs in these settings.

CHAPTER SUMMARY

- NORCs are communities not originally built for older adults but that have evolved as large numbers of older adults have either aged in place or relocated to these communities.

- The Village model is a membership-driven grassroots community organization that helps to coordinate access to affordable, prescreened services for older adults.
- More research is required to examine the outcomes for older adults in both NORCs and Villages; research related to the organizational and societal contexts that influence the sustainability of these communities is needed.
- NORCs and Villages are promising models for promoting age-friendly communities as they strive to enhance the social connectivity, independence, and well-being of older adults.

DISCUSSION QUESTIONS AND EXERCISES

1. Review the statements in the Fact or Fiction? list near the beginning of the chapter. After reading this chapter, can you identify which are true and which are false?
2. Imagine that you are approached to help with a needs assessment for a NORC. What kind of questions might you ask older residents and service providers to promote aging in place in this setting?
3. What aspects of a neighborhood would you consider most important for becoming a member of a Village?
4. Describe the research evidence about NORCs and Villages. Can you design a new program or service that might result in positive outcomes for older adults in these communities?
5. Sustainability is an issue for both NORCs and Villages. Imagine that you are asked to advocate for older adults in your community. What talking points would you share with local leaders about the need for services and supports for older adults wanting to age in place?

ADDITIONAL RESOURCES

AARP Network of Age-Friendly Communities: http://www.aarp.org/livable-communities/network-age-friendly-communities/
Beacon Hill Village: http://www.beaconhillvillage.org
NORC Blueprint: A Guide to Community Action: http://www.norcblueprint.org
SAGE Harlem NORC: http://www.lgbtagingcenter.org/
Village to Village Network: http://www.vtvnetwork.org

REFERENCES

Altman, A. (2005). The New York NORC-supportive service program. *Journal of Jewish Communal Service, 81*(3/4), 195.

Bedney, B. J., Goldberg, R. B., & Josephson, K. (2010). Aging in place in naturally occurring retirement communities: Transforming aging through supportive service programs. *Journal of Housing for the Elderly, 24*(3–4), 304–321.

Bookman, A. (2008). Innovative models of aging in place: Transforming our communities for an aging population. *Community, Work, and Family, 11*(4), 419–438. doi:10.1080/13668800802362334

Cohen-Mansfield, J., Dakheel-Ali, M., & Frank, J. K. (2010). The impact of a naturally occurring retirement communities service program in Maryland, USA. *Health Promotion International, 25*(2), 210–220.

Emlet, C. (2016). Social, economic, and health disparities among LGBT older adults. *Generations, 40*(2), 16–22.

Enguidanos, S., Pynoos, J., Denton, A., Alexman, S., & Diepenbrock, L. (2010). Comparison of barriers and facilitators in developing NORC programs: A tale of two communities. *Journal of Housing for the Elderly, 24*(3–4), 291–303. doi: 10.1080/02763893.2010.522445

Farber, N., Shinkle, D., Lynott, J., Fox-Grage, W., Harrell, R., & AARP Public Policy Institute. (2011). *Aging in place: A state survey of livability policies and practices.* AARP Public Policy Institute and National Conference of State Legislatures Research Report. Washington, DC: AARP Public Policy Institute. Retrieved from https://assets.aarp.org/rgcenter/ppi/liv-com/aging-in-place-2011-full.pdf

Fields, N. L., & Dabelko-Schoeny, H. (2015). Aging in place. In S. Krauss Whitbourne (Ed.), *Encyclopedia of adulthood and aging* (pp. 51–55). Hoboken, NJ: Wiley.

Graham, C., Scharlach, A. E., & Kurtovich, E. (2016). Do villages promote aging in place? Results of a longitudinal study. *Journal of Applied Gerontology*, 1–22. doi:10.1177/0733464816672046

Graham, C. L., Scharlach, A. E., & Wolf, J. P. (2014). The impact of the "Village" model on health, well-being, service access, and social engagement of older adults. *Health Education & Behavior, 41*(1 suppl), 91S–97S. doi:10.1177/1090198114532290

Grantmakers in Aging. (2013). *Age-friendly communities: The movement to create great places to grow up and grow old in America.* Retrieved from http://www .giaging.org/documents/130402_GIA_AFC_Primer.pdf

Greenfield, E. A. (2014). Community aging initiatives and social capital developing theories of change in the context of NORC Supportive Service Programs. *Journal of Applied Gerontology, 33*(2), 227–250.

Greenfield, E. A., & Fedor, J. P. (2015). Characterizing older adults' involvement in naturally occurring retirement community (NORC) supportive service programs, *Journal of Gerontological Social Work, 58*(5), 449–468.

Greenfield, E. A., Scharlach, A. E., Graham, C., Davitt, J., & Lehning, A. (2012). *A national overview of villages: Results from a 2012 organizational survey.* Retrieved from http://www.a1aa.org/sites/default/files/Keeping%20Seniors %20in%20Their%20Own%20Home%20Village%20Report.pdf

Greenfield, E. A., Scharlach, A., Lehning, A. J., & Davitt, J. K. (2012). A conceptual framework for examining the promise of the NORC program and Village models to promote aging in place. *Journal of Aging Studies, 26*(3), 273–284.

Greenfield, E. A., Scharlach, A. E., Lehning, A. J., Davitt, J. K., & Graham, C. L. (2013). A tale of two community initiatives for promoting aging in place: Similarities and differences in the national implementation of NORC programs and villages. *The Gerontologist, 53*(6), 928–938. doi:10.1093/geront /gnt035

Harrington, C., Ng, T., Kaye, S., & Newcomer, R. (2009). *Home and community based services: Public policies to improve access, costs and quality.* San Francisco, CA: UCSF-Center for Personal Assistance Services. Retrieved from http:// www.tilrc.org/assests/news/publications/hcbs_public_policies_to_improve _access_costs_quality%200109.pdf

Hunt, M., & Gunter-Hunt, G. (1985). Naturally occurring retirement communities. *Journal of Housing for the Elderly, 3*(3–4), 3–21.

Hunt, M. E., Arch, D., & Ross, L. (1990). Naturally occurring retirement communities: A multiattribute examination of desirability factors. *The Gerontologist, 30*, 667–674.

Ivery, J. M., & Akstein-Kahan, D. (2010). The naturally occurring retirement community (NORC) initiative in Georgia: Developing and managing collaborative partnerships to support older adults. *Administration in Social Work, 34*(4), 329–343.

Kyriacou, C., & Vladeck, F. (2011). A new model of care collaboration for community-dwelling elders: Findings and lessons learned from the NORC-health care linkage evaluation. *International Journal of Integrated Care, 11*(2), 1–20.

Lehning, A. J., Scharlach, A. E., & Davitt, J. K. (2017). Variations on the Village model: An emerging typology of a consumer-driven community-based initiative for older adults. *Journal of Applied Gerontology, 36*(2), 234–246.

Lehning, A., Scharlach, A., Price Wolf, J., Davitt, J., & Wiseman, H. (2015). Perceived challenges to the sustainability of community-based aging initiatives: Findings from a national study of Villages. *Journal of Gerontological Social Work, 58*(7–8), 684–702.

Lehning, A., Davitt, J., Scharlach, A., & Greenfield, E. (2014). *Village sustainability and engaging a diverse membership: Key findings from a 2013 national survey.* Retrieved from http://www.giaging.org/documents/Village_sustainability_study _2013.pdf

Masotti, P. J., Fick, R., Johnson-Masotti, A., & MacLeod, S. (2006). Healthy naturally occurring retirement communities: A low-cost approach to facilitating healthy aging. *American Journal of Public Health, 96*(7), 1164–1170.

McWhinney-Morse, S. (2009). Beacon hill village. *Generations, 33*(2), 85–86.

Ormond, B. A., Black, K. J., Tilly, J., & Thomas, S. (2004). *Supportive services programs in naturally occurring retirement communities.* Retrieved from https:// aspe.hhs.gov/report/supportive-services-programs-naturally-occurring-retirement -communities

Ortman, J. M., Velkoff, V. A., & Hogan, H. (2014). *An aging nation: The older population in the United States.* Current Population Reports, P25-1140. Washington, DC: U.S. Census Bureau. Retrieved from https://www.census .gov/prod/2014pubs/p25-1140.pdf

Scharlach, A. E., Davitt, J. K., Lehning, A. J., Greenfield, E. A., & Graham, C. L. (2014). Does the village model help to foster age-friendly communities? *Journal of Aging & Social Policy, 26*(1–2), 181–196. doi:10.1080/08959420. 2014.854664

Scharlach, A. E., Lehning, A. J., Davitt, J. K., Greenfield, E. A., & Graham, C. L. (2017). Organizational characteristics associated with the predicted sustainability of villages. *Journal of Applied Gerontology.* Advanced online publication. doi:10.1177/0733464817690676

Scharlach, A. E., Lehning, A. J. (2016). *Creating aging-friendly communities.* New York, NY: Oxford University Press.

Village to Village Network. (n.d.). *About.* Retrieved from http://www.vtvnetwork .org/content.aspx?page_id=22&club_id=691012&module_id=238628

Vladeck, F. (2005). Aging in place: Shaping communities for tomorrow's baby boomers—Naturally occurring retirement communities (NORCs).

In M. J. Mellor & H. Rehr (Eds.), *Baby boomers: Can my eighties be like my fifties?* (pp. 111–122). New York, NY: Springer.

Vladeck, F., & Altman, A. (2015). The future of the NORC-supportive service program model. *Public Policy & Aging Report, 25*(1), 20–22. doi:10.1093/ppar/pru050

World Health Organization. (2007). *Global age-friendly cities: A guide.* Retrieved from http://apps.who.int/iris/bitstream/10665/43755/1/9789241547307_eng.pdf

Home-Based Primary Care

The black bag may now contain a pulse oximeter, portable ECG, glucometer and digital thermometer, but both its purpose and essence remain the same. The opportunity to walk on hallowed ground and be with the patient in their most vulnerable state is one that few are fortunate enough to experience, and those who do, rediscover an art of medicine that was all but lost.

HERRITT, 2012, p. 177

LEARNING OBJECTIVES

In this chapter, you will:

- Learn about the evolution of the "house call" from the past to the present.
- Gain a better understanding of the function and potential of home-based primary care.
- Examine the existing research on home-based primary care and learn about the impact this model of care can have on homebound older adults and their families.
- Learn about the funding mechanisms for home-based primary care.
- Explore the future for home-based primary care and how this model of care might be used to augment "traditional" care models for older adults.

DIFFERENT MODELS HAVE BEEN IMPLEMENTED to help older adults remain in their homes and age in place. For some older adults, however, staying home is less of a choice and more of a necessity. Due to physical or cognitive limitations, approximately 20 percent of older adults in the United States are homebound (Musich, Wang, Hawkins, & Yeh, 2015). For this group of older adults, leaving the home to access health care resources such as physician visits or therapy appointments can be difficult and, in many cases, detrimental to their well-being. *Home-based primary care* (HBPC), formerly known as the "house call," provides medical care, case management, care coordination, and, in some cases, long-term services and support to older adults in their homes. HBPC is "an alternative way of organizing and delivering care that may better address the needs, values, and preferences of chronically ill, frail, and physically or cognitively disabled patients who have difficulty accessing traditional office-based primary care" (Totten, 2016, p. 1). Leaving the home, arranging (and often paying) for transportation, waiting for long periods of time in offices and hospitals, and seeing care providers in busy environments can be challenging and may even be impossible for some older adults with significant physical or cognitive disabilities. By bringing their services to this growing number of older adults, primary care health providers (physicians, nurse practitioners, physician assistants) are able to remove an important barrier to service for homebound older adults. HBPC involves primary care providers, but it also includes other health care professionals, such as dentists, mental health providers, nurses, and social workers. This team approach is capable of meeting the multiple needs often presented by older adults with significant health care needs.

FACT OR FICTION?

Consider the following statements.

- HBPC consist primarily of physician home visits for older adults who are experiencing acute illnesses.
- HBPC focuses on providing services to homebound older adults, many of whom have multiple conditions and difficulty leaving the home.
- HBPC is fully covered by public health insurance plans (Medicare, Medicaid), as such, there is no cost to older adults.

- HBPC visits are less expensive than traditional office visits, accounting for the cost savings of this approach.
- Researchers have clearly established that homebound older adults, their family caregivers, and the health care system in general all reap benefits from HBPC.

After reading this chapter, you will be able to affirm which statements are fact and which are fiction.

HISTORY OF THE "HOUSE CALL" IN THE UNITED STATES

Until the early 1900s, the house call was the primary setting for the delivery of health care services. Physicians routinely, and in some cases exclusively, visited patients in their homes. These house calls addressed common illnesses, such as colds and flu, as well as serious illnesses and emergencies, such as surgeries and end-of-life care (Herritt, 2012). Some physicians made as many as thirty house calls per day, and much of their time was spent on the road (Boling & Yudin, 2015). Parish health nurses and public health workers also made house calls in urban areas, augmenting the services of physicians. In rural areas, the house call was especially important and effective because patients lacked easy access to care. The physician–patient relationship was typically much closer due to the intimacy of these house calls. As one physician stated, "when I go into my patients' homes and see them in the most personal and vulnerable state, I get a sense of walking on hallowed ground. Even visits for simple problems take on a meaningful hue" (Shorter, 1991).

In the mid-1900s, the prevalence and frequency of house calls declined precipitously in the United States. Primary care via house calls dropped to 40 percent of overall visits in 1930, and house calls were down to 1 percent by 1980 (Boling & Yudin, 2015). This may seem surprising given the satisfaction both patients and physicians had with care being provided in patients' homes. A number of factors were responsible for the demise of the house call. First, the health care industry evolved to focus on efficiency of time and resources. From the provider's perspective, house calls are certainly not as efficient as the office visit. Funding also played a role in determining the way patients received services. Fee-for-service models of reimbursement made it much more profitable to schedule fifteen-minute office visits rather than home visits that could take over an hour including travel time. Home health agencies were established in the 1960s, and much of the routine care physicians had provided in house calls was assumed by paraprofessionals (see chapter 6). Fewer physicians were becoming general practitioners, opting for specialty tracks instead. This limited the pool of physicians who could and would make house calls. The decline of house calls had a detrimental impact on the physician–patient relationship as efficiency trampled the hallowed ground of the home visits once walked by physicians (Boling & Yudin, 2015; Herritt, 2012).

The modern house call, "home-based primary care" (HBPC), emerged in response to the needs of homebound older patients. The American Academy of Home Care Physicians (now the American Academy of Home Care Medicine) was established in the 1980s to advocate for HBPC. Through their advocacy efforts, Medicare increased reimbursement for physician home visits in the mid-1990s, resulting in a dramatic increase in home visits. In 1997, the Balanced Budget Act allowed for reimbursement for home visits by advanced practice nurses and nurse practitioners without requiring physician supervision. Reimbursement for physician assistants soon followed (Boling & Yudin, 2015). These regulation and reimbursement changes set the stage for clinical practices that specialized in HBPC and predominantly served older adults.

PRACTICE APPLICATION

The American Academy of Home Care Medicine (AAHCM) lists more than 280 registered health care professionals (such as physicians, nurse practitioners, and social workers) and medical groups providing HBPC in the United States. These are registered members of AAHCM, and there are undoubtedly many more providers of HBPC who are not registered with the academy. In 2012, Medicare reimbursed HBPC for 620,000 individuals (Boling & Leff, 2014). The total number of users of HBPC is much higher because many receive services through other payer sources such as private health insurance or the Veterans Administration. A recent survey of AAHCM members found that the majority of HBPC practices are located in the eastern and midwestern states, and more than 60 percent of practices primarily serve urban or suburban areas. In terms of full-time staffing, 85 percent had a physician, 73 percent had a nurse practitioner, 44 percent had a medical assistant, 37 percent had a registered nurse (RN), 32 percent had a physician assistant, and 25 percent had a social worker. More than 85 percent of the patients served were age 65 and older, and almost 80 percent of services were reimbursed through Medicare (Leff, Weston, Garrigues, Patel, & Ritchie, 2015).

Most HBPC practices employ a team approach that includes partners from multiple agencies and disciplines. For example, most HBPC practices have relationships with pharmacists, service coordinators, mental health providers, home health agencies, and Area Agencies on Aging (Boling & Yudin, 2015). HBPC has maintained the core principles of the house call of the past while advancing in complexity and possibility. In general, there are five types of HBPC house calls (Unwin & Tatum, 2011):

- Patient assessment
- Illness management for emergency, acute, or chronic conditions
- Palliative care for patients who are at the end of life
- Follow-up after hospitalization
- "Concierge services" for health promotion and disease prevention

House Calls for Seniors (see box) provides one example of services that may be provided in an HBPC practice. There is a high degree of variability in HBPC practices, and not all programs look alike.

HOUSE CALLS FOR SENIORS

House Calls for Seniors (HCS) is an HBPC provider established in the Indianapolis metro area in 1999. Using a team approach, HCS serves patients age 65 and older who are homebound due to physical, cognitive, or psychiatric impairment. They have served more than 450 older adults since the inception of the program. Patients enroll in the program for an average of two and a half years, and almost all leave due to death or nursing home placement.

Here are the typical services provided by HCS:

- A geriatrician conducts the first home visit to develop a medical care plan. The geriatrician then visits every three to four months, with most visits lasting approximately forty-five minutes.
- A nurse practitioner visits patients every four to six weeks, in between geriatrician visits. The nurse practitioner also handles any urgent or emergency visits.

(CONTINUED)

- A social worker visits patients initially to conduct a comprehensive assessment and to develop a social care plan. The social worker is then available by telephone or in person as needed.
- Weekly care meetings are held with the HBPC team to discuss patients' status and to address any concerns or needs.

HCS has the ability to conduct complex procedures using advanced technology. For example, they have a portable electrocardiogram machine to monitor heart activity, and they contract with a mobile X-ray provider. HCS also makes arrangements for home health care services (such as nursing assistants and homemaker services), medication management, durable medical equipment, and hospice services as needed. Finally, HCS has partnerships and arrangements with other health care professionals, including psychiatrists, physical and occupational therapists, podiatrists, and dentists.

Source: Adapted from Beck, Arizmendi, Purnell, Fultz, & Callahan, 2009.

CASE STUDY

Thomas is an 82-year-old white male who lives with his adult daughter, Karen, and her husband in Odessa, Texas. Thomas was married for fifty-seven years and was widowed at age 75. He was diagnosed with Alzheimer's disease four years ago and currently needs moderate assistance with his activities of daily living (for example, bathing, dressing, meal preparation). Thomas also has chronic obstructive pulmonary disease (COPD) and uses oxygen for breathing. In addition, he has arthritis, which causes considerable pain, particularly when he walks. Karen and her husband have been able to care for Thomas on their own, but his care needs are growing and he has become more and more dependent upon them.

Thomas has become increasingly fearful of unfamiliar environments, and leaving the house is now almost impossible. His family is worried that his medical conditions will worsen if he doesn't see his physician regularly. The family also has concerns about how Thomas will fare in the future if his condition warrants placement in a long-term care facility. They wonder whether a mental health professional could help address Thomas's fearfulness and reluctance to leave familiar surroundings. Thomas is currently stable, but Karen is worried that a crisis is not far off. She recently contacted the Area Agency on Aging to seek advice and help.

(CONTINUED)

Consider the following questions and exercises as they relate to this case:

1. In assessing Thomas for HBPC, what factors should you consider?
2. Compare the cost of HBPC versus other care options using the data presented in this chapter and the data provided in the Genworth Financial report: https://www.genworth.com/about-us/industry-expertise/cost-of-care.html
3. Thomas may be a good candidate for HBPC, but a service provider may or may not be available in his area. Use the HBPC provider to locate the closest provider: http://www.aahcm.org/?Locate_A_Provider
4. In addition to medical services, what other services might be beneficial to Thomas and Karen to help him age in place?

ELIGIBILITY, COST, AND FUNDING FOR HOME-BASED PRIMARY CARE

To be eligible for HBPC, older adults must be classified and certified as homebound by a primary care provider. The Centers for Medicare and Medicaid Services (CMS, 2014) put forth the following criteria for eligibility for HBPC:

- Leaving your home isn't recommended because of your condition.
- Your condition keeps you from leaving home without help (such as using a wheelchair or walker, needing special transportation, or getting help from another person).
- Leaving home takes a considerable and taxing effort.

Older adults may qualify as homebound due to a variety of conditions that limit mobility and physical strength (such as stroke, heart disease) or compromise cognitive functioning (such as Alzheimer's disease, Parkinson's disease). A recent survey found that 75 percent of homebound older adults had significant mobility issues due to chronic illnesses such as diabetes and heart failure (see figure 8.1). Approximately 50 percent of these homebound older adults were taking five or more medications and one in six had cognitive limitations (Musich et al., 2015). As the case study illustrates, multiple chronic illnesses and life circumstances can have a cumulative negative effect on an individual's ability to leave the home.

Percentage of homebound older adults with:

FIGURE 8.1   Health conditions of homebound older adults.
Source: Musich, Wang, Hawkins, & Yeh, 2015.

As with other systems of care for older adults, the cost of HBPC must be considered. In 2016, Medicare reimbursed physicians between $56 and $222 for a house call to a new patient. Nurse practitioners and physician's assistants were reimbursed between $48 and $189. Geographic location, setting (home versus congregate living), services rendered, time spent with patient, and other factors account for the variability in reimbursement rates (CMS, 2016). These standard reimbursement rates may or may not accurately capture the true cost of a house call. Providers who live in rural areas and have to travel long distances may only be able to see two or three patients in a day. Providers also look at the opportunity costs of performing house calls: one day on the road seeing five patients may be far less profitable than a day in the office seeing fifteen patients (Pedowitz, Ornstein, Farber, & DeCherrie, 2014). Although the cost of HBPC is typically higher than office or institutional-based care, emerging evidence suggests potential long-term cost savings related to reducing costly health care utilization outcomes, such as hospitalization (Totten et al., 2016).

Funding does not currently cover all older adults who are in need because HBPC is viewed as an innovative approach to care. Funding for HBPC is channeled through several sources:

- Medicare and Medicaid: Medicare and Medicaid (and certain Medicare Supplement Plans) reimburse for house calls by providers; however, these programs do not specifically and directly cover the range of services provided by HBPC. Recently, the Center for Medicare and Medicaid (CMS) funded the Independence at Home demonstration project for comprehensive HBPC. Thirteen independent practices and one consortium deliver HBPC to several thousand homebound, chronically ill patients. CMS will evaluate whether this HBPC project saves money and improves care. Future funding from Medicare will largely depend on the outcomes of this demonstration project.

- Programs for All-Inclusive Care for the Elderly: PACE provide HBPC as part of their services. PACE uses a mix of federal (CMS) and state funding to provide HBPC, respite care, adult day services, transportation, and an array of other services to help prevent "nursing home qualified" older adults from being institutionalized. Unfortunately, PACE is not available in all areas and not all older adults who might benefit from HBPC are eligible for PACE.
- Veterans Administration: The VA includes HBPC as part of their benefits to qualified veterans. The HBPC program at the VA has been associated with higher-quality care and lower health care costs. This is a growing sector of care within the VA.

DIVERSITY IN HOME-BASED PRIMARY CARE—A FOCUS ON VETERANS' HEALTH

For this focus on diversity, we spotlight the often unique needs of veterans and the role that HBPC can play in meeting these needs. Veterans are a special population that share a common, and often life-changing, experience—service in the military. The veteran population also tends to be older than the general population, with over 50 percent of male veterans age 65 and older (National Center for Veterans Analysis and Statistics, 2016). Compared with the civilian population, veterans tend to have higher rates of diabetes (21 percent versus 8 percent), cardiovascular disease (21 percent versus 6 percent), cancer (18 percent versus 6 percent), and arthritis (45 percent versus 22 percent)—the very conditions that can lead to becoming homebound (Hoerster et al., 2012). Posttraumatic stress disorder, a condition that disproportionately affects veterans, also may be linked with premature aging and higher rates of dementia—another disease that leads to becoming homebound (Lohr et al., 2015).

It is clear that veterans have special health care needs and that individualized care tailored to these needs has great potential. Shifting care from the institution to the community has been a focus of the Veterans

Health Administration for more than twenty years, and their efforts appear to be paying off. The VHA HBPC programs have been shown to reduce health care costs, reduce hospital admissions and readmissions, and reduce nursing home days (Beales & Edes, 2009; Edes et al., 2014). Veterans also express high levels of satisfaction with HBPC. The VHA HBPC programs are innovative and were some of the first programs to fully integrate mental health services, an acute issue for many older adults and a factor that may prevent them from using traditional services (Karlin & Karel, 2014). Other health care systems should look to the VHA as HBPC expands in the general population.

Perspectives from the Field

An interview with Lori Murphy, MSW, LISW-S
Social Worker, OSU Total Health and Wellness
Columbus, Ohio

What is your background and training related to home-based primary care?

I have a master's degree in social work and am a licensed independent social worker. I have fourteen years of experience in a variety of medical social work positions, most recently including five years in home-based primary care.

What are the greatest strengths of home-based primary care?

The strength of home-based primary care is the ability to connect very needy patients and their family members with an interdisciplinary team of medical professionals. The patients and family members develop close relationships with the entire care team as they all work hard to address their diverse needs. Home-based primary care provides enormous cost-savings for the health care system.

What challenges do you face in home-based primary care?

Transportation, accessible housing, and access to medical equipment are just a few examples of the gaps in resources that can create significant barriers in providing care. Coordination of care with multiple agencies is another challenge. Because of the travel and the amount of time spent with each patient in his or her home, providers struggle to treat enough patients to cover the cost of running the programs.

What do you see as the future for home-based primary care?

I believe we will continue to see more home-based primary care programs opening as our elderly population grows. I also anticipate an increase in home-based primary care for patients with diseases such as multiple sclerosis, sickle cell, and serious mental health disorders, and patients undergoing intense treatments such as chemotherapy and radiation.

RESEARCH AND EVIDENCE

In a report for the Agency for Healthcare Research and Quality (AHRQ), some of the potential benefits of HBPC for homebound older adults were outlined (Totten et al., 2016):

- Greater and easier access to care.
- Access to a variety of ancillary services, such as medication management, mental health, case management, dental, and associated therapies (physical, occupational, and speech therapies).
- A better view of the "person in environment" and the needs, challenges, and resources of the patient in his or her own home.
- Greater engagement in care and a stronger patient–provider relationship.
- More support for caregivers in need.
- Greater patient and caregiver satisfaction.
- Decreased health care utilization (hospitalizations, emergency department visits) and decreased cost of care.

Although the policy and program developers and researchers have identified these potential benefits, the research on HBPC has yet to fully demonstrate that these benefits are indeed reality.

The potential benefits of HBPC can be divided into three general categories: (a) patient benefits, (b) caregiver benefits, and (c) health care system benefits (utilization and cost). Two recent systematic reviews provide an overall picture of the effectiveness of HBPC for older adults. In a review of nine qualified studies, Stall, Nowaczynski, and Sinha (2014) found that patients in HBPC typically had high levels of satisfaction and higher levels of quality of life compared to older adults receiving regular office care. Patients were more likely to be current with their vaccinations and to have completed their advance directives. Caregivers of patients in HBPC also had higher levels of quality of life and lower levels of caregiver burden. In terms of health care utilization and cost, the reviewers found reduced hospital admission and reduced long-term care (nursing home) admission rates. There were mixed findings with regard to costs, with some studies reporting an increase and other studies reporting cost savings.

A 2016 review examined nineteen studies of HBPC interventions (Totten et al., 2016). The reviewers found that enrollment in HBPC programs was related to high levels of satisfaction and quality of life for both patients and caregivers. Findings also suggested that HBPC was able to effectively meet caregiver needs. Enrollment in HBPC programs was associated with reduced hospitalization; however, the reviewers did not find clear or significant reductions in hospital readmissions or nursing home days. There was some indication that cost savings could be achieved with certain types of HBPC approaches with specific populations of older adults, such as people with dementia and individuals with high acuity levels (in particular, see De Jonge et al., 2014).

The researchers in both systematic reviews and in other single studies are in consensus that HBPC has great potential, but the lack of standardization in HBPC and the small number of rigorous studies limits our ability to make definitive conclusions on the impact of this care approach.

Benefits for health care professionals involved with HBPC have not been measured, but entering into the lived experience of patients in their own homes suggests potential benefits. By getting to know patients in such intimate settings, providers may be better situated to holistically practice both the art and the science of health care. Health care professionals may feel more satisfied with their work, and this may, in turn, affect the quality and continuity of care and spur growth in the geriatric workforce.

An Expert Weighs In

Bruce Leff, MD
Professor of Medicine, School of Medicine
Johns Hopkins University

Research on home-based primary care is not the easiest research to conduct, but studies strongly suggest that providing home-based primary care to homebound older adults is associated with better patient and caregiver experience with care, better caregiver quality of life, and reduction in health care costs and utilization of various types including emergency department visits, hospitalizations, and long-term care. Barriers to better understanding the benefits of home-based primary care include the challenges of conducting randomized controlled trials in a frail population, lack of standardized data, and lack of standardization of this complex clinical intervention. Policy and broader societal changes needed to drive the expansion of home-based primary care include workforce development, pushing back on the societal bias against geriatrics, aging, and community-based care, and inadequate payment (reimbursement) for a service that may be one of the best values in health care. The main research priorities for home-based primary care need to focus on developing and implementing the right quality metrics for these patients and the practices that serve them, work to better define the population in need of such services, and work to design the home-based primary care system of the future, integrating, where appropriate, useful technology to augment this high-touch model of care.

THE FUTURE OF HOME-BASED PRIMARY CARE: STANDARDIZATION AND FUNDING

The future of HBPC rests on the standardization of programs, evaluating these programs with rigorous methods, and using the findings from this research to influence policy and leverage funding. The house call has long been in existence, but the current iteration of HBPC has only recently evolved. Standardization of precisely what constitutes HBPC and quality standards are not currently in place. This presents challenges in terms of maintaining quality control and evaluating the effectiveness of this approaches. Leff, Carlson, Saliba, and Ritchie (2015) recently focused their research on quality standards and presented a set of domains and standards that could be useful as HBPC continues to expand. Table 8.1 summarizes this work.

Many providers are already meeting some of the quality standards across these domains; however, some quality standards remain as unmet goals for certain providers. For example, communication between team members continues to be a challenge in HBPC—a problem that seems to exist in

TABLE 8.1   Quality Domains and Standards in Home-Based Primary Care

DOMAIN	STANDARD
Assessment	• Perform a comprehensive physical, emotional, social, and spiritual assessment of the patient. • Assess caregiver resources and challenges.
Care coordination	• Coordinate the patient's care between health care professionals.
Safety	• Manage medications. • Optimize safety and prevent falls. • Be vigilant and address for abuse and neglect.
Quality of life	• Optimize comfort and reduce burden.
Provider competency	• Competency in managing patients' and caregivers' needs in the home setting.
Goal attainment	• Align patient's and caregiver's goals with care plan. • Facilitate the development of realistic goals.
Education	• Develop an education plan and promote patient's and caregiver's understanding of care plan. • Support patient's and caregiver's self-management.
Access	• Provide timely access to routine and urgent care. • Ensure access to interdisciplinary care team.
Patient & caregiver experience	• Facilitate the development of a trusting relationship between providers, patients, and caregivers. • Manage stressors, including wait times for service.
Cost & affordability	• Match care needs with program benefits and limits. • Effectively measure health care utilization.

Source: Adapted from Leff, Carlson, Saliba, & Ritchie, 2015.

every area in which interdisciplinary teams are in place. In addition, finding and utilizing uniform outcome measures has not been done. Effectively evaluating HBPC will depend on the development and implementation of a uniform battery of outcome measures. Standardization of services, quality control, and data collection are keys to the expansion of HBPC. Expansion of HBPC funding should follow the evidence. Funding agencies, most notably CMS, will undoubtedly continue to watch as the evidence on the effectiveness of HBPC grows. Unlike many areas in health care, HBPC may eventually be the rare win-win-win-win situation for providers, patients, caregivers, and the health care system.

CHAPTER SUMMARY

- Home-based primary care (HBPC), formerly known as the "house call," provides medical care, case management, care coordination, and, in some cases, long-term services and support to older adults in their homes.
- HBPC is "an alternative way of organizing and delivering care that may better address the needs, values, and preferences of chronically ill, frail, and physically or cognitively disabled patients who have difficulty accessing traditional office-based primary care" (Totten, 2016, p. 1).
- To be eligible for HBPC, older adults must be certified as "homebound": (a) leaving home isn't recommended because of their condition; (b) their condition keeps them from leaving home without help; or (c) leaving home takes a considerable and taxing effort.
- Some health insurance plans cover house calls, but they currently do not cover the comprehensive services provided by HBPC; however, this may change with ongoing studies of HBPC.
- Research suggests that homebound older adults and their caregivers experience high levels of satisfaction with HBPC and that their overall well-being may be higher than that of older adults receiving traditional care. Although the research is not conclusive, HBPC may reduce health care utilization and costs.

DISCUSSION QUESTIONS AND EXERCISES

1. Review the statements in the Fact or Fiction? list near the beginning of the chapter. After reading this chapter, can you identify which are true and which are false?
2. The traditional "house call" was almost extinct by the mid-1900s as efficiency became the hallmark of health care. HBPC is making a comeback. In what other areas of health care for older adults (and in general) has efficiency trumped quality of care?
3. CMS continues to evaluate HBPC to determine if this is an effective and efficient method for delivering health care services to homebound older adults. Visit the Independence at Home webpage and look for updates on this promising demonstration project.
4. Research on the impact of HBPC is still in the fledging stage. Using the information presented in this chapter and your understanding of research

142 HOME-BASED PRIMARY CARE

design and data collection, design a study that effectively measures all of the potential benefits of HBPC.

5. What is your vision for the future of HBPC? In twenty years, will HBPC be the "standard way" that we deliver health care services to homebound older adults? What will be needed to move in this direction? What are the barriers?

ADDITIONAL RESOURCES

American Academy of Home Care Medicine: http://www.aahcm.org

The Commonwealth Fund, Overview of Home-Based Primary Care: http://www.commonwealthfund.org/publications/issue-briefs/2017/jun/overview-home-based-primary-care

Independence at Home demonstration project: https://innovation.cms.gov/initiatives/independence-at-home/

Programs for All-Inclusive Care for the Elderly (PACE): https://www.medicare.gov/your-medicare-costs/help-paying-costs/pace/pace.html

Veterans Administration Home-Based Primary Care: https://www.va.gov/geriatrics/guide/longtermcare/home_based_primary_care.asp

REFERENCES

Beales, J. L., & Edes, T. E. (2009). Veterans Affairs home-based primary care. *Clinics in Geriatric Medicine, 25,* 149–154.

Beck, R. A., Arizmendi, A., Purnell, C., Fultz, B. A., & Callahan, C. N. (2009). House calls for seniors: Building and sustaining a model of care for homebound seniors. *Journal of the American Geriatrics Society, 57*(6), 1103–1109.

Boling, P. A., & Leff, B. (2014). Comprehensive longitudinal health care in the home for high-cost beneficiaries: A critical strategy for population health management. *Journal of the American Geriatrics Society, 62*(10), 1974–1976.

Boling, P. A., & Yudin, J. (2015). Home-based primary care program for home-limited patients. In M. L. Malone, E. Capezuti, & R. M. Palmer (Eds.), *Geriatrics models of care: Bringing 'best practice' to an aging America* (pp. 173–181). Switzerland: Springer International.

Centers for Medicare and Medicaid Services. (2014). *CMS manual system: Pub 100–02 Medicare benefit policy.* Retrieved from www.cms.gov/Regulations-and-Guidance/Guidance/Transmittals/downloads/R192BP.pdf

Centers for Medicare and Medicaid Services. (2016). *Medicare claims processing manual.* Retrieved from https://www.cms.gov/regulations-and-guidance /guidance/manuals/internet-only-manuals-ioms-items/cms018912.html

De Jonge, K. E., Jamshed, N., Gilden, D., Kubisiak, J., Bruce, S. R., & Taler, G. (2014). Effects of home-based primary care on Medicare costs in high-risk elders. *Journal of the American Geriatrics Society, 62,* 1825–1831.

Edes, T., Kinosian, B., Vuckovic, N. H., Nichols, L. O., Becker, M. M., & Hossain, M. (2014). Better access, quality, and cost for clinically complex veterans with home-based primary care. *Journal of the American Geriatrics Society, 62,* 1954–1961.

Herritt, B. J. (2012). The house call: Past, present, and future. *University of Toronto Medical Journal, 89*(3), 175–177.

Hoerster, K. D., Lehavot, K., Simpson, T., McFall, M., Reiber, G., & Nelson, K. M. (2012). Health and health behavior differences: U.S military, veteran, and civilian men. *American Journal of Preventative Medicine, 43*(5), 483–489.

Karlin, B. E., & Karel, M. J. (2014). National integration of mental health providers in VA home-based primary care: An innovative model for mental health care delivery for older adults. *Gerontologist, 54*(5), 868–879.

Leff, B., Carlson, C. M., Saliba, D., & Ritchie, C. (2015). The invisible homebound: Setting quality-of-care standards for home-based primary and palliative care. *Health Affairs, 34*(1), 21–29.

Leff, B., Weston, C. M., Garrigues, S., Patel, K., & Ritchie, C. (2015). Home-based primary care practices in the United States: Current state and quality improvement approaches. *Journal of the American Geriatrics Society, 63,* 963–969.

Lohr, J. B., Palmer, B. W., Eidt, C. A., Aailaboyina, S., Mausbach, B. T., Wolkowitz, O. M., . . . Jeste, D. V. (2015). Is post-traumatic stress disorder associated with premature senescence? A review of the literature. *American Journal of Geriatric Psychiatry, 23*(7), 709–725.

Musich, S., Wang, S. S., Hawkins, K., & Yeh, C. S. (2015). Homebound older adults: Prevalence, characteristics, health care utilization and quality of care. *Geriatric Nursing, 36,* 445–450.

National Center for Veterans Analysis and Statistics. (2016). *Profile of veterans: 2014.* Retrieved from http://www.va.gov/vetdata/docs/SpecialReports/Profile _of_Veterans_2014.pdf

Pedowitz, E. J., Ornstein, K. A., Farber, J., & DeCherrie, L. V. (2014). Time providing care outside visits in a home-based primary care program. *Journal of the American Geriatrics Society, 62*(6), 1122–1126.

Shorter, E. (1991). *Doctors and their patients: A social history.* New York, NY: Routledge.

Stall, N., Nowaczynski, M., & Sinha, S. K. (2014). Systematic review of outcomes from home-based primary care programs for homebound older adults. *Journal of the American Geriatrics Society, 62,* 2243–2251.

Totten, A. M., Foy White-Chu, E., Wasson, N., Morgan, E., Kansagara, D., Davis-O'Reilly, & Goodlin, S. (2016). *Home-based primary care interventions.* AHRQ Publication No. 15(16)-EHC036-EF. Retrieved from https://effectivehealthcare.ahrq.gov/ehc/products/590/2183/home-based-care-report-160216.pdf

Unwin, B. K., & Tatum, P. E., III. (2011). House calls. *American Family Physician, 83*(8), 925–931.

Assisted Living and Housing with Services

Assisted living offers a chance to positively alter the LTC [long-term care] land-scape if it can combine three ingredients: a homelike residential environment, a true service capacity, and a philosophy of consumer choice, dignity, and normal lifestyle—all wrapped up in a package that middle-class and low-income people can afford, and public entities can afford to subsidize.

KANE, 2001, p. 300

LEARNING OBJECTIVES

In this chapter, you will:
- Gain an understanding of the history and philosophy of assisted living.
- Explore the types of care and services offered in assisted living.
- Learn about other models of housing with services.
- Review existing and emerging research on resident outcomes in assisted living.
- Explore future directions in assisted living and other housing with service models.

HOME-BASED PRIMARY CARE (HBPC) OFFERS many older adults with functional limitations or cognitive impairment the opportunity to receive medical care, case management, and care coordination in their homes. HBPC is an alternative to traditional office-based primary care, but some older adults may require a residential setting that offers care beyond what can be provided in their own home, including around the clock supervision. *Assisted living* (AL) is broadly defined as a residential care setting that provides older adults with assistance and supervision with personal care and health care as well as support for activities of daily living. The foundation of AL is a philosophy of care that promotes dignity, independence, and privacy for residents. AL typically serves older adults for whom home care does not provide enough support but who do not need the high level of care provided by nursing homes. Most residents in AL pay privately to live in these settings, and others have their payments subsidized by Medicaid. *Housing with services* is also considered residential care; however, this type of setting is usually considered independent living and is focused on providing housing and services such as meals, housekeeping, transportation, and social activities. Housing with services settings do not typically provide assistance with medication, activities of daily living, or other health-related services.

FACT OR FICTION?

Consider the following statements.

- Assisted living and nursing homes are rooted in a similar philosophy of care.
- Assisted living settings serve a large number of older adults with dementia or memory impairment.
- There is currently no unifying definition of assisted living.
- Service coordinators are not typically associated with the housing with services model.
- Service-enriched housing provides health and social services to older adults who live in privately subsidized buildings.

After reading this chapter, you will be able to affirm which statements are fact and which are fiction.

HISTORY AND CURRENT STATE OF ASSISTED LIVING AND HOUSING WITH SERVICES

Before the 1965 enactment of Medicare and Medicaid, residential settings that provided supportive care for older adults existed under a variety of names including boarding homes and homes for the aged (Cohen, 1974).

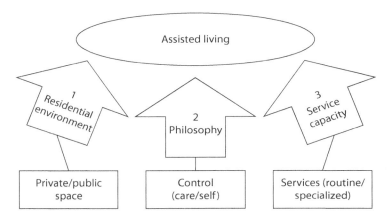

FIGURE 9.1 Core components of assisted living.
Sources: Adapted from Kane, Kane, & Ladd, 1998; Wilson, 2007.

After 1965, many residential settings converted to nursing homes and became regulated by the state and federal government. However, some residential settings did not want to provide long-term medical services and either did not want to conform or were unable to conform to state and federal regulations. The early models of assisted living were designed to be an alternative to nursing facilities for older adults seeking a less restrictive setting for long-term care (figure 9.1). During the 1980s, AL emerged as a form of housing and services that included a residential style physical environment, service capacity for routine and specialized services, and a philosophy of care that emphasized resident choice (Wilson, 2007).

The first use of the term *assisted living* was in a 1985 proposal to the state of Oregon to fund a pilot study of a new residential setting for nursing home–level Medicaid recipients (Wilson, 2007). At this time, states varied in how they defined the services provided by AL, including the amount of disability allowed of its residents (that is, the level of care needed). Because of this variability and concern for how AL should be defined, as well as how it should be regulated, AARP, a nonprofit organization that advocates for older adults' quality of life, commissioned a national study in 1992 that proposed a working definition of AL as a group residential setting not licensed as a nursing facility that provides or arranges personal care for residents that meets their functional requirements and need for routine nursing services (Kane & Wilson, 1993).

In 2001, the Assisted Living Workgroup, a national coalition of nearly fifty organizations representing AL providers, consumers, and other stakeholders, came together at the behest of the U.S. Senate Special Committee on Aging to develop a uniform definition of AL to ensure consistent quality in these settings across the country. After eighteen months, the workgroup failed to pass a vote on a single definition of AL (Assisted Living Workgroup, 2003). Today there remains no uniform definition of AL, and each state regulates and monitors these settings to comply with local laws (Argentum, 2016).

In 2014, it was estimated that 30,200 AL and similar residential care communities were in operation, serving approximately 835,200 residents (Caffrey, Harris-Kojetin, & Sengupta, 2015). The availability of AL varies, however, as the average capacity in the highest performing states was sixty-two units per 1,000 people age 65 and older compared with eleven units per 1,000 people age 65 and older in the lowest performing states (Mollica, Houser, & Ujvari, 2012). The charge for AL also varies, with Arkansas having the lowest monthly base rate of $2,156 and Washington, D.C. having the highest average monthly base rate of $5,757 (MetLife Mature Market Institute, 2012). Monthly rates typically include "room and board" and at least two meals per day, housekeeping services, and assistance with some activities of daily living. AL services may also include twenty-four-hour supervision/assistance, exercise and wellness programs, medication management/assistance, and transportation (National Center for Assisted Living, n.d.). Some AL settings specialize in serving residents with Alzheimer's disease or other forms of dementia. Although most residents pay privately for AL, most states participate in Medicaid programs to subsidized the cost for low-income older adults through the Home and Community-Based Services Waiver (Carlson, Coffey, Fecondo, & Newcomer, 2010). Estimates suggest that between 13 and 23 percent of residents had at least some services paid for by Medicaid, depending on the size of the community (Sengupta, Harris-Kojetin, & Caffrey, 2015).

The majority of residents in AL are age 85 and older, female, and non-Hispanic white. A profile of the services AL residents require includes these items (Harris-Kojetin et al., 2016; National Center for Assisted Living, n.d.):

- 62 percent need help with bathing
- 47 percent need help with dressing

- 39 percent need help with toileting
- 20 percent need help with eating
- 30 percent need help transferring from/to the bed
- 40 percent have Alzheimer's disease or dementia
- 46 percent have cardiovascular disease
- 23 percent have depression
- 17 percent have diabetes

AL is often considered a "housing with services model"; however, other models exist to provide support to older adults in residential settings. Typically, "housing with services" encompasses all forms of accommodation designed specifically for older adults where the housing provider is responsible for delivering one or more types of care services. Settings such as retirement communities and continuing care retirement communities fall under the umbrella of housing with services.

Retirement communities developed in the 1960s to offer post–World War II retirees a housing option with resort-style amenities geared toward leisure and entertainment (such as golf courses). Health care services were not typically part of retirement communities, and these settings primarily cater to older adults who are independent and have few health care or medical problems. A *continuing care retirement community* (CCRC) provides a continuum of services from independent living, to assisted living, to skilled nursing and nursing home care within a single campus (figure 9.2).

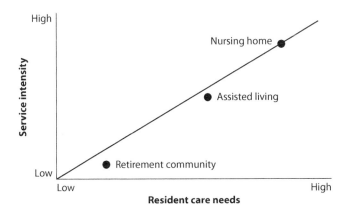

FIGURE 9.2 Types of residential care by service intensity and resident need.

CCRCs offer multiple levels of care, and residents can move between the different levels as their needs change. Continuing care retirement communities are usually very expensive and require an upfront entry fee payment. In 2010, the average CCRC entrance fee was $248,000 per year, but fees can range from $20,000 to more than $1 million (Stone, 2013). Although retirement communities and CCRCs provide housing with services, these settings are unaffordable for many older adults who wish to access home- and community-based services and avoid moving to a nursing home.

Options exist for older adults who are not able to afford costly retirement communities or CCRCs. Congregate housing developments in the 1980s and 1990s began to offer housing with services for older adults with low to moderate incomes. The term *service-enriched housing* describes living arrangements that provide health and social services to older adults who live in publicly subsidized buildings for low-income older adults (Castle & Resnick, 2016). These settings typically include a service coordinator who assists residents with counseling, education, advocacy, and, if needed, home health care contracted with an outside agency. The primary role of the service coordinator is to assist residents in accessing the services that may help them live independently in the community. This often includes (1) assessing residents health and social needs; (2) identifying, accessing, and coordinating services; (3) referring residents to other service providers; (4) building partnerships with service providers; and (5) serving as a member of an interdisciplinary care team (Weiss, Malone, & Walsh, 2015).

MODELS OF CARE IN ASSISTED LIVING AND HOUSING WITH SERVICES

The philosophical underpinnings of AL were developed in the 1980s in response to consumers wanting a type of housing for older adults that was distinct from nursing homes. Core principles included respect for resident independence, choice, and privacy in a noninstitutional setting. These core values continue to inform the AL industry, and the current philosophy is to provide personalized care in a setting that treats residents with dignity, provides privacy, and encourages resident autonomy (Argentum, 2016).

In the 1990s, four models of AL emerged: the hybrid model, the hospitality model, the housing model, and the health care model (Wilson, 2007). The *hybrid model* emphasized apartment-style housing, which provided or made available a wide variety of services for the personal and health-related needs of residents. The hybrid model focused on resident choice, autonomy, and independence. The *hospitality model* focused on concierge services such as housekeeping, meals, activities, and transportation with less provision of personal or health care–related services. The *housing model* specialized in adding services to already existing publicly subsidized housing for older adults. For example, case managers often helped coordinate the delivery of services from outside providers. Finally, the *health care model* of AL focused on the clinical aspects of care, such as medication administration, and often added residential "wings" to nursing facilities that served as "feeders" to these facilities (Wilson, 2007). The health care model was less focused on the independence and autonomy of its residents than other models of care. In addition to these four models of AL, the *social model* of care emerged, which focused on AL as a homelike environment with respect for the dignity, privacy, autonomy, and individuality of residents (Kane & Wilson, 2001). The social model of care was developed in contrast to the medical model of care, which was often used to define hospital and nursing home settings. Today most states incorporate the social model of care in their regulatory requirements for AL (Eckert et al., 2009). This philosophy emphasizes that the AL resident is a valued customer who should be made to feel at home and given the right to make decisions about how and when to receive services (Wylde, 2008).

Staff requirement in AL settings vary from state to state. Research suggests that the total average hours for nursing care is 2.6 hours per day; however, licensed staff members only spend 0.5 hours of nursing care per resident, which suggests that aides provide the majority of resident care in ALs (Harris-Kojetin, Sengupta, Park-Lee, & Valverde, 2013). Other reports suggest that 85 percent of ALs have a licensed nurse on-site for more than eight hours each day; 27 percent have licensed nurses available twenty-four hours per day (National Center for Assisted Living, 2010). Across most states, AL management staff decide the level of staffing that adequately meets the needs of residents. AL also employs other staff positions such as administrators, marketing directors, dining, housekeeping, maintenance, and activity coordinators. Social workers in AL may serve in various roles, including as mental health assessor/counselor and resident advocate, as well as provide support to the family and resident during the transition to AL (Fields, Koenig, & Dabelko-Schoeny, 2012; Koenig, Lee, Fields, & Macmillan, 2011).

A growing issue in AL is the number of residents with dementia or cognitive impairment, which ranges from 40 percent to 90 percent (Carder, 2017). Approximately 22 percent of AL settings are designated for dementia care and have designated floors or sections referred to as "special care units" (Harris-Kojetin et al., 2016). Special care units may be secured by alarms with locked doors to prevent residents from wandering or leaving the AL. Research on the effectiveness of dementia care units in maintaining residents' health and well-being is mixed (Zimmerman et al., 2013). When planning a move to an AL, it is important for individuals with dementia and their families to consider the ability and willingness of the AL to provide memory care. There is a wide variation in the extent to which ALs will serve residents with behavioral issues related to late stage dementia such as wandering or end-of-life care.

Older adults who are unable to afford the costs of AL and who do not have low enough incomes to qualify for Medicaid face the dilemma of having to move from their home or apartment due to the need for additional supports and services and relocate to a setting such as a nursing home. Many of these older adults wish to age in place and continue to live in the community in spite of age or health-related changes that may make this difficult (Fields & Dabelko-Schoeny, 2015). Approximately 1.9 million older adults live in publicly assisted housing (Federal Section 202 and 236 programs, Low Income Housing Tax Credit properties) and are in need of health care and other home- and community-based services to help them successfully age in place (Stone, 2013). Service-enriched housing models and programs link residents with health and supportive services for aging in place. These models may include the provision of a service coordinator as well as formal partnerships with adult day centers, hospitals, health centers, and Area Agencies on Aging. Two models are the Congregate Housing Services Program (CHSP), created by the U.S. Department of Housing and Urban Development (HUD) to provide service-enriched housing for older adults including meals, transportation, homemaking, shopping, and service coordination; and the Supportive Services Program in Senior Housing (SSPSH), created by the Robert Wood Johnson Foundation, that uses service coordinators to implement services in housing for low-income older adults (Pynoos, Liebig, Alley, & Nishita, 2005). Research suggests that service-enriched housing is a promising model for aging in place; however, because these programs require

CASE STUDY

Phil Sherman, age 78, was diagnosed with Alzheimer's disease a year ago. He is a retired construction worker and currently lives with his wife of fifty-two years in their home in a suburb of Dallas, Texas. The diagnosis of Alzheimer's disease came as a shock to Phil and his family because he is an otherwise active, independent, and healthy individual. However, his family had noticed that he had become extremely forgetful and he did get lost while driving on several occasions in his neighborhood. His family health care provider has recommended that he no longer drive. During the past month, Phil woke up at 2 AM, dressed, and tried to leave the house, stating that he was "getting ready to go to work."

Phil's two adult sons living in another state are concerned that he is at risk for wandering because of his dementia. They also are worried about their mother taking care of Phil on her own. They have encouraged her to begin looking at assisted living communities that provide memory care. She is open to the idea, but Phil is strongly against moving to an assisted living facility for fear of losing his independence and autonomy. The family also is very worried about how to pay for assisted living.

As the staff person at the Area Agency on Aging on the phone with Mrs. Sherman, consider these statements and questions in relation to this case.

1. What types of services and supports does Phil currently need or anticipate needing due to his diagnosis of Alzheimer's disease?
2. What type of assisted living facility would be able to accommodate Phil's level of care needs both now and as his dementia progresses?
3. What are the expectations of the family in terms of the services and supports offered by AL?
4. What types of financial challenges might Phil's family face in moving him to assisted living?

collaboration with multiple agencies with different goals and eligibility requirements, there are challenges to implementing and sustaining these types of housing with supportive services (Castle & Resnick, 2016).

PRACTICE APPLICATIONS

All states require AL settings to assess whether or not a resident's needs can be met and to create a care plan for services that meet the resident's needs and preferences (Carder, O'Keefe, & O'Keefe, 2015). Typically, AL settings require a physician to approve that an older adult live in the AL. Some states use a standardized assessment form, and others permit AL providers to use their own forms with some oversight from the state. Some states require a preadmission assessment before a resident is admitted to ensure that the AL setting is able to meet the care needs of the individual. The regulations of each state describe the allowable health conditions of residents in AL as well as the staffing requirements for certain diagnoses. For example, state-specific admission guidelines may indicate that an on-site licensed nurse or nursing supervisor is required to administer certain medications.

Once a resident is admitted to the AL facility, a comprehensive assessment usually includes the physical, cognitive, emotional, and psychosocial domains. Licensed professionals such as nurses typically conduct these assessments. Observing the resident, interviewing the resident, and performing a physical evaluation of the resident are all part of the assessment process. Family members of the resident may be interviewed as a part of the assessment as well. Resident assessments in AL settings vary, but most include demographic questions as well as questions about medical conditions, functional ability, medication use, communication, hearing and vision, moods and behaviors, and continence. Because one of the key philosophies of AL is to promote autonomy, the purpose of the assessment is often to capture what services the resident needs to remain as independent as possible and to assess the ways in which what the AL facility can provide will maximize a resident's functioning.

The information collected during the assessment is used to inform the resident service plan (also known as a care plan). A service plan is a tool that identifies a resident's care needs/goals and interventions to meet those care needs/goals. Most states require that every resident in AL have an individualized service plan. Some states require that the service plan be updated annually and when a resident's care needs significantly change. Service plans usually address the following:

- Assistance required to support activities of daily living (dressing, grooming, bathing)
- Use of mobility devices such as walkers and canes
- Dietary requirements

- Continence care
- Medication management
- Medical care for specific diagnoses such as diabetes
- Assistance needed to attend the dining room or activities such as someone to escort the resident
- Behavioral needs such as wandering
- Psychosocial needs
- Need for physical, occupational, or speech therapy

Perspectives from the Field

An interview with Christine Serdinak, LSW, CEAL, LNHA
Senior Executive Director, The AbbeWood Senior Living Community
Elyria, Ohio

What is your professional background and training?

I am a licensed social worker with additional education and training for working with children and older adults. For the last twenty-three years, I have worked with older adults. I'm currently the Senior Executive Director at a 165-unit independent and assisted living community.

What are the challenges facing assisted living?

With the transition of health care and who is paying for it, the patient population has shifted. Hospital patients go to a skilled nursing center, and the folks who were in long-term care are now in assisted living. People are living beyond the years for which they had financially prepared, and the care and environment they desire may not match what they can afford.

What do you see as the future of assisted living?

Because the patient population has shifted, assisted living facilities will have to be licensed for Medicaid to accommodate the need. AL is becoming more like a nursing home without the Medicare and Medicaid audits. The rules will become stricter in the future.

*What advice would you give to someone interested in working
in assisted living?*

I would definitely recommend a conversation and possibly a day of job
shadowing. Most people think they can handle death, but when faced with
it find it is not for them. The staff members not only need to be caregivers
but social workers, customer service representatives, sales driven, and
willing to jump in wherever needed. Job shadowing would allow one to live
and breathe this atmosphere.

DIVERSITY IN ASSISTED LIVING—A FOCUS ON RACIAL AND ETHNIC MINORITY RESIDENTS

Current residents in AL settings are primarily non-Hispanic white women
in their mid-eighties; however, demographic trends "are contributing to
increased use of AL, including by African American and rural families,
who have traditionally 'cared for their own'" (Perkins, Ball, Whittington,
& Hollingsworth, 2012, p. 3). As the Hispanic and Asian populations
continue to grow, we may see these groups of older adults turning to AL
for care. Researchers have begun to examine the experiences of racial and
ethnic minority older adults in AL and have found that their experiences
can be different from their white counterparts, particularly when there are
socioeconomic disparities. Lower-income older adults tend to have fewer
options in selecting an AL setting and lower feelings of control (Ball et al.,
2005; Ball, Perkins, Hollingsworth, Whittington, & King, 2009). Sense of
control, in particular, has emerged as an important component of quality
of life in AL and other residential settings (Koehn, Mahmood, & Stott-
Eveneshen, 2016). Given the relationship of race and socioeconomic status
in the United States, older adults from racial and ethnic minorities appear
to be at the greatest risk of compromised control and autonomy in AL.
As practitioners, cultural competence begins with an awareness of these
potential disparities.

In some AL facilities, cultural competence is at the forefront in their
approach to care. Aegis Gardens, located in Fremont, California, is one such
facility. Although Aegis Gardens is open to all ethnicities, the majority of
residents are Chinese American, and care reflects Chinese culture and traditions. Residents participate in Chinese cultural activities such as tai-chi,

calligraphy, and mahjong. Staff members speak Mandarin, Cantonese, and English. Residents celebrate both Chinese and American holidays. Aegis Gardens is considered a culturally sensitive community because it provides an environment for residents to interact and socialize with others who share the same cultural background, language, belief system, and interests. Culturally sensitive housing is growing in demand as many older adults from diverse ethnic backgrounds are opting to live independently rather than with their adult children.

RESEARCH AND EVIDENCE

Leading researchers in the field indicate that AL is the fastest growing long-term care sector in the United States. From 2007 to 2010, the number of AL beds increased by approximately 18 percent (from 1.05 million to 1.2 million beds), and the number of beds in nursing homes decreased (Mollica et al., 2012). AL settings have become an important platform for the delivery of housing and supportive services for growing numbers of older adults wishing to age in place (Grabowski, Stevenson, & Cornell, 2012). Growth in the number of AL facilities is likely to continue because older adults and their family members view these settings as more "home-like" than nursing homes and because the social care model in AL emphasizes resident independence and autonomy. However, research suggests that AL residents have complex care needs and multiple chronic health conditions that often result in the need for increased health care services (McNabney et al., 2014). Nearly half of AL residents are discharged from these settings due to health concerns, and many residents who are discharged from AL end up moving to a nursing home (National Center for Assisted Living, 2010). Discharges from AL to nursing homes are often related to family concerns, financial issues, or medical needs (Hyde, Perez, Doyle, Forester, & Whitfield, 2014). Although the overarching philosophy of AL is to provide a less restrictive model of long-term care, studies suggest that greater emphasis on the complex health care needs of AL residents may be needed as well as more comprehensive resident assessment upon admission (Fields, 2016). Finally, due to a lack of a uniform definition of assisted living, research on outcomes in these settings is difficult to interpret.

As for other models of housing with services, evidence suggests that the provision of resident services through service coordinators results in positive health outcomes for older adults wishing to age in place in community settings (Weiss et al., 2015). Studies further suggest that the use of service coordinators improves resident and housing manager relationships (Levine & Johns, 2008). The Staying at Home (SAH) program was implemented in publicly subsidized housing for low-income older adults (Castle & Resnick, 2016), and services included care coordination, advance planning, medication management, and a health care diary provided by an intervention team consisting of a social worker, a registered nurse, and a physician, as needed. Study findings suggest that the SAH program improves residents' health and health outcomes including lowering the likelihood of unscheduled hospital stays, nursing home transfers, ER use, and inpatient use. However, the SAH program was implemented by a not-for-profit health care provider with vast resources, which limits the reproducibility of the program. Overall, more research is needed to examine service-enriched program outcomes as a potential housing with services strategy for supporting the aging in place of low- to moderate-income older adults in the community.

An Expert Weighs In

Sheryl Zimmerman, PhD
Mary Lily Kenan Flagler Bingham Distinguished Professor
Associate Dean for Research and Faculty Development, School of Social Work
The University of North Carolina at Chapel Hill

Assisted living has grown and evolved over the last decades—specifically, growing 97 percent during the 1990s, in part due to the perception that moving into a nursing home was a "dreaded event." Although initially envisioned as a supportive care environment to promote quality of life, changes across the health care system have resulted in assisted living caring for residents with higher acuity and health care needs than originally expected. Indeed, national data indicate that many assisted living residents have hypertension, diabetes, chronic obstructive pulmonary disease, and coronary heart disease, as well as depression and dementia. Therefore, medical and psychosocial care are important in the future of assisted living. In addition to medical care needs, it is important to address dementia care in assisted living—most especially the use of "off-label" antipsychotic medications to address behaviors among people with dementia—and the overall provision of person-centered care, lest these settings adopt an institutional model of care.

Two medical care issues also loom large in the future of assisted living: the use of long-term care medical practices to provide care to residents, and affiliation with hospitals. All four of these areas—specialty medical care, affiliation with hospitals, antipsychotic use, and person-centered care—warrant research as assisted living moves into the future.

THE FUTURE OF ASSISTED LIVING AND HOUSING WITH SERVICES

AL providers face the need to provide supports and services to residents with more complex and chronic care needs than in the past. The lack of uniformity of how AL is defined is of growing concern to policy makers, researchers, practitioners, and consumers. However, the debate continues as to whether AL settings that create care standards and regulations similar to those of nursing homes will lose their distinctive philosophical emphasis on resident independence, privacy, and autonomy. Furthermore, although AL is less costly than nursing home care, many older adults cannot afford to pay privately and may not be eligible for Medicaid waivers. Finally, as baby boomers age, research suggests that they are likely to be interested in a variety of housing options with supportive services that may include assisted living, continuing care retirement communities, and housing for older adults; however, some of these options may be out of reach for low- to moderate-income older adults (Robinson, Shugrue, Fortinsky, Gruman, & Williamson, 2014). The future of AL settings and housing with services will greatly depend on their affordability, accessibility, and availability.

CHAPTER SUMMARY

- Although no uniform definitions exist, assisted living is broadly defined as a residential care setting that provides older adults with assistance and supervision with personal and health care as well as support with activities of daily living.
- Housing with services is usually considered independent living and is focused on providing housing and services such as meals, housekeeping, transportation, and social activities.

- Service-enriched housing describes living arrangements that provide health and social services to older adults who live in publicly subsidized buildings for low-income older adults.
- AL is the fastest growing long-term sector in the United States.
- A growing number of residents in AL have a diagnosis of dementia or cognitive impairment.
- Research suggests that the provision of resident services through service coordinators results in positive health outcomes for older adults wishing to age in place in their communities.

DISCUSSION QUESTIONS AND EXERCISES

1. Review the statements in the Fact or Fiction? list near the beginning of the chapter. After reading this chapter, can you identify which are true and which are false?
2. Imagine that you are approached to help with a preadmission assessment for a potential AL resident. What kind of questions might you ask both the older adult and his or her family members?
3. How is the philosophy of AL different from that of a nursing home?
4. Describe the research evidence about AL and housing with services.
5. Discuss the pros and cons of creating a uniform definition of AL.

ADDITIONAL RESOURCES

Aegis Gardens: http://www.aegisliving.com/aegis-living-of-aegis-gardens/
American Seniors Housing Association: https://www.seniorshousing.org
Assisted Living Federation of America: https://www.argentum.org
National Center for Assisted Living: https://www.ahcancal.org/ncal/Pages/index
.aspx

REFERENCES

Argentum. (2016). *State regulations and licensing.* Retrieved from http://www
.argentum.org/alfa/State_Regulations_and_Licensing_Informat.asp
Assisted Living Workgroup. (2003). *Assuring quality in assisted living: Guidelines for federal and state policy, state regulation, and operations.* Final Report to the U.S. Senate Special Committee on Aging. Retrieved from http://www.theceal
.org/images/alw/ALWReport-Definition-and-Core-Principles.pdf

Ball, M.M., Perkins, M.M., Hollingsworth, C., Whittington, F.., & King, S.V. (2009). Pathways to assisted living: The influence of race and class. *Journal of Applied Gerontology, 22*(1), 81–108.

Ball, M.M., Perkins, M.M., Whittington, F.J., Hollingsworth, C., King, S.V., & Combs, B.L. (2005). *Communities of care: Assisted living for African Americans.* Baltimore, MD: Johns Hopkins University Press.

Caffrey, C., Harris-Kojetin, L., & Sengupta, M. (2015). *Variation in operating characteristics of residential care communities, by size of community: United States, 2014.* Retrieved from https://www.cdc.gov/nchs/data/databriefs/db222.pdf

Carder, P. C. (2017). State regulatory approaches for dementia care in residential care and assisted living. *The Gerontologist.* Advance online publication. doi: 10.1093/geront/gnw197

Carder, P. C., O'Keeffe, J., & O'Keeffe, C. (2015). *Compendium of residential care and assisted living regulations and policy.* Retrieved from https://aspe.hhs.gov /basicreport/compendium-residential-care-and-assisted-living-regulations -and-policy-2015-edition

Carlson, E., Coffey, G., Fecondo, J., & Newcomer, R. (2010). Medicaid funding for assisted living care: A five-state examination. *Journal of Housing for the Elderly, 24*(1), 5–27.

Castle, N., & Resnick, N. (2016). Service-enriched housing: The Staying at Home program. *Journal of Applied Gerontology, 35*(8), 857–877.

Cohen, E. (1974). An overview of long-term care facilities. In Elaine Brody (Ed.), *Social work guide for long-term care facilities* (pp. 11–26). Washington, DC: U.S. Government Printing Office.

Eckert, J. K., Carder, P. C., Morgan, L. A., Frankowski, A. C., & Roth, E. G. (2009). *Inside assisted living: The search for home.* Baltimore, MD: Johns Hopkins University Press.

Fields, N. L. (2016). Exploring the personal and environmental factors related to length of stay in assisted living. *Journal of Gerontological Social Work, 59*(3), 205–221.

Fields, N. L., & Dabelko-Schoeny, H. (2015). Aging in place. In Susan Krauss Whitbourne (Ed.), *Encyclopedia of Adulthood and Aging* (pp. 51–55). Hoboken, NJ: Wiley.

Fields, N. L., Koenig, T., & Dabelko-Schoeny, H. (2012). Resident transitions to assisted living: A role for social workers. *Health & Social Work, 37*(3),147–154.

Grabowski, D., Stevenson, D., & Cornell, P. (2012). Assisted living expansion and the market for nursing home care. *Health Services Research, 47*(6) 2296–2315.

Harris-Kojetin, L., Sengupta, M., Park-Lee, E., & Valverde, R. (2013). Long-term care services in the United States: 2013 overview. *Vital and Health Statistics, 3*(37). Retrieved from http://www.cdc.gov/nchs/data/nsltcp/long_term_care_services_2013.pdf

Harris-Kojetin, L., Sengupta, M., Park-Lee, E., Valverde, R., Caffrey, C., Rome, V., & Lendon, J. (2016). *Long-term care providers and services users in the United States: Data from the national study of long-term care providers, 2013–2014.* Retrieved from https://www.cdc.gov/nchs/data/series/sr_03/sr03_038.pdf

Hyde, J., Perez, R., Doyle, P., Forester, B., & Whitfield, T. (2014). The impact of enhanced programming on aging in place for people with dementia in assisted living. *American Journal of Alzheimer's Disease & Other Dementias, 30*(8), 733–737.

Kane, R. A. (2001). Long-term care and a good quality of life: Bringing them close together. *Gerontologist, 41*(3), 293–304.

Kane, R. A., & Wilson, K. B. (1993). *Assisted living in the United States: A new paradigm for residential care for frail older persons?* Washington, DC: AARP Public Policy Institute.

Kane, R. A., & Wilson, K. B. (2001). *Assisted living at the crossroads: Principles for its future.* Portland, OR: Jessie F. Richardson Foundation.

Koehn, S. D., Mahmood, A. N., & Stott-Eveneshen, S. (2016). Quality of life for diverse older adults in assisted living; The centrality of control. *Journal of Gerontological Social Work, 59*(7–8), 512–536.

Koenig, T. L., Lee, J. H., Fields, N. L., & Macmillan, K. R. (2011). The role of the gerontological social worker in assisted living. *Journal of Gerontological Social Work, 54*(5), 494–510.

Levine, C., & Johns, A. (2008). *Multifamily property managers' satisfaction with service coordination.* Retrieved from https://www.huduser.gov/Publications/PDF/Multifamily_prop.pdf

McNabney, M. K., Onyike, C., Johnston, D., Mayer, L., Lyketsos, C., Brandt, J., ... Samus, Q. (2014). The impact of complex chronic diseases on care utilization among assisted living residents. *Geriatric Nursing, 35*(1), 26–30.

MetLife Mature Market Institute. (2012). *Market survey of long-term care costs.* Retrieved from https://www.metlife.com/assets/cao/mmi/publications/studies/2012/studies/mmi-2012-market-survey-long-term-care-costs.pdf

Mollica, R. L., Houser, A. N., & Ujvari, K. (2012). *Assisted living and residential care in the states in 2010.* Washington, DC: AARP Public Policy Institute.

National Center for Assisted Living. (n. d.) *Residents.* Retrieved from https://www.ahcancal.org/ncal/facts/Pages/Residents.aspx

National Center for Assisted Living. (2010). *2009 overview of assisted living.* Washington, DC: Author.

Perkins, M. M., Ball, M. M., Whittington, F. J., & Hollingsworth, C. (2012). Relational autonomy in assisted living: A focus on diverse care settings for older adults. *Journal of Aging Studies, 26*(2), 214–225.

Pynoos, J., Liebig, P., Alley, D., & Nishita, C. M. (2005). Homes of choice: Towards more effective linkages between housing and services. In J. Pynoos, P. H. Feldman, & J. Ahrens (Eds.), *Linking housing and services for older adults: Obstacles, options and opportunities* (pp. 5–49). Binghamton, NY: The Haworth Press.

Robinson, J., Shugrue, N., Fortinsky, R., Gruman, C., & Williamson, J. (2014). Long-term supports and services planning for the future: Implications from a statewide survey of baby boomers and older adults. *The Gerontologist, 54*(2), 297–313.

Sengupta, M., Harris-Kojetin, L., & Caffrey, C. (2015). *Variation in residential care community resident characteristics, by size of community: United States, 2014.* Retrieved from https://www.cdc.gov/nchs/data/databriefs/db223.pdf

Stone, R. (2013). What are the realistic options for aging in community? *Generations (San Francisco, California), 37*(4), 65–71.

Weiss, L. J., Malone, M., & Walsh, K. (2015). *Value of enhanced service coordination for American Association of Service Coordinators.* Retrieved from https://c.ymcdn.com/sites/www.servicecoordinator.org/resource/resmgr/Files/Useful_Links/Value_of_Enhanced_Service_Co.pdf

Wilson, K. B. (2007). Historical evolution of assisted living in the United States, 1979 to the present. *The Gerontologist, 47*(suppl 1), 8–22.

Wylde, M. A. (2008). The future of assisted living. Residents' perspectives, 2006–2026. In S. M. Golant & J. Hyde (Eds.), *The assisted living residence: A vision for the future* (pp. 169–197). Baltimore, MD: Johns Hopkins University Press.

Zimmerman, S., Anderson, W. L., Brode, S., Jonas, D., Lux, L., Beeber, A. S., . . . & Sloane, P. D. (2013). Systematic review: Effective characteristics of nursing homes and other residential long-term care settings for people with dementia. *Journal of the American Geriatrics Society, 61*(8), 1399–1409.

10

Adult Day Services

I have completely free hands from 9 o'clock in the morning until 4 in the afternoon and I can do whatever I like—not at all being dependent upon her. I can go here, there and everywhere—but then I just think what this has been doing for her—as I was telling you earlier—she looks forward to going [to day care]—obviously she feels good there and she returns [home] pleased, happy and grateful.

I can go on keeping him at home, as long as I have the support of my family, and not least the day-care facility. (Statements of family caregivers)

GUSTAFSDOTTIR, 2014, pp. 350-351

LEARNING OBJECTIVES

In this chapter, you will:

- Gain an understanding of the history and evolution of adult day services.
- Explore the different models of care and services offered in adult day services.
- Identify the characteristics of older adult participants and their family caregivers in adult day services.
- Learn about the roles of the different professionals practicing in adult day services.
- Review existing and emerging research on the impact and effectiveness of adult day services.
- Explore future directions for this growing service sector.

MANY SERVICES AND BENEFITS ARE offered in assisted living and housing with services, but assisted living may not be an affordable, available, or desirable option for some older adults and their families. These families face a dilemma: they need care beyond the limited hours offered through home care but don't necessarily want or require residential/institutional care. Adult day services straddle the line between home care and residential/institutional care. *Adult day services* (ADS), also referred to as adult day care, support the health, nutritional, social, and daily living needs of adults with functional limitations in a group setting during daytime hours (National Adult Day Services Association [NADSA], 2017a). ADS primarily serve older adults with cognitive and physical limitations, but they also serve younger adults with intellectual and developmental disabilities. Family caregivers benefit from ADS by receiving a break from caregiving duties (referred to as "respite"). This enables caregivers to work, to rest, and to remain engaged in life outside of their caregiving responsibilities. In recent years, ADS has begun to offer rehabilitation services for older adults. The number of ADS centers has grown in recent years, but many consider it to be an underutilized service within the spectrum of home- and community-based services (HCBS).

FACT OR FICTION?

Consider the following statements.

- Adult day services for older adults are not the same as day care for children, although the two types of care are grouped at times in intergenerational centers.
- Research has clearly demonstrated the effectiveness of adult day services for older adults and their caregivers.
- Adult day services are staffed primarily by volunteers drawn from the community.
- Adult day services are not highly regulated on the federal level, resulting in challenges in quality control and evaluation.
- There is a lack of diversity in adult day service participants, primarily because these services are targeted to higher-income families.
- Adult day services are funded directly by both Medicaid and Medicare.

After reading this chapter, you will be able to affirm which statements are fact and which are fiction.

HISTORY AND CURRENT STATE OF ADULT DAY SERVICES

Congregate settings serving older people existed in the United States prior to the 1960s, but ADS did not emerge as a provider of health care until the late 1960s and early 1970s. The adult day service model is based on the geriatric day hospitals in England. The first geriatric day hospital was transplanted to North Carolina and later to Pennsylvania. Early ADS programs focused on socialization and resembled senior centers. By the end of the 1970s, the Health Care Financing Administration listed almost 300 ADS programs. With concerns about cost containment for long-term care growing in the early 1980s, Congress passed Section 2176 of the Medicaid Waiver program, which enables states to receive matching federal funds when nursing home level care is delivered in the community—for example, in an ADS—at a lower cost. Other funding sources provided in the late 1970s and early 1980s included Title XX of the Social Security Act and Title III of the Older Americans Act. These policies provided funding through block grants for supportive and nutritional services delivered in a community-based environment (Dabelko, Koenig, & Danso, 2008).

As awareness and funding grew, the number of ADS centers increased. By the 1980s, it was estimated that 1,400 ADS centers were in operation (NADSA, 2017b). Public funding for ADS continued to grow in the 1990s and 2000s as public awareness was raised about the devastating effects of Alzheimer's disease and related dementias and the financial, physical, and emotional burden of family caregiving. As the number of baby boomers reaching older age increased, consumers began to want more choice in long-term care services and to receive care in the least restrictive environment possible. A 2002 census identified 3,400 centers in the United States (Partners in Caregiving, 2001–2002), and by 2014 an estimated 4,800 ADS centers were in operation, serving more than 280,000 participants and their families on any given day (Harris-Kojetin et al., 2016).

MODELS OF CARE AND SERVICES PROVIDED
IN ADULT DAY SERVICES

Historically, ADS have been characterized as either medical models, social models, or combined models of care (Weissert, 1976, 1977). Centers operating medical programs emphasized skilled assessment, treatment, and rehabilitation. Social models focused on socialization and preventive services, and combined models had elements of both social and medical models depending on individual participant needs. In 2002, approximately 37 percent of ADS centers were based on the medical model, 21 percent on the social model, and 42 percent on a combination of the medical and social models (Partners in Caregiving, 2001–2002). In 2010, more than 95 percent of ADS centers reported that they offered assistance with toileting and 89 percent offered blood pressure monitoring—certainly health-related services. Rather than continuing this classification system, it might be best to consider ADS as facilities that offer a wide range and combination of services that meet the holistic needs of participants and family caregivers.

So precisely what types of services do ADS centers provide? Services can be broken down into five general categories: transportation, nutrition, socialization and recreation, health care (including physical, mental health, and rehabilitation services), and caregiver support. Individual care plans lie at the heart of person-centered care and are the blueprints that outline the individual care needs and treatment of ADS participants. As expected, almost every center offers care planning, and these plans are updated on a regular basis, typically every three to six months (MetLife Mature Market Institute, 2010). As with congregate sites, getting older adults to the ADS center requires transportation services, and by 2010, more than three-quarters of ADS centers offered transportation to and from the facility. Nutrition services have long been a staple in ADS centers. In 2010, it was found that almost every ADS center offered meals to participants, most (85 percent) at no extra cost (MetLife Mature Market Institute, 2010). Opportunities for socialization and recreation are another core service provided by ADS. Social isolation and loneliness have been associated with higher levels of mental and physical health problems in older adults, as well as a higher risk of mortality (Hawkley & Cacioppo, 2010; Steptoe, Shankar, Demakakos, & Wardle, 2013). Three-quarters of ADS programs offer music, art, and pet therapy programs. Just under three-quarters of ADS programs offer intergenerational programming activities that bring different age groups together. More than 90 percent of ADS programs employ activity therapists who are trained to facilitate therapeutic interventions (MetLife Mature Market Institute, 2010). Social workers, nurses, and direct care staff also contribute to social and recreational programs.

Health care is another core provision in ADS and an area in which centers have become more capable and sophisticated in recent years. The most basic care generally revolves around activities of daily living (ADLs) and instrumental activities of daily living (IADLs), those activities that occur within the fabric of daily life. In 2010, more than 90 percent of ADS centers provided assistance with walking, toileting, transferring and sit-to-stand movements, and eating. Other basic services, such as bathing, were offered at more than half of all ADS centers, and more than 80 percent offered blood pressure monitoring, weight monitoring, medication management, and diabetes monitoring (MetLife Mature Market Institute, 2010). Almost half of ADS centers offered physical, occupational, and speech therapies in 2014, in some cases at no extra cost (Harris-Kojetin et al., 2016). Some centers provide podiatry, hearing, dental, and vision services on-site. Reflective of the growing capacity of ADS centers to address complex care needs, in 2010 approximately half of centers offered medication injections, wound care, catheter and colostomy care, and tube feeding (MetLife Mature Market Institute, 2010). Some centers are beginning to offer post acute care (rehabilitation care following hospitalization). Recognizing the need for holistic services, many ADS centers also provide mental health services to older adult participants in the form of medication management and counseling (Dabelko-Schoeny, Anderson, & Guada, 2013). More recent data indicate that approximately one-third of ADS centers provide mental health or counseling services (Harris-Kojetin et al., 2016). Bridging the physical and mental health domains, dementia care has been and continues to be a focus and strength in ADS. As the population struggling with dementia continues to grow, ADS will increasingly be called upon to provide community-based care.

Finally, ADS provides respite to family caregivers and enables them to work, rest, socialize, exercise, and engage with life. Although some may view caregiver respite as an indirect or collateral benefit, respite is a primary focus of ADS and is seen as equal to the benefits provided to participants. Respite benefits caregivers physically, emotionally, socially, and financially. ADS centers also offer key direct services to family caregivers. In 2010, 71 percent of ADS centers offer educational programs, 58 percent offer caregiver support groups, and 40 percent offer individual counseling (MetLife Mature Market Institute, 2010). Many ADS centers view family caregivers as partners in care and recognize that the health and well-being of family caregivers is critical to the health and well-being of the care recipient. In the future, there may be a growth in services provided to family caregivers in ADS as policy makers realize the central role caregivers play in home- and community-based care.

CASE STUDY

Angela is a 74-year-old African American woman who lives with her daughter, Valerie, in suburban Chicago. Angela was born and raised in the city and worked as a teacher's aide at an elementary school for more than thirty years. She retired in her sixties and lived with her husband until his death five years ago. After Angela's husband died, her emotional and physical health began to decline, and her family noticed signs of forgetfulness and confusion. Two years ago, Angela reluctantly agreed to move in with Valerie and her family. Angela was recently diagnosed with probable Alzheimer's disease along with an existing diagnosis of diabetes.

Over the past two years, Valerie has struggled to provide care to her mother while balancing full-time work and raising her children. She fears for her mother's safety during the daytime, particularly in terms of her wandering away from home and her high risk for falls. Valerie often leaves work during lunchtime to run home and check on her mother. These worries are beginning to take a toll on Valerie's emotional and physical well-being and her work performance. A friend suggests that she check out the adult day center that her own father attends. Valerie decides to go with her mother to visit the adult day center on her day off.

As the intake professional at the adult day center, consider the following statements and questions in relation to this case.

1. What questions and areas of concern will you will need to focus on in your assessment of Angela?
2. Angela will be the participant in your program, but you also are concerned with Valerie's well-being. What are your concerns and what might be some of Valerie's concerns? What support services could you offer Valerie?
3. Angela is clearly confused as to what is happening, and she appears reluctant to be a part of the adult day program. What techniques or interventions might help Angela adjust to this transition?
4. Create a care plan for Angela that addresses her physical, emotional, and social well-being. Incorporate ideas for helping Valerie care for her mother when she is home.

PRACTICE APPLICATION

In 2014, ADS centers reported that 64 percent of participants were age 65 and older and 59 percent (including younger adults) were women. Again, it is important to note that ADS also serves younger adults with IDD and other disabling conditions. In terms of race and ethnicity, approximately 44 percent of participants were non-Hispanic white, 20 percent were Hispanic, 17 percent were non-Hispanic black, and 19 percent were non-Hispanic other. This is considerably more diverse than the overall population (approximately 80 percent non-Hispanic white) and more diverse than other environments of care, such as home health, nursing homes, and hospice care. ADS centers reported that between 24 and 40 percent of participants required assistance with bathing, dressing, toileting, or eating (Harris-Kojetin et al., 2016). In 2010, more granular level data were collected by MetLife Mature Market Institute (2010) on the health conditions of ADS participants. The most prevalent conditions of participants were dementia, hypertension, physical disabilities, cardiovascular disease, and diabetes (figure 10.1). The most common reasons for enrolling in ADS were decreased functional ability, the need for caregiver respite, declines in caregivers' ability to provide care, and increased behavioral challenges presented by the care recipient.

Staffing in ADS centers is necessarily interdisciplinary. In 2010, it was reported that almost 60 percent of ADS directors had backgrounds and

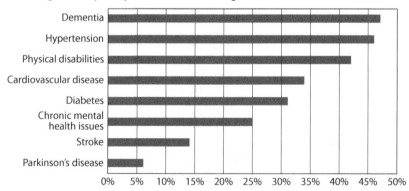

FIGURE 10.1 Health conditions of ADS participants.

Source: MetLife Mature Market Institute, 2010.

education in the helping disciplines, including nursing, social work, and activities/recreation therapy. Approximately 30 percent of ADS directors came from the business and health care management and administration disciplines (MetLife Mature Market Institute, 2010). Staffing in ADS centers tends to consist primarily of direct care workers (DCW), typically nursing assistants and aides, and professional staff including registered nurses (RN), licensed practical nurses (LPN), social workers, and activity therapists. In 2014, 60 percent of ADS centers employed at least one RN, 45 percent employed at least one LPN, 70 percent employed at least one nursing assistant, 43 percent employed at least one social worker, and 88 percent employed at least one activities director on staff (Harris-Kojetin et al., 2016). The ratio of DCWs to participants improved from one DCW for every eight participants in 2002 to one DCW for every six participants in 2010 (MetLife Mature Market Institute, 2010). Physical, occupational, and speech therapists frequently provide services and may be present on a daily basis in centers that offer post acute rehabilitation. Physicians, dentists, and podiatrists provide periodic visits to ADS centers, which is one of the advantages of congregate care settings. Professionals can make one stop and visit multiple patients in a cost- and time-effective manner (Harris-Kojetin et al., 2016). This also benefits family caregivers who do not need to take extra time off to escort their loved ones to appointments.

Perspectives from the Field

Beth Meyer-Arnold RN, MS
Principal, Cygnet Innovations Group LLC
Milwaukee, Wisconsin

What is your professional background and training?

I have a BS and an MS in nursing and community health with a gerontology focus.

What is your role in ADS?

I was the director of an ADS for twenty-five years and now work as a consultant in the industry.

*What challenges have you faced in working with older
adults in ADS?*

ADS will always have the challenge of responding to the current needs of participants. Long-term care is very focused on nursing home and other residential settings and hasn't really learned that people want to stay at home. This may be the fault of adult day services too, as we have not advocated as well as we could for the value of ADS.

What do you see as the future for ADS?

The future of ADS depends on our ability to articulate our contributions to the health of citizens and to the efficiencies and effectiveness of the health care system. How well can we work with managed care organizations? How can we be a value to the primary physicians in their offices? Can we keep people out of expensive emergency room visits? Can we rehab older adults after a fall? If we can do these things, then we have a future as a prominent partner in the health of all Americans.

*What advice would you give to someone interested
in working in ADS?*

Find a mentor and ask that person to help you with challenging and emerging service situations. Ask for help in motivating your staff to work as a team. Learn about person-centered dementia care and practice it every day. Expect more from your team and from your participants—they will all surprise and delight you!

FUNDING OF ADULT DAY SERVICES

ADS is one of the most affordable forms of HCBS, averaging approximately $65 for a full day. Although comparisons are challenging due to differences in rates and services, ADS is generally considered less expensive than home health care ($20/hour), assisted living ($3,500/month), and nursing home care ($212–$240/day; Genworth Financial, 2014). Costs for ADS have not increased dramatically, as have other sectors of health care even though the services offered in ADS have grown in number and complexity. The affordability of ADS is beneficial to families and society, but the expenses of providing care often exceed current fees. The expenses associated with providing care totaled close to $69 per day in 2010 (MetLife Mature Market Institute, 2010). In the vast majority of cases, ADS programs struggle to keep fees low and to control the costs of providing care.

Funding for ADS is more complex than most other forms of HCBS and varies widely from state to state. Medicare does not pay for ADS; however, Medicaid does pay for ADS for lower-income older adults with nursing home level of care needs. In many states, Medicaid funding is directed to ADS through Home and Community-Based Services Waiver programs. These programs are designed to give states flexibility in spending funds on the care of older adults with the aim of diverting funding from institutional care such as nursing homes to community care. The Veterans Administration also provides funding for ADS and in 2010 was listed as the second largest source of public funds. Approximately one-quarter of funding for ADS centers comes straight from the pockets of participants and their families (private pay). The remainder of the funding for ADS is made up of public funding, grants, donations, organization funding, and private insurance (figure 10.2). As you might expect, funding has been identified as the most pressing current and future concern for ADS centers (Anderson, Dabelko-Schoeny, & Tarrant, 2012).

Some ongoing funding initiatives use Medicare funding to cover ADS for older adults. Programs for All-Inclusive Care for the Elderly (PACE) provide HCBS (including ADS) for older adults (age 55 and older in this case) who otherwise would require nursing home care. The key to the

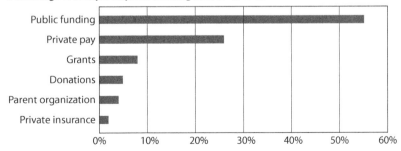

Percentage of ADS participants needing assistance with:

FIGURE 10.2 Sources of funding for ADS.
Source: MetLife Mature Market Institute, 2010.

PACE model is the availability and use of Medicare funding in a flexible manner rather than having funds delineated for certain types or settings of care. PACE organizations must meet certain requirements set forth by the Centers for Medicare and Medicaid Services (CMS) to be eligible for funding. In 2013, there were 113 PACE programs serving older adults in thirty-two states—a relatively small number of programs. Although limited in scope, evidence suggests that this flexible, person-centered approach to funding and providing care may be a cost-effective alternative to traditional fee-for-service approaches (Wieland, Kinosian, Stallard, & Boland, 2013).

DIVERSITY IN ADULT DAY SERVICES—A FOCUS ON CULTURALLY COMPETENT CARE

As current statistics indicate, ADS centers have one of the most diverse client bases of any of the service platforms in HCBS. ADS also has a long history of honoring and serving diverse populations. One exemplary program that started more than forty-five years ago is the On Lok ADS program in Northern California. This was one of the first ADS programs in the country to recognize the importance of tailoring services to specific groups within the older adult population. Started in 1972, On Lok focused primarily on the unmet needs of older adults of Chinese descent. On Lok provides a welcoming environment, culturally competent staff, and culturally sensitive and appropriate programming in terms of language, traditions, customs, and preferences. The On Lok approach is reflected in a growing number of ADS programs across the country. For example, the United Community Center (Centro de la Comunidad Unida) in Milwaukee, Wisconsin, offers programs geared toward the Latino population. Staff are bilingual, meals are prepared that celebrate Latino traditions, and programming is sensitive to the histories and preferences of the Latino population they serve.

Perhaps because of the community-embedded approach of ADS and programs such as On Lok, the ADS industry has been especially adept at meeting the needs of diverse older adults. As the older adult population in the United States grows increasingly diverse, it is imperative that ADS centers continue to address the unique cultural needs of participants and their family members. For example, ADS centers should design and deliver programs and services that take into account cultural and religious traditions, food preferences, language and language barriers, gender roles, sexual orientation (such as LGBT elders), potential mistrust of health care professionals/formal care providers, the importance of informal care/family caregiving among minority populations, and culture imbedded in relationships and human interaction (Black et al., 2017). More so than most other systems of care, ADS centers appear to be well-positioned to meet the needs of older adults and their families in a fashion that is both person- and family-centered and culturally informed.

RESEARCH AND EVIDENCE ON THE IMPACT OF ADULT DAY SERVICES

Over the past several decades, the evidence that supports the benefit of ADS has grown gradually and steadily. Gaugler and Zarit (2001) conducted a systematic review of research in ADS from 1975 to 2000. The authors concluded that "adult day programs appear to exert positive impacts on some domains of client functioning, but not on others" (p. 32). There was a lack of consistency in the results of the studies particularly related to the impact of ADS on health status/outcomes, participant behavior, and functional status (that is, independence with activities of daily living). Gaugler and Zarit did find a consensus that ADS use was positively related to improved mood and morale and a high level of satisfaction with services. The 2001 systematic review found that with "sustained and regular utilization, adult day services have a positive impact on caregivers' stress and negative mental health" (p. 35). The number of days and the constancy of attendance appear to play a role in the effectiveness of ADS for caregivers. The impact of ADS on health care utilization was tentative but suggested that ADS attendance does not necessarily delay nursing home placement nor serve as an alternative to nursing home care.

Over a decade later, a second systematic review was conducted, again looking at the effectiveness of ADS (Fields, Anderson, & Dabelko-Schoeny, 2014). This research again found that ADS attendance was related to improvements in psychosocial well-being, such as mood, engagement, and "problem behaviors." The impact of ADS attendance on physical well-being was more complex and appeared to be program specific. For example, a study evaluating a fall prevention program in ADS found a reduction in falls in the treatment group compared with the control group receiving ADS services as usual (Diener & Mitchell, 2005). The 2014 review revealed additional evidence that ADS can have positive benefits for family caregivers, such as reducing stress and burden and improving general well-being. Evidence of the positive impact of ADS for caregivers of people with dementia has grown, particularly when targeted interventions were offered such as comprehensive care management and dementia care-specific training (Gitlin, Reever, Dennis, Mathieu, & Hauck, 2006). In contrast to the 2001 review, evidence has begun to suggest that ADS utilization may delay nursing home placement, particularly when the caregiver is an adult child (Kim, Zarit, Femia, & Savla, 2012). Additional research is needed to fully understand the relationships between ADS use and delays in institutionalization. Research since 2000 has begun to look at other indices of health care utilization, and the results are promising. For example, one study found that older adults who use ADS for rehabilitation services were less likely to be readmitted to the hospital than older adults who were discharged to nursing homes or to home health care (Jones et al., 2011).

More recent research has begun to shed additional light on the benefits of ADS, particularly with regard to respite provided to family caregivers. Researchers at the Center for Healthy Aging at the Pennsylvania State University have examined the relationship between ADS attendance and caregiver stress using biomarkers, such as cortisol and sleep patterns. Their findings suggest that ADS use helps to moderate sleep duration and cortisol levels resulting in "better days" for caregivers when their family members are enrolled in ADS (Leggett, Liu, Klein, & Zarit, 2016; Liu, Almeida, Rovine, & Zarit, 2016). Other researchers have found additional evidence suggesting links between ADS use and delayed institutionalization (Kelly, Purveen, & Gill, 2016). Such findings are critical as ADS evolves and as policy makers and funding agencies consider shifting attention toward HCBS and away from institutional care.

An Expert Weighs In

Shannon E. Jarrott, PhD
Professor, College of Social Work
The Ohio State University
Columbus, Ohio

Research has shaped ADS in a few ways. First, most research surrounding ADS use has addressed the impact of respite on family caregivers; most studies report benefits and push researchers now to study the impact on participants. Second, researchers have introduced innovative approaches and services, often grounded in theory, that are now commonplace at ADS centers, such as person-centered care, music therapy, and intergenerational programming. Third, research suggests that use of ADS services has grown but is still underutilized, which points to an imperative to study health benefits to ADS participants that equate to financial benefits for families and insurers. Research using standardized outcome measures is important for advancing our knowledge. As a result, limited data are available on the health and well-being of ADS participants. The gap in knowledge about the impact of ADS on participants may contribute to families' reluctance to choose ADS for a loved one.

ADS research will continue to explore innovative programming and design initiatives (such as the physical environment) that add to a menu of therapeutic services that benefit participants, families, and staff. A shift to participant outcome research will highlight best practices for providers and promote standards of care that foster aging in place for participants, ease caregiver burden, and increase organizational stability. Future research will pull back the curtain on ADS; the "best kept secret" in elder care will no longer be a secret.

THE FUTURE OF ADULT DAY SERVICES

Not unexpectedly, the future complexion and growth of ADS is largely tied to funding. If the current funding structure remains unchanged, ADS centers will continue to provide services for older adults in the community. However, centers will struggle to piece together their funding, and the true potential of ADS may never be realized. Expanded Medicare funding for ADS is the key to realizing this potential. Efforts to secure expanded Medicare funding for ADS have not been met with success in the past. The Medicare Adult Day Services Act (H.R. 3043), introduced in Congress in 2009, called for expanded Medicare support for the "substitution" of ADS for services typically provided by home health care and by nursing homes. The bill met with opposition from the home health and nursing home industries and was not enacted. In 2013, a slightly modified version of the bill (H.R. 3334) was introduced again, calling for Medicare coverage for ADS. This legislation also failed to be ratified; however, a similar bill (H.R. 1383) was introduced in 2015 and sits with the Subcommittee on Health. ADS centers remain one of the most cost-effective service platforms in HCBS, and the populations served and the ability to meet complex care needs have seen exponential growth. Whether funding agencies recognize the potential of ADS centers to meet the challenges and opportunities presented by our aging society remains to be seen.

CHAPTER SUMMARY

- ADS centers support the health, nutritional, social, and daily living needs of older adults with functional limitations in a group setting during daytime hours.
- ADS centers provide important respite and support services for family caregivers.
- ADS centers provides a wide array of services, including transportation, opportunities for socialization, and the prevention and treatment of chronic and acute health conditions.
- At an average of approximately $65 per day, ADS is a cost-effective care option for older adults and their families.
- ADS appear poised to grow in the coming years as the baby boom generation ages and anticipated demand for HCBS increases; however, the lack of Medicare funding may prevent ADS from reaching its full potential.

DISCUSSION QUESTIONS AND EXERCISES

1. Review the statements in the Fact or Fiction? list near the beginning of the chapter. After reading this chapter, can you identify which are true and which are false?
2. Imagine you are a member of an interdisciplinary team that cares for individuals attending an ADS center. What kind of questions might you need to ask prospective participants and their family caregivers upon enrollment in the program?
3. Develop a care plan for a newly enrolled ADS participant with moderate dementia, urinary incontinence, and a history of depression.

4. The evidence that ADS has a positive impact on participants and reduces costly service utilization such as emergency department visits and hospitalization is mixed. Design a study that could further build our understanding of the potential benefits of ADS.

5. Imagine that you are giving a tour of an ADS facility to a prospective family caregiver. What kinds of information would you provide about the services and supports provided for both caregivers and participants?

6. ADS benefits are not currently reimbursed by Medicare. Imagine that you are speaking with your congressperson—what talking points would you share about the benefits of ADS that warrant Medicare coverage?

ADDITIONAL RESOURCES

LeadingAge: https://www.leadingage.org

National Adult Day Services Association (NADSA): http://www.nadsa.org

National Association of States United for Aging and Disabilities (NASUAD): http://www.nasuad.org

National PACE Association: www.npaonline.org

On Lok: www.onlok.org

United Community Center (Centro de la Comunidad Unida): www.unitedcc.org

REFERENCES

Anderson, K. A., Dabelko-Schoeny, H. I ., & Tarrant, S. D. (2012). A constellation of concern: Exploring the present and the future challenges for adult day services. *Home Health Care Management & Practice, 24*(3), 132–139.

Black, H. K., Rubinstein, R. L., Frankowski, A. C., Hrybyk, G., Nemec, M., & Tucker, G. G. (2017). Identity, semiotics, and use of symbols in adult day services. *Gerontologist*. Advance online publication. doi:10.1093/geront /gnx074

Dabelko, H. I., Koenig, T. L., & Danso, K. (2008). An examination of the adult day services industry using the resource dependence model within a values context. *Journal of Aging & Social Policy, 20*(2), 201–217.

Dabelko-Schoeny, H., Anderson, K. A., & Guada, J. E. (2013). Adult day services: A service platform for delivering mental health care. *Aging & Mental Health, 17*(2), 207–214.

Diener, D. D., & Mitchell, J. M. (2005). Impact of a multifactorial fall prevention program upon falls of older frail adults attending an adult health day care center. *Topics in Geriatric Rehabilitation, 21*(3), 247–257.

Fields, N. L., Anderson, K. A., & Dabelko-Schoeny, H. I. (2014). The effectiveness of adult day services for older adults: A review of the literature from 2000 to 2011. *Journal of Applied Gerontology, 33*(2), 130–163.

Gaugler, J. E., & Zarit, S. H. (2001). The effectiveness of adult day services for disabled older people. *Journal of Aging & Social Policy, 12*(2), 23–47.

Genworth Financial. (2014). *Genworth 2014 cost of care survey: Home care providers, adult day health facilities, assisted living facilities and nursing homes.* Retrieved from https://www.genworth.com/dam/Americas/US/PDFs/Consumer/corporate/130568_032514_CostofCare_FINAL_nonsecure.pdf

Gitlin, L. N., Reever, K., Dennis, M. P., Mathieu, E., & Hauck, W. W. (2006). Enhancing quality of life of families who use adult day services: Short- and long-term effects of the Adult Day Services Plus program. *Gerontologist, 46*(5), 630–639.

Gustafsdottir, M. (2014). The family's experience of sharing the care of a person with dementia with the services in specialized day-care units. *Dementia and Geriatric Cognitive Disorders Extra, 4,* 344–354.

Harris-Kojetin, L., Sengupta, M., Park-Lee, E., Valverde, R., Caffrey, C., Rome, V., & Lendon, J. (2016). Long-term care providers and services users in the United States: Data from the National Study of Long-Term Care Providers, 2013–2014. *Vital Health Statistics, 3*(38). Retrieved from https://www.cdc.gov/nchs/data/series/sr_03/sr03_038.pdf

Hawkley, L. C., & Cacioppo, J. T. (2010). Loneliness matters: A theoretical and empirical review of consequences and mechanisms. *Annals of Behavioral Medicine, 40,* 218–227.

Jones, K. R., Tullai-McGuinness, S., Dolansky, M., Farag, A., Krivanek, M. J., & Matthews, L. (2011). Expanded adult day program as a transition option from hospital to home. *Policy, Politics, & Nursing Practice, 12*(1), 18–26.

Kelly, R., Puurveen, G., & Gill, R. (2016). The effect of adult day services on delay to institutional placement. *Journal of Applied Gerontology, 35*(8), 814–835.

Kim, K., Zarit, S. H., Femia, E. E., & Savla, J. (2012). Kin relationship of caregivers and people with dementia: Stress and response to intervention. *International Journal of Geriatric Psychiatry, 27,* 59–66.

Leggett, A. N., Liu, Y., Klein, L. C., & Zarit, S. H. (2016). Sleep duration and the cortisol awakening response in dementia caregivers utilizing adult day services. *Health Psychology, 35*(5), 465–473.

Liu, Y., Almeida, D. M., Rovine, M. J., & Zarit, S. H. (2016). Modeling cortisol daily rhythms of family caregivers of individuals with dementia: Daily stressors and adult day services. *Journals of Gerontology: Psychological and Social Sciences.* Advance online publication. doi: 10.1093/geronb/gbw140

MetLife Mature Market Institute. (2010). *The MetLife national study of adult day services.* Retrieved from http://www.metlife.com/assets/cao/mmi/publications /studies/2010/mmi-adult-day-services.pdf

National Adult Day Services Association. (2017a). *About adult day services.* Retrieved from http://www.nadsa.org/learn-more/about-adult-day-services/

National Adult Day Services Association. (2017b). *Historical highlights.* Retrieved from http://nadsa.org/learn-more/historical-highlights/

Partners in Caregiving. (2001–2002). *National study of adult day services.* Retrieved from http://www.rwjf.org/pr/product.jsp?id=20940

Steptoe, A., Shankar, A., Demakakos, P., & Wardle, J. (2013). Social isolation, loneliness, and all-cause mortality in older men and women. *Proceedings of the National Academy of Sciences, 110*(15), 5797–5801.

Wieland, D., Kinosian, B., Stallard, E., & Boland, R. (2013). Does Medicaid pay more to a Program of All-Inclusive Care for the Elderly (PACE) than for fee-for-service long-term care? *Journals of Gerontology: Biological Sciences & Medical Sciences, 68*(1), 47–55.

Weissert, W. G. (1976). Two models of geriatric day care. *Gerontologist, 16*(5), 420–427.

Weissert, W. G. (1977). Adult day care programs in the United States: Current research projects and a survey of 10 centers. *Public Health Reports, 92*(1), 49–56.

Hospice Care in Community Settings

A few conclusions become clear when we understand this: that our most cruel failure in how we treat the sick and the aged is the failure to recognize that they have priorities beyond merely being safe and living longer; that the chance to shape one's story is essential to sustaining meaning in life; that we have the opportunity to refashion our institutions, our culture, and our conversations in ways that transform the possibilities for the last chapters of everyone's lives.

ATUL GAWANDE, 2014

LEARNING OBJECTIVES

In this chapter, you will:

- Gain insight into the introduction and development of hospice care in the United States.
- Explore and compare the different models of care and services offered in hospice.
- Identify the characteristics of hospice patients and the challenges of reaching and serving certain populations.
- Learn about the roles of the different professionals practicing in hospice.
- Review existing and emerging research on the impact of hospice.
- Explore the future of hospice in the face of changing societal attitudes toward end-of-life care.

MODERN U.S. SOCIETY HAS NOT been particularly effective at allowing older adults and those who are seriously ill to self-define the end of their life. Focusing on curing disease often overshadows the importance of allowing those at the end of life to die a peaceful death with some degree of control and choice. For many, and especially for older adults, dying in the comfort of home, or experiencing a "good death," is not what the future holds. More than two-thirds of adults age 85 and older die in either the nursing home or the hospital; only one-fifth die at home (Centers for Disease Control and Prevention [CDC], 2011). This trend is beginning to change, and fewer older adults are dying in institutions and more older adults are dying at home. Hospice is one home- and community-based service (HCBS) that has played a role in this shift. Hospice is a model of care that provides comprehensive services at the end of life with the goals of patient and family comfort, alleviation of pain, and support during and after the dying process. Typically, hospice care is provided to individuals with less than six months to live. As the National Hospice and Palliative Care Organization (NHPCO, 2015) succinctly states, "Hospice focuses on caring, not curing" (p. 3). "Palliative care" and "hospice" are often used interchangeably, and both focus on comfort; however, there are distinctions in meaning. *Hospice* focuses on care at the end of life, whereas *palliative care* can be administered to provide comfort at any time during the course of an illness.

FACT OR FICTION?

Consider the following statements.

- Hospice is primarily provided at inpatient facilities and, in rare cases, in the home setting.
- Caring for people at the end of life goes back centuries, but the modern hospice movement did not begin until the 1960s.
- Hospice care is provided primarily by nursing and medical professionals because the goal is to treat underlying conditions and illnesses.
- Hospice has had challenges in reaching and providing services to certain groups, such as African Americans and Native Americans.
- For-profit hospices tend to have higher satisfaction rates because they are driven toward excellence by market forces and competition.

After reading this chapter, you will be able to affirm which statements are fact and which are fiction.

HISTORY OF HOSPICE IN THE UNITED STATES

Providing comfort care to the dying goes back centuries in time, but the modern hospice movement can be traced back only decades to one influential physician, Dame Cicely Saunders. In 1967, Dame Saunders founded the first hospice in London, and it is still in operation. During this same period, Elisabeth Kubler-Ross (1969) wrote *On Death and Dying*, a widely read and seminal book on death and dying that calls for specialized care for the terminally ill and emphasizes choice in the way that we die. In 1974, the first hospice in the United States was founded in Connecticut by Florence Ward, an early colleague of Saunders. The hospice was based on the model created by Saunders and was influenced by the discussion and tone set by Kubler-Ross in her work on and advocacy for compassionate end-of-life care (Connor, 2007). This is echoed in the words of Dame Saunders: "You matter because you are you, and you matter to the end of your life. We will do all we can, not only to help you die peacefully, but also to live until you die" (St. Christopher's, 2017).

Three early legislative and funding events helped to establish hospice as an accepted government-funded health care option (NHPCO, 2016). In 1979, the Health Care Financing Administration (now known as the Centers for Medicare and Medicaid Services [CMS]) supported a demonstration project to evaluate the effectiveness of hospice and scope of services. Three years later, in 1982, Congress granted initial approval of temporary funding for a Medicare hospice benefit. Rather than focusing on the mission of hospice, the federal government viewed hospice as a potential cost-containment approach to end-of-life care (Gage et al., 2000). Congress approved permanent funding for a Medicare hospice benefit in 1984 after seeing that this approach to end-of-life care could reduce health care expenditures. At the same time, states were granted the option of funding for a Medicaid hospice benefit. The hospice benefit was approved for funding through the Veterans Administration for veterans and the Indian Health Service for American Indians and Alaskan Natives in the mid-1980s.

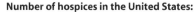

Number of hospices in the United States:

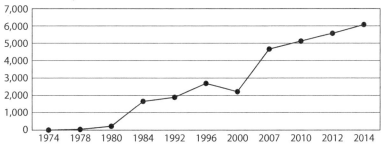

FIGURE 11.1   Hospice providers in the United States.
Source: Gage et al., 2000; NHPCO, 2015.

The hospice "industry" has expanded rapidly since 1974. Early estimates of the number of hospice programs in the United States were included in a report on the hospice industry (Gage et al., 2000). Only 58 hospices were in existence in 1978, but that figure had increased fourfold by 1980. Permanent funding for hospice in 1984 increased the number of hospices to 1,694, and by 1992 there were 1,935 hospices. Growth leveled out in the late 1990s (2,722 in 1996) but increases continued steadily into the twenty-first century (figure 11.1). By 2014, hospices were in operation in all fifty states, Washington, D.C., and other U.S. territories, and an estimated 6,100 hospices served 1.7 million hospice patients and their families (NHPCO, 2015). Recent movements (for example, Death with Dignity) have worked to expand options for the terminally ill and to increase the acceptance of death and are partially behind the expansion of hospice. Patient-, person-, and family-centered care, the demand for patient choice, and changing attitudes toward death have all played a role and will continue to drive the evolution of hospice and end-of-life care.

PRACTICE APPLICATION

Entrance into hospice begins with an assessment and determination of eligibility (termed "certification"). CMS provides a basic set of criteria to enable individuals and families to elect the hospice benefit. In 2013, 91 percent of hospice patients were covered by Medicare or Medicaid and their eligibility was governed by these criteria. For hospice patients covered by other payment sources, such as private insurance or self-pay, these same eligibility criteria are generally applied:

- The hospice provider or primary care provider (limited to physicians and trained nurse practitioners) must certify that the patient is terminally ill with a life expectancy of six months or less.
- The patient (or his or her health care proxy) must accept palliative care instead of curative approaches.
- The patient (or his or her health care proxy) must sign a statement electing hospice services and declining other curative treatments. (CMS, 2015)

Based on NHPCO guidelines, hospice organizations develop "local coverage determinations" (LCDs) outlining general clinical and disease-specific criteria to aid physicians in determining whether a patient has a life expectancy of six months or less. In general, patients must display a decline in clinical status such as weight loss, infection, poorly controlled nausea, diarrhea, or increasing pain. Problematic changes in laboratory results and low scores should also be considered, such as reductions in oxygen saturation. Increases in emergency department visits and hospitalizations are indicators that hospice may be appropriate. Declines in functional status, increased dependency, and low scores on performance tests (such as the Karnofsky Performance Scale or the Palliative Performance Scale) are also used in determining eligibility. In addition, patients must meet disease-specific criteria related to their primary diagnosis. For example, cancers must be at certain stages (metastases), and the condition must be worsening despite therapies and treatments (NHPCO, 2010a).

Typically, hospice benefits are extended to patients in ninety-day periods. At the end of each period, physicians must recertify that patients are terminally ill with a life expectancy of six months or less. Hospice benefits are available to those living longer than six months, but these patients must be recertified every sixty days. Patients can stop hospice services at any time. For patients whose illness is no longer deemed terminal and who no longer need hospice, health care would resume under the same format as prior to the terminal illness. For example, a patient's cancer may go into remission, and he or she may no longer need hospice. However, the patient still may have complex medical needs, and these needs would be met with "care as usual" (CMS, 2015).

Implementing these general and disease-specific eligibility criteria and determining whether a patient has six months to live can be incredibly challenging for health care professionals. More problematic, however, is the fact that most hospice patients receive services for only two weeks or less (NHPCO, 2015). This calls into question whether such a brief time fully allows patients and families to benefit from hospice services. The fact is that most older adults do not use hospice at the end of life. Only 32.3 percent of 65 and older Medicare decedents used hospice in 2010, and undoubtedly other individuals and families would have benefited from hospice services (Aldridge, Canavan, Cherlin, & Bradley, 2015). The health care system and health care professionals bear some of this responsibility, but the election of hospice benefits is far more complex. Patients and families grapple with the difficult decision of moving from the curative to the palliative mind-set and accepting the finality of death. The decision to elect hospice is influenced by the level of understanding of the prognosis, past experiences with the illness and with health care in general, decision-making styles, and communication and relationships with their health care providers. Scholars have suggested that a shared decision-making process might be most effective in the optimal timing of hospice election (Romo, Wallhagen, & Smith, 2016).

CASE STUDY

Janet is an 88-year-old white woman who has been living with end stage renal disease for a year. She was widowed over fifteen years ago and has lived in an assisted living facility for the past four years. Janet has a son and daughter who live nearby and another daughter who lives across the country. Janet selected her eldest daughter, who lives out of town, to be her health care proxy. The dialysis treatments have taken a toll on Janet both physically and emotionally, and she has expressed a wish to stop dialysis. Her two children who live locally have witnessed and shared in her struggles and agree that this might be time to shift to hospice care. Her eldest daughter and health care proxy disagrees and states, "We can't just let Mom die."

Janet's case has been referred to you, a nurse case manager, to see if hospice might be an option. As the nurse case manager, your job is to assess the patient and the family, to educate them on hospice and end-of-life decision making, and to help them receive the most appropriate care in the given circumstances. When you enter Janet's room at the assisted living facility, you feel the tension in the air as

(CONTINUED)

you sit down with Janet and her adult children. You introduce yourself and begin to learn more about Janet, her family, and the difficult decisions they now face.

Consider the following questions related to this difficult, but common, case.

1. Who is the client in this situation—Janet, her health care proxy, her other two children, or the entire family system?
2. What ethical principles are at play in this situation?
3. Write down the statements and phrases you would use to describe hospice to this family.
4. How would you respond to the statement, "We can't just let Mom die"?
5. What online information and educational resources are available to families?

HOSPICE SERVICES, PROVIDERS, AND PATIENTS

Adopting language from the Social Security Act, the scope of hospice is officially defined as "services provided to a terminally ill individual . . . under a written plan established and periodically reviewed by the individual's attending physician and by the medical director (and by the interdisciplinary group)." These services include:

- Nursing care provided by or under the supervision of a registered professional nurse.
- Physical or occupational therapy, or speech-language pathology services.
- Medical social services under the direction of a physician (or qualified nurse practitioner).
- Services of a home health aide and homemaker.
- Medical supplies (including drugs and biologicals) and the use of medical appliances.
- Physicians' services.
- Short-term care (including both respite care and procedures necessary for pain control and acute and chronic symptom management) in an inpatient facility. (Note: Respite care may be provided only on an intermittent, nonroutine, and occasional basis and may not be provided consecutively over longer than five days.)
- Dietary counseling.
- Counseling with respect to adjustment to death. (CMS, 2016)

The law goes on to note that these services may be provided on a "24-hour, continuous basis only during periods of crisis and only as necessary to maintain the terminally ill individual at home" (CMS, 2016). Most hospice care is intermittent unless there is a crisis. Hospice is far different from intensive care, for example, where staff are continuously on hand administering or anticipating treatment. This may come as a surprise to some family members, especially those who view dying as a time of crisis requiring medical intervention.

Although hospice services are comprehensive, they typically will *not* cover the following:

- Treatment intended to cure a terminal illness or related conditions. (Note: Patients do have the right to stop hospice care at any time.)
- Prescription drugs (except for symptom control or pain relief).
- Care from any provider that wasn't set up by the hospice medical team.
- Room and board except short-term respite care.
- Care in an emergency room, inpatient facility care, or ambulance transportation, unless it's either arranged by the hospice team or is unrelated to the terminal illness and related conditions. (CMS, 2015)

Hospice services can be delivered in a variety of locations, including private residences, congregate housing (such as assisted living facilities), nursing homes, hospitals, and specifically designated hospice facilities. Unfortunately, there is a common misperception that a person must relocate to a designated hospice facility to receive end-of-life care. Most hospice patients receive services until the end of their lives in their own private homes or in their rooms in assisted living facilities or nursing homes. Only about one-third of hospice patients die in hospice facilities. Hospices can be free-standing/independent organizations (57.4 percent), part of a hospital system (20.5 percent), part of a home health agency (16.9 percent), or part of a nursing home (5.2 percent). Most hospices are rather moderate in size, with 78.7 percent admitting 500 or fewer patients per year and 45.6 percent admitting 150 or fewer patients per year. Mean daily census figures (the average number of patients served on any given day) were estimated at 137.7 patients per day in 2013 (NHPCO, 2015). Tax status has been changing rapidly over the last twenty years, and there are more for-profit than nonprofit hospices today. This is one of the biggest changes in

THE FOR-PROFIT QUESTION

In 1992, only 13 percent of Medicare-certified hospices were for-profit. Ten years later, 47 percent of Medicare-certified hospices were for-profit. Today, well over half of all hospices are operated as for-profit ventures, and the growth in the industry has almost entirely been attributed to the for-profit sector (NHPCO, 2015). What does this shift from almost entirely nonprofit to majority for-profit mean for the hospice movement and for hospice consumers? The quality of care in for-profit and nonprofit hospices is similar (Halabi, 2014), but for-profit hospices tend to offer a narrower range of services and focus on mandatory services that offer the best profit margin. In addition, for-profit hospices are less likely to admit patients with anticipated short stays, which are less profitable (American Society of Clinical Oncology, 2008). Halabi (2014) suggests that the focus on profit runs counter to the original mission of hospice and argues that "the commercialization of hospice care has resulted in the expansion of monetary and business incentives to the care network that used to work toward patient welfare free from these distorting influences (p. 451). As with other sectors in health care, the future orientation of the hospice industry may be driven more by economics than by patient welfare and evidence-based best practices.

hospice, and questions persist as to whether for-profit status detracts from the "noble mission" and focus of hospice (see box).

Hospice is one of the most inter- and multidisciplinary programs within the spectrum of HCBS. From medical and nursing services, to social and spiritual care, to home health aide and volunteer services, hospice is designed to meet the often complex, multifaceted needs of patients and families at the end of life. Professionals, paraprofessionals, administrative staff, and volunteers all have distinct roles, and cooperation and coordination are key to the successful implementation of hospice services. It is important to note that these roles are shared, and the lines between disciplines is blurred. Physicians and nurses often provide emotional support and perform psychosocial assessments, social workers and spiritual counselors can be conduits for medical concerns, and volunteers and home health aides may be the most important providers of comfort care, social support, and emotional support within the entire team. The care plan serves as the written roadmap for providing person-centered care, and all of the disciplines in hospice play a role in developing this plan. Care plans typically include patient/family goals, diagnoses and assessments, interventions to achieve goals, and coordination with outside agencies and resources. NHPCO (2010b) suggests that the interdisciplinary team review the care plan every fifteen days or as needed as patient and family needs change.

Hospice services are available to any age group; however, the vast majority of hospice patients are older adults. Approximately 84 percent of hospice patients are age 65 and older and over 40 percent are age 85 and older. Women (56.4 percent) are more likely than men (45.3 percent) to receive hospice services (NHPCO, 2015). In the earlier years of hospice, most hospice patients had a primary diagnosis of cancer, but this has changed over the years. In the latest available figures (NHPCO, 2015), cancer accounted for just over one-third of primary diagnoses for hospice (figure 11.2). Dementia diagnoses for hospice patients has risen (from 12.8 percent in 2012 to 15.2 percent in 2013), as have diagnoses for chronic conditions such as heart disease (from 11.2 percent in 2012 to 13.4 percent in 2013) and lung disease (from 8.2 percent in 2012 to 9.9 percent in 2013). Amyotrophic lateral sclerosis (ALS) and HIV/AIDS account for only a small percentage of primary diagnoses in hospice (0.4 percent and 0.2 percent in 2013, respectively).

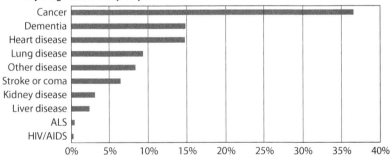

FIGURE 11.2 Primary diagnoses of hospice patients.
Source: NHPCO, 2015.

Perspectives from the Field

An interview with Sami J. Douglas, MSW
Director of Social Services in Hospice
and
Penny Jankovich, RN
Director of Nursing in Hospice
Missoula, Montana

*How does multidisciplinary teamwork play into your work
in hospice?*

Interdisciplinary (or multidisciplinary) teamwork is the foundation
of hospice services. The hospice nursing staff view a patient through a
"physical lens." The hospice social work staff view a patient through an
"emotional lens." The hospice spiritual care staff view a patient through
a "spiritual lens." Collectively, the ongoing assessments of each of these
disciplines inform the development and modification of an individualized
plan of care.

What has been the most rewarding aspect of working in hospice?

As hospice practitioners, we are both acutely aware that we are invited
into a family's life at a most vulnerable time. We do not take this trust for
granted. Being offered the gift of trust is truly the most profound reward of
our work.

*What advice would you give to someone interested
in working in hospice?*

For both of us, our hospice work is a calling and not simply a job. Our
hearts are engaged each and every day through the work we do; therefore,
it is imperative that we make a commitment to our own self-care as a personal, professional, and ethical responsibility. Seek mentorship and clinical
supervision from hospice professionals. Self-awareness is key; one must be
able to manage not only complex patient/family emotions but one's own
emotions related to end of life as well.

DIVERSITY IN HOSPICE—A FOCUS ON AMERICAN INDIANS/ ALASKAN NATIVES

Race and ethnic diversity among hospice patients is not representative of the U.S. population, and this is an issue of concern: 75.9 percent of hospice patients were white in 2015, 7.6 percent were black, 7.1 percent were Hispanic, 3.1 percent were Asian/Pacific Islander, and 0.3 percent were American Indian/Alaskan Native (NHPCO, 2015). A number of factors account for the relatively low use of hospice by racially/ethnically diverse individuals and families. These include personal and cultural values that conflict with the hospice philosophy, lack of awareness of hospice services, lack of availability of hospice services, mistrust of the health care system, language barriers, and historical discrimination (Cagle, LaMantia, Williams, Pek, & Edwards, 2015; Park, Jang, Ko, & Chiraboga, 2016; Washington, Bickel-Swenson, & Stephens, 2008). Some of these same factors affect low-income individuals and individuals from historically marginalized groups, such as the lesbian, gay, bisexual, and transgender populations (Farmer & Yancu, 2015; O'Mahoney et al., 2008).

Disparities in hospice utilization are particularly glaring for American Indians and Alaskan Natives (AI/AN). For example, researchers found that only 2.8 percent of end-of-life patients at one Indian Health Service hospital in New Mexico used their Medicare hospice benefit compared to a state average of 30.8 percent (Domer & Kauer, 2008). Lack of access, geographic isolation, poverty, and lack of cultural awareness and competence have all been cited as reasons for these disparities in hospice use for AI/AN patients (Domer & Kauer, 2008). Fortunately, models of successful hospices have emerged that help bring hospice and palliative care services to the AI/AN population. The Zuni Home Health Care Agency (ZHHCA) serves the Zuni Pueblo Indians, and they kept the views of their community at the forefront when designing their hospice and end-of-life care programs. The ZHHCA conducted an initial needs assessment to gauge the community's desires and preferences for hospice services. Language and communication were found to be critically important. Using respectful language and presenting information in the presence of the family were important techniques. Having community members educate health care professionals about their culture and beliefs was also helpful in providing sensitive and appropriate end-of-life care.

Hiring staff members who are part of the tribe and training staff on culturally sensitive care were critical elements of the success of this program
(Finke, Bowannie, & Kitzes, 2004).

RESEARCH AND EVIDENCE

Evaluating the effectiveness of hospice differs somewhat from the evaluation of other approaches of HCBS for older adults. In hospice, almost
all of the patients die—an outcome that is generally viewed as a failure
in curative, preventative approaches. Systematic reviews have summa-
rized the impact of hospice and palliative care on patients, families, and
the health care system in some domains (Agency for Healthcare Research
Quality [AHRQ], 2012; Candy, Holman, Leurent, Davis, & Jones, 2011;
Zimmerman, Riechelmann, Krzyzanowska, Rodin, & Tannock, 2008).
Researchers have found evidence that moderately supports the conclu-
sion that palliative and hospice care provides effective pain management.
Palliative and hospice care also results in higher levels of patient and family
caregiver satisfaction. Hospice care, in particular, appears to be effective in
helping patients die in the home setting, which in turn may be related to
satisfaction and quality of life. In terms of emotional well-being, it is not
clear that palliative and hospice care alleviates the distress associated with
dying. Singular studies suggest that hospice holds great promise and has
a capacity to positively affect patients and family members by providing
grief and depression screenings and subsequent therapeutic interventions
(Ghesquiere et al., 2015).

The literature on health care utilization and cost is also mixed, but the
evidence suggests hospice has the potential to save money. One systematic
review found that hospice care, specifically in community settings, was
associated with reductions in health care utilization and cost (Candy et al.,
2011). A more recent review found that palliative care approaches at the
end of life were significantly less costly than comparative approaches (Smith,
Brick, O'Hara, & Normand, 2014). Other studies have echoed the findings
that hospice care saves money, primarily through reduced hospital stays
(Zuckerman, Stearns, & Sheingold, 2016). One group of researchers found
that these cost savings ranged from $2,561 to $6,430 when comparing hospice enrollees to matched non–hospice users (Kelley et al., 2013). On the

other hand, researchers have not found cost savings as hospice patients lived longer and continued to consume health care resources (Campbell, Lynn, Louis, & Shugarman, 2004; Meng, Dobbs, Wang, & Hyer, 2013). We are beginning to grasp the potential benefits of hospice, but much research is left to be done as health care systems change, new approaches and options emerge, and the needs and desires of patients and families evolve.

An Expert Weighs In

Sara Sanders, MSW, PhD
Associate Professor and Director, School of Social Work
University of Iowa
Iowa City, Iowa

With the birth of hospice care in the United States approximately fifty years ago, attention to end-of-life care has blossomed. Multiple trends are occurring nationally that present exciting opportunities for hospice programs to meet the needs of patients and families. Palliative care is growing in both hospitals and in communities as patients are seeking better pain management and symptom control as well as improved communication with their provider.

Currently four states (Oregon, Washington, California, and Vermont) have Death with Dignity laws, and Montana has Death with Dignity by court decision. Another twenty-four states have considered Death with Dignity laws, or steps are being taken to present Death with Dignity legislation. As more Death with Dignity laws are passed, hospice programs nationally will expand their service delivery models to accommodate this additional end-of-life care option.

Illinois passed medical marijuana legislation on January 1, 2016, and for states with similar legislation, education for hospice providers about the utilization of medical marijuana is necessary. Additional areas that require our attention and additional research include expanding lengths of stay, which currently is seventeen days, greater outreach to diverse populations, expansion of cultural competency training for staff and volunteers, and expanding evidence-based protocols for both pharmacological and non-pharmacological interventions.

THE FUTURE OF HOSPICE

As with other areas of health care, policy will most certainly drive the future of hospice. As others have noted, one of the most pressing areas of concern are policies that restrict access and create barriers to hospice services (Aldridge Carlson, Barry, Cherlin, Mc Corkle, & Bradley, 2012; Wallace, 2015). For example, it is difficult to predict the course of certain diseases (such as Alzheimer's disease), and many patients could benefit from hospice services even if their life expectancy cannot be accurately determined or may exceed six months. Patients often are not referred until the final days or weeks of life and may not fully benefit from hospice services. In addition, patients and families may be hesitant to forgo curative treatments as specified in the current eligibility criteria for the hospice benefit. For example, cancer patients on chemotherapy are typically required to stop treatments as they shift to hospice care. Some emerging policies and options may expand the reach of hospice, such as open-access policies that allow patients to enroll in hospice prior to fulfilling all of the eligibility criteria. The goal is to transition the patient to hospice and to optimize the timing of services to allow for the full benefit of hospice services. Another approach, concurrent services, allows hospice patients to receive continued curative care at the same time that they are receiving hospice care (Wallace, 2015). Others have suggested reframing hospice and palliative care as "primary care" that could and should be delivered by all health care professionals and be a part of care as usual (Murray, 2015). These types of expansions are likely to continue as the baby boomers and future generations express their voices and choices about living to the end of their life.

CHAPTER SUMMARY

- Hospice provides comprehensive comfort, palliative, and supportive care to patients and families at the end of life.
- The goals of hospice care are to alleviate pain, to provide emotional and spiritual support to patients and families, to facilitate comfort during the dying process, to provide choice in terms of one's own death, and to reduce expensive costs at the end of life.

- To be eligible for hospice, an individual's medical provider must "certify" that the patient has six months or less to live, and the person must forgo curative treatment.
- Eighty-four percent of hospice patients are age 65 and older, and 40 percent are age 85 and older.
- Most hospice care is delivered in patients' own residences—and this is where they eventually die.

DISCUSSION QUESTIONS AND EXERCISES

1. Review the statements in the Fact or Fiction? list near the beginning of the chapter. After reading this chapter, can you identify which are true and which are false?
2. Understanding roles and boundaries is important when working on a multidisciplinary hospice team. Go online and compare the codes of ethics of the following professionals:
   a. Social workers (https://www.socialworkers.org/pubs/code/code.asp)
   b. Nurses (http://www.nursingworld.org/codeofethics)
   c. Physicians/Medical professionals (http://www.ama-assn.org/ama/pub /physician-resources/medical-ethics/code-medical-ethics.page)
3. What are some steps that could increase the length of service and thus the overall benefit of hospice services?
4. Do you ever envision hospice care as being "care as usual" at the end of life? What would facilitate this shift? What would prevent or deter this shift?

ADDITIONAL RESOURCES

American Academy of Hospice and Palliative Medicine: http://aahpm.org
Death with Dignity Movement: https://www.deathwithdignity.org
Hospice Foundation of America: https://hospicefoundation.org/End-of-Life -Support-and-Resources
National Association for Home Care & Hospice: http://www.nahc.org
National Hospice and Palliative Care Organization: https://www.nhpco.org
National Palliative Care Research Center: http://www.npcrc.org
St Christophers hospice, London: http://www.stchristophers.org.uk/

REFERENCES

Agency for Healthcare Research Quality. (2012). *Improving health care and palliative care for advanced and serious illness*. Retrieved from http://effectivehealthcare .ahrq.gov/search-for-guides-reviews-and-reports/?pageaction=displayproduct &productID=1303

Aldridge, M. D., Canavan, M., Cherlin, E., & Bradley, E. H. (2015). Has hospice use changed? 2000–2010 utilization patterns. *Medical Care, 53*(1), 95–101.

Aldridge Carlson, M. D., Barry, C. L., Cherlin, E. J., McCorkle, R., & Bradley, E. H. (2012). Hospices' enrollment policies may contribute to underuse of hospice care in the United States. *Health Affairs, 31*(12), 2690–2698.

American Society of Clinical Oncology. (2008). The debate in hospice care. *Journal of Oncology Practice, 4*(3), 153–157.

Cagle, J. G., LaMantia, M. A., Williams, S. W., Pek, J., & Edwards, L. J. (2015). Predictors of preference for hospice care among diverse older adults. *American Journal of Hospice & Palliative Care Medicine*. Advance online publication. doi: 10.1177/1049909115593936

Campbell, D. E., Lynn, J., Louis, T. A., & Shugarman, L. R. (2004). Medicare expenditures associated with hospice use. *Annals of Internal Medicine, 140*, 269–272.

Candy, B., Holman, A., Leurent, B., Davis, J., & Jones, L. (2011). Hospice care delivered at home, in nursing homes and in dedicated hospice facilities: A systematic review of quantitative and qualitative evidence. *International Journal of Nursing Studies, 48*, 121–133.

Centers for Disease Control and Prevention. (2011). *Location of death for decedents Aged ≥85 years: United States, 1989–2007*. Retrieved from http://www.cdc .gov/mmwr/preview/mmwrhtml/mm6037a9.htm

Centers for Medicare & Medicaid Services. (2015). *Medicare benefit policy manual*. Retrieved from https://www.cms.gov/Regulations-and-Guidance/Guidance /Manuals/downloads/bp102c09.pdf

Centers for Medicare & Medicaid Services. (2016). *Hospice*. Retrieved from https://www.cms.gov/Medicare/Medicare-fee-for-service-payment/hospice /index.html

Connor, S. R. (2007). Development of hospice and palliative care in the United States. *Omega, 56*(1), 89–99.

Domer, T., & Kauer, J. S. (2008). Palliative practice in Indian health. *South Dakota Medicine, Special Edition*, 36–40.

Farmer, D. F., & Yancu, C. N. (2015). Hospice and palliative care for older lesbian, gay, bisexual and transgender adults: The effect on history, discrimination, health disparities and legal issues on addressing service needs. *Palliative Medicine and Hospice Care, 1*(2), 36–43.

Finke B., Bowannie T., & Kitzes J. (2004). Palliative care in the Pueblo of Zuni. *Journal of Palliative Medicine, 7*(1), 135–143.

Gage, B., Miller, S. C., Coppala, K., Harvel, J., Laliberte, L., Mor, V., & Teno, J. (2000). *Important questions for hospice in the next century.* Retrieved from http://aspe.hhs.gov/daltcp/reports/impques.pdf

Gawande, A. (2014). *Being mortal: Medicine and what matters in the end.* New York, NY: Metropolitan Books.

Ghesquiere, A. R., Aldridge, M. D., Johnson-Hurzeler R., Kaplan, D., Bruce, M. L., & Bradley, E. (2015). Hospice services for complicated grief and depression: Results from a national survey. *Journal of the American Geriatrics Society, 63,* 2173–2180.

Halabi, S. (2014). Selling hospice. *Journal of Law, Medicine & Ethics, 42*(4), 442–454.

Kelley, A. S., Deb, P., Du, Q., Aldridge C., Melissa D., & Morrison, R. S. (2013). Hospice enrollment saves money for Medicare and improves care quality across a number of different lengths-of-stay. *Health Affairs, 32,* 552–561.

Kubler-Ross, E. (1969). *On Death and Dying.* New York, NY: Macmillan.

Meng, H., Dobbs, D., Wang, S., & Hyer, K. (2013). Hospice use and public expenditures at the end of life in assisted living residents in a Florida Medicaid waiver program. *Journal of the American Geriatrics Society, 61,* 1777–1781.

Murray, S. A. (2015). Palliative care as a primary care issue. In E. Bruera, I. Higginson, C. F. von Gunten, & T. Morita (Eds.), *Textbook of palliative medicine and supportive care* (2nd ed., pp. 83–90). Boca Raton, FL: CRC Press.

National Hospice and Palliative Care Organization. (2010a). *Initial certification of the hospice terminal illness: Compliance tip sheet.* Retrieved from http://www .nhpco.org/sites/default/files/public/regulatory/Initial_Certification _TerminalIllness_TipSheet.pdf

National Hospice and Palliative Care Organization. (2010b). *Patient and family-centered care standards.* Retrieved from http://www.nhpco.org/sites/default /files/public/quality/Standards/PFC.pdf

National Hospice and Palliative Care Organization. (2015). *NHPCO's facts and figures: Hospice care in America.* Retrieved from http://www.nhpco.org /resources

National Hospice and Palliative Care Organization. (2016). *History of hospice care.* Retrieved from http://www.nhpco.org/history-hospice-care

O'Mahoney, S., McHenry, J., Snow, D., Cassin, C., Schumacher, D., & Selwyn, P. A. (2008). A review of barriers to utilization of the Medicare Hospice Benefit in urban populations and strategies for enhanced access. *Journal of Urban Health, 85*(2), 281–290.

Park, N. S., Jang, Y., Ko, J. E., & Chiraboga, D. A. (2016). Factors affecting willingness to use hospice in racially/ethnically diverse older men and women. *American Journal of Hospice and Palliative Medicine, 33*(8) 770–776.

Romo, R. D., Wallhagen, M. I., & Smith, A. K. (2016). Viewing hospice decision making as a process. *American Journal of Hospice and Palliative Medicine, 33*(5), 503–510.

Smith, S., Brick, A., O'Hara, S., & Normand, C. (2014). Evidence on the cost and cost-effectiveness of palliative care: A literature review. *Palliative Medicine, 28*(2), 130–150.

St. Christopher's website. (2017). *Tributes to Dame Cicely Saunders.* Retrieved from http://www.stchristophers.org.uk/about/damecicelysaunders/tributes

Wallace, C. (2015). Hospice eligibility and election: Does policy prepare us to meet the need? *Journal of Aging & Social Policy, 27,* 364–380.

Washington, K. T., Bickel-Swenson, D., & Stephens, N. (2008). Barriers to hospice use among African Americans: A systematic review. *Health & Social Work, 33*(4), 267–274.

Zimmermann, C., Riechelmann, R., Krzyzanowska, M., Rodin, G., & Tannock, I. (2008). Effectiveness of specialized palliative care: A systematic review. *Journal of the American Medical Association, 299*(14), 1698–1709.

Zuckerman, R. B., Stearns, S. C., & Sheingold, S.H. (2016). Hospice use, hospitalization, and Medicare spending at the end of life. *The Journals of Gerontology: Series B, 71*(3), 569–580. doi: 10.1093/geronb/gbv109

International Perspectives on Home- and Community-Based Services

For many years, when we were still really children, we stopped playing "My Generation" because we thought we were too old. That was The Who themselves buying into the wrong interpretation of the lyric "I hope I die before I get old," which is more about a state of mind than actual age.

PETE TOWNSHEND, 2006

LEARNING OBJECTIVES

In this chapter, you will:

- Understand the broad picture of the aging world population.
- Explore the green care farm approach to caring for older adults in the community.
- Learn about the dementia village concept currently in operation in the Netherlands.
- Gain an understanding of how the physical activity on prescription program works in Sweden.
- Critically examine the factors that facilitate and retard development and implementation of innovative approaches to home- and community-based services in the United States.

WHEN BRITISH ROCKERS THE WHO sang their classic anthem "My Generation" in 1965, the bandmates were in their twenties. The surviving members of the band and their "generation" are now in their seventies and are part of a rapidly aging world. As the World Health Organization (WHO, 2015; an entirely different WHO) reported, "for the first time in history most people can expect to live into their 60s and beyond" (p. 3). Indeed, it appears that most people in the world are not dying before they "get old"! Across every region of the world, populations are aging, and this trend is expected to continue for several decades. By 2050, the proportion of those over age 60 across the world will have grown from 12 percent to 22 percent, and by 2020 this group of older adults will outnumber children under the age of 5 (WHO, 2015). Two major factors account for this dramatic shift in demographics: increases in life expectancy and decreases in fertility rates. Life expectancy across all regions of the world has increased since 1950, and this trend is projected to continue (figure 12.1). By 2050, the life expectancy of the world population will have increased by almost twenty years on average. At the same time, world fertility rates present a reverse image (figure 12.2). People are having fewer children in almost every region, regardless of income level (WHO, 2015).

Examining the world by region paints a much clearer picture of the aging of the world's population. Populations in all regions of the world are

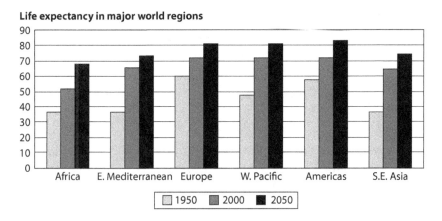

Life expectancy in major world regions

FIGURE 12.1 Changes in life expectancy.
Source: Adapted from WHO, 2015.

Births per woman 1960–2010

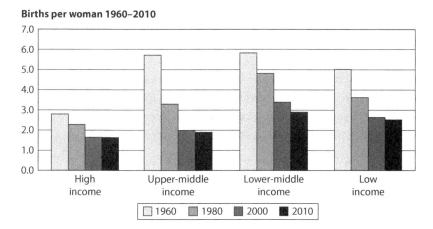

FIGURE 12.2 Fertility rates.

Source: Adapted from WHO, 2015.

aging, but the rates are not uniform. Table 12.1 breaks down the number and percentage of those age 65 and older and provides projected changes in 2030 and 2050 in six major world regions. In Africa, for example, the percentage of the overall population age 65 and older is projected to almost double (3.5 percent to 6.7 percent) by the year 2050. In Asia, Europe, and Latin America, the percentage of those age 65 and older is

TABLE 12.1 Population Age 65 and Older by Region

REGION	POPULATION 65+ (MILLIONS)			% OF REGIONAL POPULATION 65+		
	2015	2030	2050	2015	2030	2050
Africa	40.6	70.3	150.5	3.5	4.4	6.7
Asia	341.4	587.3	975.3	7.9	12.1	18.8
Europe	129.6	169.1	196.8	17.4	22.8	27.8
Latin America	47.0	82.5	139.2	7.6	11.8	18.6
North America	53.9	82.4	94.6	15.1	20.7	21.4
Oceania	4.6	7.0	9.5	12.5	16.2	19.5

Source: Adapted from He, Goodkind, & Kowal, 2016.

projected to grow by approximately 10 percent. In North America, that growth is significant, yet much smaller when compared with other major regions, a little over 6 percent (He, Goodkind, & Kowal, 2016). The aging U.S. population is often referred to as the "Silver Tsunami." If that is the case, the wave is much bigger and presents much greater challenges in other major regions of the world.

Some of the more pressing challenges include finding answers to these questions:

- With dependency ratios (the number of older adults divided by the number of working age adults) increasing, who is going to care for this growing number of older adults?
- How are governments going to finance the care needs of this group?
- Can societies create innovative approaches to caring for older adults in the community rather than in more costly and less desirable institutions?

In this chapter, we turn our attention to home- and community-based services (HCBS) for older adults on the international level. HCBS present many opportunities for innovative and potentially cost-effective approaches to meeting the needs of older adults across the world. Rather than providing a broad overview, we focus on three approaches currently in place in Europe: the green care farm, the dementia village, and physical activity on prescription programs. These programs were selected based on their (a) innovative nature and design, (b) lower or comparable cost versus traditional or institutional approaches, and (c) potential for adaptation and adoption in the United States.

FACT OR FICTION?

Consider the following statements.

- The growing number of older adults globally presents challenges, but the dependency ratio should be of equal or greater concern.
- In the green care farm model, farm production is key, and most older adults with dementia are not well-suited for these settings.
- European models of dementia villages are currently being developed in the United States.

- In physical activity on prescription programs, older adults and their families face penalties and higher insurance premiums if they don't complete the exercise programs.
- Two of the most challenging barriers to adapting and adopting innovative approaches to care for older adults in the United States are the rigid nature of the U.S. health care system and the litigious nature of U.S. society.

After reading this chapter, you will be able to affirm which statements are fact and which are fiction.

GREEN CARE FARMS

The benefits of engaging with nature have long been touted as a remedy to a wide array of health problems, both physical and mental. As societies have modernized and industrialized, however, fewer and fewer people have access to natural environments, and health care systems have turned away from natural approaches and rely primarily on medical interventions. In the last few decades, however, programs have been developed that incorporate nature into care plans for individuals with special needs. Emerging in Europe in the early 1990s, *green care farms* (GCFs) are actual working farms where adults with disabilities (most notably, older adults with dementia) engage in activities ranging from feeding and caring for animals to harvesting vegetables and preparing fresh meals. The intention of GCFs is to provide meaningful and therapeutic activities and experiences to clients in noninstitutional, natural settings. GCFs also offer opportunities for community engagement, social inclusion, skill building, and even paid employment for clients in sheltered work programs. The "therapy" on GCFs is often referred to as "hidden therapy" because the benefits are derived from activities that don't resemble traditional therapeutic approaches. The respite provided by GCFs is also a much-needed benefit for family caregivers. Finally, the farms benefit as they receive reimbursement for the provision of these services (de Bruin, Oosting, van der Zijpp, Enders-Slegers, & Schols, 2010). The GCF model has expanded across Europe and into Asia. For example, more than 1,000 GCFs are in operation in the Netherlands and in Norway.

The GCF model has been used with a wide array of participants, including younger adults with intellectual and developmental disabilities, individuals with mental health and addictions issues, and older adults with physical and cognitive limitations. In this review, we focus primarily on GCFs for older adults with dementia—one of the primary populations served by GCFs. As in the United States, traditional HCBS across the world include home health care and adult day services. In countries where GCFs are in operation, however, older adults with dementia and their families are given the option of attending a GCF as an alternative to the traditional HCBS model.

The key here is that attendance at GCFs is a choice made by the health care consumer. Once an older adult and his or her family make this choice, the older adult is matched with a farm and a program of activities that meet his or her interests and abilities. The older adult then attends the GCF program from one to five days a week, depending on the person's level of interest and need and available funding. Care farms are financed differently in each country, but funding generally comes from government sources along with a sliding scale of private co-payments.

GCFs vary widely in designs, environments, and activities offered. "Care farming is a truly complex intervention. Farms differ in terms of the type of farming activities (e.g., horticulture and livestock farming), other activities (e.g., gardening, conservation, woodwork and metal work) and well-being and skills interventions provided (e.g., health promotion, counselling and skills qualifications)" (Elsey et al., 2014, p. 1). The key to the GCFs is matching the activities to the abilities and desires of the older adult. One of the benefits of the farm environment is that there are activities for almost every ability level. A "typical day" on a GCF might look like this:

- Transportation is provided from the older adult's home to the GCF.
- The older adult is greeted by the farmer and her or his fellow participants.
- Participants engage in a scheduled morning activity. This could include planting vegetables, feeding animals, or collecting and sorting eggs or produce.
- Participants help prepare lunch and then eat in a congregate setting. Preparing and sharing lunch is critical to building community and facilitating social engagement.
- After a brief rest after lunch, participants engage in a scheduled afternoon activity.
- Participants are thanked for their contributions and transported home.

A growing body of research has focused on the effects of GCFs on older adults with dementia. Early studies found that older adults with dementia who were engaged with GCFs tended to show fewer behavioral problems, required fewer psychotropic drugs, and had an enhanced sense of well-being (Milligan, Gatrell, & Bingley, 2004; Rappe, Kivelä, & Rita, 2006; Schols & van der Schriek-van Meel, 2006). More recent studies echoed these findings and found benefits for older adults with dementia ranging from enhanced sense of social inclusion and participation to improved dietary intake (de Bruin et al., 2010, 2015). Research on GCFs is ongoing; we have only scratched the surface in understanding the benefits of this approach.

An Expert Weighs In

Simone de Bruin, PhD
Senior Researcher, Department for Quality of Care and Health Economics
Dutch National Institute for Public Health and the Environment
Centre for Nutrition, Prevention, and Health Services
Netherlands

As a researcher, I have studied the impact of green care farms for over ten years in the Netherlands and across Europe, and I've been a senior researcher at the Centre for Nutrition, Prevention, and Health Services since 2009. So far, we don't know much about the impact of green care farms in the long term (for example, nutritional status or physical functioning) or on outcomes such as behavioral symptoms and medication use (for example, psychotropic drugs). Both in the Netherlands and Norway new studies are being conducted that focus on some of these gaps.

Green care farms may be beneficial for people with dementia for several reasons. First, the homelike and noninstitutional environment at green care farms may evoke memories and stimulate the senses so that people with dementia may easily feel at home. Second, the variety of environments at green care farms make it possible to choose and to participate in activities that best fit clients' preferences and abilities. Third, having a choice may provide a strong sense of autonomy and identity, and the availability of useful and meaningful activities (such as feeding animals, gardening, preparing meals) may enable people with dementia to feel useful. Fourth, the opportunities to be active at green care farms may enhance the mobility of people with dementia.

The GCF model only recently came to the United States, and only one small program based on the European model is currently in operation in rural Montana. A recent evaluation of this program concluded that the GCF model is feasible within the U.S. health care system and that the benefits for participants and family members reflect those found in European studies. However, there are some substantial barriers to implementing the GCF model in the United States, including the rigidity of the U.S. health care system, an overdeveloped focus on liability and risk, and negative societal views on the abilities and potential of older adults with dementia (Anderson, Chapin, Reimer, & Siffri, 2017). We hope the potential of this innovative HCBS approach will provide the necessary buoyancy to overcome these hurdles. A brief interview with Maarten Fischer, the director of the first GCF program in the United States based on the European model, follows.

Perspectives from the Field

An interview with Maarten Fischer, MS
Director of Lifeside Farms (GCF)
Kalispell, Montano

*What is your professional background as it relates
to green care farms?*

I have more than fifteen years of experience implementing and operating green care farms and sustainable agriculture projects in both the United States and Europe.

*How do green care farms foster a sense of purpose
for older adults?*

On the farms, everyone has a chance to contribute and gain a sense of purpose. A long-term care facility manager once told me that he could decrease health-related issues and cost by 50 percent if he could give people a sense of purpose.

What have been the reactions of family members?

People often say that their loved ones spend half the week looking forward to the farm day and the other half of the week talking about what happened there. In traditional forms of respite, caregivers often feel a stigma of guilt, but this is not the case with us because the participants have just as much of a fun day off as the caregiver or family members.

*What do you see as the future of green care farming
in the United States?*

Our concept can be copied to other areas of the country, but I do think it works best when managers are from a local or regional level. It took flight in many European countries, and I really do hope it will in the United States too. If it does, it would be wise to develop a national standard early in the process to ensure quality and safety for all involved in it.

HOGEWAY: THE DEMENTIA VILLAGE APPROACH

The Netherlands is also home to another innovative approach to caring for older adults with dementia in the community. *Hogeway is a purpose-built, gated community specifically designed for older adults with dementia.* Located in a small town twenty miles from Amsterdam, Hogeway was opened in 2008 at a cost of €19.3 million (approximately US$30 million in 2008). Currently, Hogeway serves 152 older adults with moderate to severe dementia in twenty-three houses with six or seven residents per house (Glass, 2014). The stated mission of Hogeway is twofold:

- To relieve the anxiety, confusion, and often considerable anger people with dementia can feel by providing an environment that is safe, familiar, and human.
- To maximize quality of life, to keep older adults with dementia engaged and active, and to focus on strengths and abilities rather than deficits and disabilities. (Goodwin, 2015, p. 28; Henley, 2012)

How does Hogeway go about achieving these goals, and what elements set this approach apart from traditional dementia care? First, the built environment was specifically designed for people with dementia and purposely built to resemble typical homes and communities. Residents live in two-story houses and share bathrooms and kitchens. Residents are encouraged to decorate their rooms with their own possessions and have their own pets. The neighborhood also resembles a traditional community. There is a grocery store where residents can shop, a theater, a concert hall, health care clinics, and even a café/pub where residents can have a drink and socialize. Residents are not required to pay for their purchases, and staff are on hand to help them if they need assistance. The grounds are laid out for exploration, the doors are not locked, and there are no dead-end walkways. The built environment has a direct relationship to the social environment. Residents are grouped in their houses based on their past lifestyles. For example, older adults from urban environments may live in a more modernized house and share in meals and activities that reflect their past life in the city. Residents from rural areas whose past lives were less "cosmopolitan" may live in a house that is decorated to reflect country living and meals, and activities that reflect that culture. These shared experiences help build community and encourage a sense of belonging (Jenkins & Smythe, 2013). Finally, the staff are specially trained to support the mission of Hogeway and to intrude as little as possible on the normal lives of residents. In fact, the staff do not wear uniforms and blend in with the village (Glass, 2014). Residents at Hogeway often live in this community until they die. Staff increase support as needed as diseases progress, and the end of life is normalized to every extent possible.

Although the Hogeway concept is compelling, there is a lack of research and little direct evidence beyond anecdotal stories to validate the advantages of this approach over traditional nursing homes. There is, however, a well-developed body of research confirming that built and social environments can affect the quality of life and well-being of older adults with dementia. For example, a recent evidence-based review of 169 studies of environmental design and dementia found that "offering residents an environment that does not have an institutional design but has a homelike appearance and allows for individual transformations has positive effects on behavior, well-being, social abilities, and care outcomes" (Marquardt, Bueter, & Motzek, 2014, p. 147). Hogeway's focus on creating a homelike environment may help contribute to a higher quality of life for residents. We also know that efforts to promote personhood and to stimulate socialization can improve the lives of older adults with dementia. Hogeway's approach of matching residents on lifestyle and preference and offering purposeful activities (such as shopping) is closely aligned with the principles of the personhood movement in dementia care. We can draw inferences from the research literature, however, and rigorous research is needed to shed light on the impact the Hogeway approach has on residents, family members, and staff. The evidence on cost is clear: the cost per resident is no greater than standard nursing home care in the Netherlands (Hurley, 2012).

Some have raised ethical concerns about "therapeutic lying," the creation of "make believe" communities for older adults with dementia. However, those who have visited Hogeway seem to think differently. As Jenkins and Smythe (2013) observed, "the Hogeway environment is a deliberate and artificial creation, yet it does not feel deceitful" (p. 18). One scholar cited the work Tom Kitwood (1998), a visionary in dementia care, in summarizing her reactions to Hogeway: "Hogeway was immensely impressive and extremely moving, providing the nearest I have ever seen to the care that engenders Kitwood's 'trustful serenity'" (Godwin, 2015, p. 31). Other countries seem to agree, and efforts are under way in Germany and Switzerland to create dementia villages based on Hogeway. Hogeway has begun to receive increased international and national attention as well. For example, Dr. Sanjay Gupta profiled Hogeway on CNN in 2013, and the video has since had well over one million viewers. Concepts are discussed and current news and reports are posted and updated on the Hogeway website as well.

As we move away from institutionalization and toward HCBS for older adults in the United States, Hogeway offers a unique, innovative, and humane approach to dementia care. Efforts to incorporate elements of the dementia village concept are under way here as well. For example, Glenner Town Square in San Diego is being built with storefronts that resemble a small downtown, including a post office, barbershop, diner, and movie theater. This is an adult day program and not a residential facility, but the approach is similar to the dementia village concept in that it strives to create a homelike atmosphere and to foster reminiscence and purpose through familiar environments and meaningful activities. More dementia village–inspired approaches can be expected in the United States given the high level of interest in this innovative concept and the growing level of need for dementia care.

PHYSICAL ACTIVITY ON PRESCRIPTION

Physical activity and exercise have many benefits for older adults, including improved physical and mental health, higher functioning, greater independence, and less health care utilization and cost (lower use of medications, fewer hospitalizations). Simply put, physically active and fit older adults have healthier (lower morbidity) and longer (lower mortality) lives than their more sedentary counterparts. In some health care systems, the importance of physical activity and fitness for all populations (including older adults) has been recognized, codified, and funded as an integral prevention and treatment modality. One of these *physical activity on prescription* (PAP) programs is the Fysick aktivitet pa Recept (FaR) program in Sweden. Similar programs exist in other European countries, including Denmark, the Netherlands, and Finland (Raustorp & Sundberg, 2014).

In Sweden, the PAP program emerged in the 1980s on the county level and was established nationally in 2001. As the name implies, licensed health care providers (physicians, nurses, physiotherapists) can prescribe physical activity for patients of all ages when exercise is seen as potentially beneficial. The Swedish PAP program is far more than simply a prescription. In the guidelines provided by the Swedish government, PAP includes individualized counseling about physical activity, collaboration between the health care provider and the physical activity provider, and follow-up monitoring and evaluation. A key innovation of the Swedish PAP program is the variety of physical activities that can be prescribed based on need and preference. For example, the physical activity providers can be private sports clubs, personal trainers, walking clubs, municipal facilities (such as swimming pools or tennis courts), or individual exercise programs such as bicycling. Ongoing monitoring and counseling is an important component of PAP because it helps individuals stay on track (Raustorp & Sundberg, 2014). The final key to the Swedish PAP program is the fact that the activity program is paid for partially, and in some cases entirely, through the health care system. The cost is not completely borne by the patient, thereby making it easier to access the physical activity program and increasing the likelihood that the patient will adhere to the prescribed plan. The case study provides an example of how the PAP program can work for an older adult.

CASE STUDY

Luuk is a 68-year-old man living on the outskirts of Amsterdam, Netherlands. He lives with his wife of forty years and has four adult children who live around the city. Luuk retired two years ago after working for thirty-six years as a carpenter and a homebuilder. He now has a lot of time on his hands and admits to feeling "a bit lost." Luuk has been feeling fatigued lately, and his wife has noticed that he is not as "happy go lucky." He seems disinterested in many of the activities he enjoyed in the past, and he has gained twenty pounds since retiring. Luuk recently visited his physician at the urging of his wife.

The physician asks Luuk to tell her a little about his background and the presenting problem. After ruling out any physical problems (other than his weight gain), the physician determines that Luuk meets the diagnostic criteria for depression. The physician presents the following treatment options: (a) a pharmacological approach, (b) a therapeutic approach that includes counseling, (c) a combined pharmacological and therapeutic approach, or (d) a physical activity on prescription (PAP) program. Luuk states that he prefers not to take medications and that "talk therapy" is not for him. He had never heard of the PAP program, but he agrees to give it a try.

Consider the following questions as they relate to Luuk's situation.

1. What are the biopsychosocial treatment goals for Luuk?
2. After explaining how the PAP program works, what is the next step in developing a PAP plan for Luuk? (Hint: Luuk likes to swim.)
3. There is a swimming club in Luuk's town. How might the physician work with the swim club as part of Luuk's PAP plan? Could the swim club be used to monitor adherence to the PAP plan?
4. What are some of the keys to successfully making lifestyle changes a part of a person's routine? (See http://www.apa.org/helpcenter/lifestyle-changes.aspx.)

The research on exercise clearly identifies myriad benefits for all age groups, but questions persist as to whether individuals will adhere to prescribed physical activity and whether the benefits justify the cost. A systematic review of PAP programs found moderate increases in physical activity and moderate improvements in fitness levels. The researchers also found that PAP is feasible and acceptable to both providers and patients. Finally, there was evidence that PAP programs can be cost-effective, but the evidence was sparse (Sorensen, Skovgaard, & Puggaard, 2006). More recent studies, including those focusing on older adults, have found increased levels of physical activity and physical capacity, improved body composition, and gains in health-related quality of life (Kallings et al., 2009; Leijon, Bendtsen, et al., 2009; Moren, Welmer, Hagstromer, Karlsson, & Sommerfeld, 2016; Olsson et al., 2015). PAP programs can have adherence levels similar to those of pharmacological approaches, although patients must be well enough and motivated to participate in the physical activities (Leijon, Faskunger, et al., 2011). As in prior studies, the cost-effectiveness of PAP programs has yet to be firmly established, and evaluation is quite complex when benefits such as improved mood are considered. Researchers have called for long-term follow-up to examine factors such as health care utilization and mortality (Rome, Persson, Ekdahl, & Gard, 2009).

This brings us to our final question, "Is the PAP approach feasible within the U.S. health care system?" Certain realities must be considered in addressing this question. First, the U.S. health care system focuses heavily on treatment rather than prevention. Although PAP is viewed as a treatment in European health care systems, exercise tends to be viewed as a preventative measure in the United States. Second, there may be some resistance to funding PAP in the United States. Exercise tends to be viewed as an individual responsibility—similar to the way we view diet. Paying for someone to join a gym or for a personal trainer runs contrary to societal expectations, even if it saves money in the long run. Finally, the U.S. health care system relies heavily on pharmacological approaches, and health care professionals are not well-trained in prescribing, coordinating, and following up on lifestyle changes. There are some indications that prevention is gaining traction in the United States. For example, many health insurance companies offer wellness programs that provide incentives for physical activity. As we learn more about PAP programs, particularly in terms of long-term cost savings, the U.S. health care system may see that an "ounce of prevention is worth a pound of cure."

CHAPTER SUMMARY

- Every region on the globe is experiencing population aging, and it has been projected that the world population over age 60 will grow from 12 percent to 22 percent by the year 2050.
- A plethora of innovative approaches to HCBS internationally could be adopted or adapted for use in the United States.

- Green care farms are alternatives to traditional adult day services where older adults (particularly those with dementia) participate in the therapeutic setting and activities of actual working farms.
- The dementia village approach creates an actual neighborhood where older adults with dementia can experience day-to-day life much like other older adults in the community while receiving the care and help that they need.
- Physical activity on prescription programs provide older adults (and others) with actual prescriptions for exercise programs that are tailored to their needs and preferences.

DISCUSSION QUESTIONS AND EXERCISES

1. Review the statements in the Fact or Fiction? list near the beginning of the chapter. After reading this chapter, can you identify which are true and which are false?
2. As the demographics indicate, the world is aging due to increased life expectancy and decreased fertility rates. What factors contribute to increased life expectancy? Can you speculate on the forces that are driving down fertility rates?
3. Green care farms are an innovative and intriguing form of HCBS. Do you think this approach would be effective with older adults with urban backgrounds and lifestyles?
4. What are some of the challenges that might be encountered in starting a dementia village in the United States?
5. Physical activity on prescription programs are part of the fabric of the health care systems in countries such as Sweden. Why are such preventative approaches rare in the United States?
6. The World Health Organization holds periodic forums to share and discuss innovations in aging. Visit the WHO website and take a look at the different programs that exist around the world.

ADDITIONAL RESOURCES

Dementia Village Advisors: http://dementiavillage.com
Exercise Is Medicine: http://www.exerciseismedicine.org
Hogeway profile on CNN (2013): https://www.youtube.com/watch?v=LwiOBlyWpko
Hogeway: http://hogeweyk.dementiavillage.com/en/

Multifunctional Agriculture in Europe: http://www.maie-project.eu/index.php?id=48

Prescription for Activity: http://www.prescriptionforactivity.org

Social Farming Across Borders: http://www.socialfarmingacrossborders.org/seupb

WHO Forums on Aging: http://www.who.int/kobe_centre/ageing/innovation
-forum/en/

REFERENCES

Anderson, K. A., Chapin, K. P., Reimer, Z., & Siffri, G. (2017). On fertile ground: An initial evaluation of green care farms in the United States. *Home Health Care Services Quarterly, 36*(1), 1–15.

de Bruin, S. R., Oosting, S., van der Zijpp, A., Enders-Slegers, M-J., & Schols, J. (2010). The concept of green care farms for older people with dementia. *Dementia, 9*(1), 79–128.

de Bruin, S. R., Sttop, A., Molema, C. C. M., Vaandrager, L., Hop, P. J. W. N., & Baan, C. A. (2015). Green care farms: An innovative type of adult day service to stimulate social participation of people with dementia. *Gerontology & Geriatric Medicine*. Advance online publication. doi: 10.1177/2333721415607833

Elsey, H., Bragg, R., Elings, M., Cade, J. E., Brennan, C., Farragher, T., . . . Murray, J. (2014). Understanding the impacts of care farms on health and well-being of disadvantaged populations: A protocol of the Evaluating Community Orders (ECO) pilot study. *British Medical Journal Open, 4*, 1–10.

Glass, A. P. (2014). Innovative seniors housing and care models: What we can learn from the Netherlands. *Senior Housing & Care Journal, 22*(1), 74–81.

Godwin, B. (2015). Hogeway: A 'home from home' in the Netherlands. *Journal of Dementia Care, 23*(3), 28–31.

He, W., Goodkind, D., & Kowal, P. (2016). *An aging world: 2015*. Retrieved from https://www.census.gov/content/dam/Census/library/publications/2016/demo/p95-16-1.pdf

Henley, J. (2012, August 27). The village where people have dementia—and fun. *The Guardian*.

Hurley, D. (2012, May 17). 'Village of the demented' draws praise as new care model. *Neurology Today*, 12–13.

Jenkins, C., & Smythe, A. (2013). Reflections on a visit to a dementia care village. *Nursing Older People, 25*(6), 14–19.

Kallings, L. V., Sierra-Johnson, J., Fisher, R. M., de Faire, U., Stahle, A., Hemmingsson, E., & Hellenius, M.L. (2009). Beneficial effects of individualized physical activity on prescription on body composition and cardiometabolic risk factors: Results from a randomized controlled trial. *European Journal of Cardiovascular Prevention and Rehabilitation, 16*(1), 80–84.

Kitwood, T. (1998). Toward a theory of dementia care: Ethics and interaction. *Journal of Clinical Ethics, 9*(1), 23–34.

Leijon, M. E., Bendtsen, P., Nilson, P., Festin, K., & Stahle, A. (2009). Does a physical activity referral scheme improve the physical activity among routine health care patients? *Scandinavian Journal of Medicine & Science in Sports, 19*(5), 627–636.

Leijon, M. E., Faskunger, J., Bendtsen, P., Festin, K., & Nilsen, P. (2011). Who is not adhering to physical activity referrals, and why? *Scandinavian Journal of Primary Health Care, 29*(4), 234–240.

Marquardt, G., Bueter, K., & Motzek, T. (2014). Impact on the design of the built environment on people with dementia: An evidence-based review. *Health Environments Research & Design Journal, 8*(1), 127–157.

Milligan, C., Gatrell, A., & Bingley, A. (2004). Cultivating health: Therapeutic landscapes and older people in northern England. *Social Science & Medicine, 58*(9), 1781–1793.

Moren, C., Welmer, A. K., Hagstromer, M., Karlsson, E., & Sommerfeld, D. K. (2016). The effects of "physical activity on prescription" in persons with transient ischemic attack: A randomized controlled study. *Journal of Neurologic Physical Therapy, 40*(3), 176–183.

Olsson, S., Borjesson, M., Ekblom-Bak, E., Hemmingsson, E., Hellenius, M-L., & Kallings, L. V. (2015). Effects of Swedish physical activity on prescription model on health-related quality of life in overweight older adults: A randomized controlled trial. *BMC Public Health, 15*, 687.

Rappe, E., Kivelä, S., & Rita, H. (2006). Visiting outdoor green environments positively impacts self-rated health among older people in long-term care. *Horttechnology, 16*(1), 55–59.

Raustorp, A., & Sundberg, C. J. (2014). The evolution of physical activity on prescription (FaR) in Sweden. *Schweizerische Zeitschrift fur Sportmedizin und Sporttraumatologie, 62*(2), 23–25.

Rome, A., Persson, U., Ekdahl, C., & Gard, G. (2009). Physical activity on prescription (PAP): Costs and consequences of a randomized, controlled trial in primary healthcare. *Scandinavian Journal of Primary Health Care, 27*(4), 216–222.

Schols, J. M., & van der Schriek-van Meel, C. (2006). Day care for demented elderly in a dairy farm setting: Positive first impressions. *Journal of the American Medical Directors Association, 7*(7), 456–459.

Sorenson, J. B., Skovgaard, T., & Puggaard, L. (2006). Exercise on prescription in general practice: A systematic review. *Scandinavian Journal of Primary Health Care, 24,* 69–74.

Townshend, P. (2006). Exclusive interview: *The Who's Pete Townshend.* Retrieved from http://www.artistdirect.com/nad/news/article/0,,3833778,00.html

World Health Organization. (2015). *World report on ageing and health.* Retrieved from http://apps.who.int/iris/bitstream/10665/186463/1/9789240694811 _eng.pdf?ua=1

13

Technology in Home- and Community-Based Services

I can and do, write prescriptions for her many medical problems, but I have little to offer for the two conditions that dominate her days: loneliness and disability. She has a well-meaning, troubled daughter in a faraway state, a caregiver who comes twice a week, a friend who checks in on her periodically, and she gets regular calls from volunteers with the Friendship Line. . . . What she needs is a robot caregiver. . . . That may sound like an oxymoron. In an ideal world, it would be: each of us would have at least one kind and fully capable human caregiver to meet our physical and emotional needs as we age. But most us do not live in an ideal world, and a reliable robot may be better than an unreliable or abusive person, or than no one at all.

LOUISE ARONSON, 2014

LEARNING OBJECTIVES

In this chapter, you will:

- Learn about older adults' and family caregivers' use of the Internet and social media to improve their health outcomes.
- Gain insight into the capabilities and applications of smart home technologies for community-dwelling older adults.
- Understand the role that robots currently play in the care of older adults and the future for this technology to meet growing demand.
- Explore the ethical considerations of using technology to care for older adults.

INNOVATIVE AND RELATIVELY LOW-TECHNOLOGY APPROACHES are meeting the needs of older adults today, but technology has the potential to creatively address many of the challenges and opportunities of aging populations. Some argue that the challenges we now face with the aging population are the result of advances in technology and our ability to stave off death and to "artificially" prolong our lives. This may be the case, but technology also may hold the key to solving many of the dilemmas associated with caring for the growing number of older adults. Technology can fill the gaps when our human capital is exhausted or unable to meet the needs of older adults. As technology advances, we may find that robots, sensors, and artificial intelligence exceed the capacity of humans and, in some respects, is preferable for both caregivers and care recipients. In this chapter, we focus on three primary areas associated with technology: (a) the use of technology (such as online resources and social media) by older adults and caregivers for information, resources, and support; (b) gerontechnology and smart home technology; and (c) service robots for older adults. As we explore each of these areas, keep in mind the speed at which technology has developed in the past several decades. The technological advances we see today provide a glimpse into the future, and they will undoubtedly seem rudimentary as we become more savvy and sophisticated.

FACT OR FICTION?

Consider the following statements.

- Rates of Internet and social media use are typically very low for older adults.
- Smart home technology is out of reach for many older adults due to cost and a lack of technical skills.
- Older adults tend to live in older homes that are not amenable to smart home technology adaptation.
- Robots currently have the capacity to replace family caregivers.
- Ethical concerns regarding the use of robots in caring for older adults include issues of privacy, deception, human dignity, and distributive justice.

After reading this chapter, you will be able to affirm which statements are fact and which are fiction.

INTERNET AND SOCIAL MEDIA USE BY OLDER ADULTS
AND CAREGIVERS

As the old saying goes, "information is power." For older adults and their caregivers, the Internet and social media offer a wealth of information and resources that can better equip and empower them to care for themselves and for each other in home- and community-based settings. According to the Pew Research Center (2017a), 88 percent of adults in the United States use the Internet. Internet use is not limited to young people: more than half (54 percent) of those age 65 and older and more than three-quarters (77 percent) of those age 50 to 64 (the most common age range for caregivers) use the Internet. Of the total population of Internet users, 72 percent say they used the Internet for health-related information. This includes searching for information on health conditions, treatments, and health care professionals. Caregivers even more than noncaregivers are heavy users of the Internet for health-related purposes (figure 13.1). The Pew Research Center (2017b) reports that 34 percent of older adults use social media and networking sites such as Facebook. This is more than 3 times the percentage that was reported in 2010 (11 percent) and 17 times the percentage that was reported in 2005 (2 percent). Finally, nearly one-quarter of adults consult social media for peer-to-peer support regarding

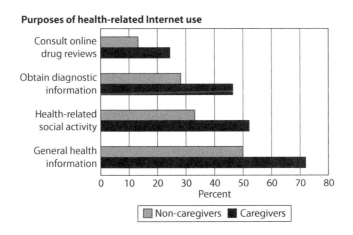

FIGURE 13.1 Caregivers versus non-caregivers health-related Internet use.

Source: Adapted from Pew Research Center, 2016.

a health condition (Pew Research Center, 2013). Clearly, the Internet and social media are increasingly playing a role in health care.

The Internet enables us to access a vast sea of information. This information can help older adults and their caregivers learn more about their health-related issues, find health care providers, locate home- and community-based services such as adult day centers, and ultimately help inform their health care decisions. For example, a general search using the term "Parkinson's disease" returned almost 12 million results. The first page of results included advertisements and links for organizations such as the Michael J. Fox Foundation and the American Parkinson's Disease Association, links to health care sites such as the Mayo Clinic and the National Institute of Neurological Disorders and Stroke (NINDS), links to news stories on individuals with Parkinson's disease, and links to sites such as Wikipedia and WebMD.com. These search results reflect well-vetted sources of information. A click on the NINDS link pulls up a plethora of information on the disease, including approved diagnostic criteria, results from clinical trials, peer-reviewed research articles and reports, and links to agencies and organizations that can provide assistance and support. A click on the Wikipedia link provides information in a clear format; however, be aware that this source allows users to edit the pages. The quality of information on the Internet can vary widely. As researchers have noted, older adults and caregivers who do cursory searches for information may find information that has not been vetted, or information that is biased such as on pharmaceutical sites (Anderson, Nikzad-Terhune, & Gaugler, 2009).

In addition to information, older adults and caregivers can find interventions and support in the community—in this case the "online community." These interventions and support come in a variety of formats, including online support groups, interactive blogs, online social communities and networks (such as Facebook), and online professional counseling. The National Parkinson Foundation provides an online forum "for open discussion among Parkinson's patients and caregivers." The Michael J. Fox Foundation has an active Facebook page where users can find information, share their experiences, and find support. Researchers have found that online interventions and social media provide a number of important benefits. For example, a recent systematic review found that online interventions for caregivers can decrease depression, increase feelings of competency, self-efficacy, and confidence in decision making, and reduced caregiver burden and strain (Boots, de Vugt, van Knippenberg, Kempen, & Verhey, 2014). In some cases, online support groups may be superior to in-person groups, particularly given the time constraints and the transportation issues often facing older adults and their caregivers (Namkoong et al., 2012). As Internet and social media use continues to grow, we may see more and more individuals turning to online communities for support.

Traditionally, the Internet and social media were not viewed as home- and community-based services (HCBS). Now the Internet has become an important tool for linking older adults with the information and services they need to continue to live in the community. In addition, online communities can be a source of support and strength for older adults with health care needs and for caregivers struggling to provide care. Individuals who are better informed and more involved in their health care experience tend to have better outcomes (Bornkessel, Furberg, & Lefebvre, 2014). Engaging with others online provides valuable support to older adults and their caregivers and has a positive impact on health behaviors and outcomes (Hamm et al., 2013). Most important, the information and support individuals receive through the Internet and social media can encourage and empower older adults and their caregivers to become "owners" of their health care choices and decisions (Nikzad-Terhune, Anderson, & LaBey, 2015). As Internet and social media use continues to grow, new ways to leverage the power of this technology to improve the lives and facilitate aging in the community will undoubtedly be discovered.

GERONTECHNOLOGY AND SMART HOME TECHNOLOGY

Gerontechnology (technology for older adults) refers to the use of a variety of monitors, sensors, and electronic devices designed to improve the lives of older adults and their caregivers. *Smart home technology* is the systematic use of gerontechnology in a residence to provide monitoring, surveillance, and assistance. Ultimately, the goal of these systems is to help older adults remain in the home and community with as much independence as possible. A wide variety of technological approaches can be used in smart homes for older adults. You are probably familiar with some of these devices, such as emergency response systems that became familiar to many through the "Help, I've fallen and I can't get up" television commercial, but other technologies are just emerging and may surprise you with their complexity and capabilities. Two basic categories of gerontechnology—safety and health—along with selected examples commonly used in smart homes are examined in this chapter. We conclude by discussing ethical concerns, barriers to adoption, and the future of gerontechnology for enhancing HCBS.

Safety Technology

Safety technology are "alarms and personal response systems [that] collect data to detect acute events, monitor chronic risks and detect adverse events" (Piau, Campo, Rumeau, Vellas, & Nourhashemi, 2014, p. 99). These technologies can be as simple as an alarm an older person presses when he or she falls or a pressure sensor embedded in a carpet that alerts a caregiver when an older adult steps out or falls out of bed. Other simple technologies such as video monitors provide live links to caregivers to track the movements and safety of older adults in the home. Using these simple approaches in creative ways can improve the lives of both caregivers and older adults. For example, placing cameras in the bathroom at ankle height allows family members to know when their older family member is in the bathroom and if there has been a fall. This protects the older adult's dignity while allowing for simple safety monitoring in one of the more dangerous places in the home. Accelerometers and body position indicators are other fall prevention/detection technologies. Safety technologies can monitor home conditions such as lighting, temperature, doors and locks (to address home safety and wandering/elopement), and appliances such as ovens, stoves, and sinks (water overflow monitors). More advanced safety technology can track movements throughout the house to help establish routines. Deviations from a routine could denote safety issues. Many of these safety technologies are particularly applicable to older adults with cognitive impairment and the myriad safety issues that accompany this condition.

Health Technology

Health technology uses some of the same approaches as safety technology, but the goal is to monitor and promote health. Again, these technologies can be simple or quite advanced in their design and function. For example, some applications provide reminders and health coaching for older adults regarding medications, exercise, health appointments, and activities of daily living (for example, bathroom breaks). Some of these applications allow the use of a familiar voice, such as a spouse or adult child, to help personalize the reminders and coaching. More advanced smart medication bottles can now visually, audibly, and electronically remind older adults when to take their medications and transmit data to caregivers, health care providers, and pharmacists regarding medication adherence and when refills are needed. (Search the Internet using the term "smart pill bottle" to explore the creative approaches to this health technology.) More advanced health technologies can remotely collect vital signs (weight, blood pressure, and so on) of older adults in their homes and transmit this information to caregivers and health care providers. Online and video technologies link older adults directly with health care providers to enable virtual home visits. An interesting example of both safety and health technologies combined in smart home applications can be seen in a brief video from the National Science Foundation (see link at the end of the chapter.)

An Expert Weighs In

Jenay Beer, PhD, MS
Assistant Professor, Computer Science and Engineering
College of Social Work, College of Engineering and Computing
University of South Carolina

For this chapter, please see these videos by aging and technology expert, Dr. Jenay Beer. Either follow these links or perform Internet searches using the key words "Jenay Beer TEDx."

- https://youtu.be/5ppyWqFdc1Q
- https://youtu.be/M5RuAhWphO0

Perspectives from the Field

An interview with Jarod T. Giger, PhD, MSW
Assistant Professor College of Social Work
College of Medicine, Center for Health Services Research
College of Public Health, Graduate Center for Gerontology
University of Kentucky

*How receptive are older adults and family members to smart
home technologies?*

Anecdotally and empirically there is an appetite among older adults and their family members for smart home technologies. Although smart home technology is not a "silver bullet" in terms of aging or aging in place, the use of smart home technology, which tends to be unobtrusive and passive, has obvious appeal due to its real-time ability to capture in-home data on key health domains such as sleep, ADLs, ambulation, and physical activity.

*How can we negotiate between safety and privacy in the use
of smart home technologies?*

If you ask older adults whether they have privacy concerns regarding smart home technology, they very well may say they do. But if you follow that question up with "If smart home technology can help you live independently longer in the residence of your choice, would you be comfortable with the potential privacy concerns?" I suspect older adults might give you a very different answer.

*What do you see as the greatest barriers to expanding the use of
smart home technologies?*

Antiquated or paternalistic thinking and behaviors toward older adults and technology present the greatest barriers. The science suggests that older adults can be trained to use technology, but the prevailing belief is that older adults do not use and cannot learn how to use technology, including smart home technology.

*What do see as the future of smart home technologies
for older adults?*

In twenty years, smart home technology will be considered standard care. Data-driven customized care will be the norm, and smart home technology will be at the center of the discussion.

Smart Homes

What does the research say about the impact of gerontechnologies and smart homes on the lives of older adults and their caregivers? These technologies are emerging and evolving rapidly, so research on their effectiveness is limited. Methodological issues include a lack of randomized controlled trials, and research has been skewed toward qualitative over quantitative approaches. Indications suggest that gerontechnologies can be beneficial in monitoring health, maintaining independence, increasing feelings of security (for both older adults and caregivers), and facilitating aging in place. Researchers in systematic reviews warn that this body of evidence is thin and that important benchmarks—such as reducing falls, lowering the risk of disability, or increasing health-related quality of life— have yet to be met (Lui, Stroulia, Nikolaidis, Miguel-Cruz, & Rincon, 2016; Morris et al., 2013). Gerontechnologies also have not been determined to be cost-effective. This lag in and lack of quality research should not be confused with a lack of effectiveness; rather, it should direct future research and development of these promising technologies.

Finally, we must consider the barriers to the use of smart home technology and the future of gerontechnologies as a part of HCBS. Recent systematic reviews and analyses reveal that privacy is a primary concern for older adults in accepting gerontechnology into their homes (Wilson, Hargreaves, & Hauxwell-Baldwin, 2015; Yusif, Soar, & Hafeez-Baig, 2016). This is not surprising given the potentially intrusive nature of cameras and monitors in the home. Stigmatization also is an issue as older adults may view technological devices as signs of dependence rather than facilitators of independence. Older adults are concerned with whether to trust the gerontechnology and whether these devices will actually improve or add value to their lives. Finally, cost is a concern as gerontechnology can be expensive and most residences need to be adapted to fully become smart homes. A recent survey found that family caregivers were willing to pay an average of approximately $70 per month for smart home technology, which is probably not a large enough investment to reap the full benefits of this technology (Schulz et al., 2016). In looking toward the future, one thing is clear: technology will continue to advance and become more intertwined in all of our lives. For example, an international agency predicted that the installation of smart home devices and appliances (such as refrigerators that allow you to monitor the contents remotely) would triple worldwide, from 4 billion in 2016 to 12 billion in 2020 (International Energy Agency, 2017).

ROBOTS!

When someone mentions robots, what images are conjured up in your mind? Perhaps you think of R2-D2 or C-3PO from *Star Wars* fame or, for those with some years, maybe you envision Robot B-9 from *Lost in Space*. If so, you are not far off from the current reality of service robots for older adults. "A robot is an actuated mechanism programmable in two or more axes with a degree of autonomy, moving within its environment, to perform intended tasks" (International Federation of Robotics (2016). *Service robots* are differentiated from industrial robots in that they are designed to serve the needs of humans, in this case older adults. The idea of using robots to care for older adults is relatively new, with the first service robots coming into commercial use in the mid-2000s. Given the caregiver shortages worldwide and particularly in Asia, development of service robots has rapidly evolved with more than a hundred prototypes in development around the globe (Bedaf, Gelderblom, & De Witte, 2015). We review some of activities robots can do with and for older adults, but we encourage you to go online and learn more about the current state and future projections regarding this promising technology.

Service robots for older adults generally fall into two categories: health care robots and social or socially assistive robots. "A healthcare robot is a robot with the aim of promoting or monitoring health, assisting with tasks that are difficult to perform due to health problems or preventing further health decline" (Robinson, MacDonald, & Broadbent, 2014, p. 576). *Health care robots* can help with a variety of tasks, including the following:

- Provide reminders regarding medications, health measurements, appointments, and activities of daily living (for example, bathing, toileting).
- Monitor the older adult regarding health-related activities such as medication adherence, fall detection, exercise, movement, and safety (such as falls, wandering).

- Provide information regarding health, health and emergency services, advice/coaching, and controlling the environment (for example, lights, temperature).
- Lift, transfer (such as from wheelchair to the commode), and assist with mobility. (Bedaf et al., 2015, p. 90)

Health care robots come in a variety of forms, largely based on the functions they serve. For example, robots that assist only with eating typically are small devices with an articulating arm. Robots that assist with mobility have an exoskeleton that provides support, stability, and power. To understand the variety of health care robots, search online images using the search term "healthcare robots."

Social robots provide companionship, social engagement, and emotional support for older adults. Where health care robots target physical health, social robots focus on addressing issues related to social isolation, boredom, and loneliness. More specifically, social robots can fill the following roles:

- Interact with older adults and form supportive relationships.
- Facilitate communication (engage in conversations or read to the older adult) and social engagement.
- Provide opportunities for recreation, entertainment, and cognitive stimulation.
- Provide therapeutic activities (such as tactile stimulation or "animal-assisted" therapy) for older adults with dementia. (Bedaf et al., 2015, p. 90)

Social robots can take many forms, from animals to humanoid shapes. PARO, one of the most popular social robots, is shaped like a baby harp seal with white fur and actuated head, eyes, and flippers. PARO is hardly a toy and is capable of responding to light, sound, and touch and providing interactive comfort and companionship to older adults with dementia. In a systematic review, researchers found that social robots can enhance the well-being of older adults and decrease the burden on their caregivers (Kachouie, Sedighadeli, Khosia, & Chu, 2014). However, real concerns remain about the impact that robot caregivers and other technologies may have on human relationships between older adults and family members. The age-old question remains, "Will robots replace humans?" Probably not, but they may reduce human interaction, and that is certainly a concern. Additional and

CASE STUDY

Misaki is a 94-year-old widowed woman who lives independently in a continuing care retirement community in Tokyo, Japan. Misaki is in remarkably good health and has experienced very little physical or cognitive decline with age. Although her overall health is good, she has been diagnosed with osteoporosis and arthritis and takes medications to control the impact of these chronic conditions. Emotionally, Misaki has a positive outlook on life and has developed resilience through her experiences and her faith. Misaki has one adult son, Hiraku, who recently relocated for work to Osaka—300 miles away from Tokyo.

With his move, Hiraku has become increasingly concerned about his mother's safety. He recently spoke to a friend who purchased a robot and installed smart home monitoring technology for his mother's home. Hiraku eventually meets with Misaki to discuss options. Misaki has mixed emotions regarding the technology and feels that these "machines" will compromise her independence and privacy. Due to cultural norms, Misaki does not explicitly state her feelings. Hiraku picks up on his mother's nonverbal cues and tries to convince her that this is the wave of the future. Eventually, they agree to start with a medication reminder system and an emergency call system. The robot will have to wait for another day!

1. What ethical principles are at play in this case study?
2. What are some of the cultural considerations of Japanese society that you would need to be familiar with in working with this family?
3. Follow this link (http://www.bbc.com/news/world-asia-31901943) to read and view a BBC report on the shortage of caregivers in Japan. Will robotic technology be ready to fill this shortage of caregivers?
4. Some question whether to encourage immigration of workers to provide care or to pursue the continued development of robots. What are the pros and cons of these two approaches?

more rigorous research is needed to better understand the impact of these ever-evolving technologies and their interface with the human world.

There has been much discussion regarding the ethics of using robots to care for older adults, and this is an important consideration as capabilities and applications of robots expand. Vallor (2011) lists these ethical concerns:

- Objectifying older adults as problems that can be solved with technology.
- The potential restriction of "capabilities, freedom, autonomy, and/or dignity of older adults."

- The possibility that robots could reduce or replace engagement with real humans, including family and friends.
- Intruding upon the privacy of older adults.
- Deceiving and infantilizing older adults, particularly those with dementia. (p. 254)

Issues of access and affordability also touch on the ethical considerations of equity and distributive justice (see box). As with other technologies, we must be careful to value the personhood of older adults and to be aware of the ethical issues associated with service robots.

In addition to the ethical concerns highlighted by Vallor (2011), other barriers exist to the use and acceptance of robots by older adults and

THE DIGITAL DIVIDE

Technology certainly holds promise for augmenting or, in some cases, replacing human capacities to care for older adults. Robots, smart home technology, and the use of information technology are increasingly available to older adults and their caregivers; however, the ability to access these technological resources is limited to those who can understand and afford these options. The "digital divide" refers to disparities in access and ability to use technology, such as computers, the Internet, and many of the gerontechnologies discussed in this chapter. Recent research by the Pew Research Center (2016) stratified the U.S. population with regard to their readiness to use technology. Women, members of minority ethnic and racial groups, individuals age 50 and older, individuals living in rural communities, individuals in lower-income households, and individuals with lower levels of formal education were among the least prepared to adopt technology and the least likely to use the Internet for learning. More specifically, only 6 percent of those age 65 and older were considered to be digitally ready. Although 65 percent of whites were considered digitally ready, only 12 percent of blacks and 13 percent of Hispanics fell into this category. Finally, only 16 percent of individuals living in rural communities were considered digitally ready—far below the readiness of urban (39 percent) and suburban (45 percent) dwellers. We must keep these disparities in mind and realize that the benefits of these advances are far out of the reach of a significant portion of the older adult population.

their caregivers. Cost is undoubtedly a major barrier. Complex, multitask, health care robots are prohibitively expensive, but simple health care robots, such as robots that assist with eating and social robots, tend to be less expensive. For example, Pepper, a humanoid robot that can read and respond to human emotions sells for approximately $1,600 in Japan (see link at the end of the chapter). Acceptance of robots also is a barrier to use. Researchers have found that older adults and their caregivers are more likely to accept robotic assistance if the robot is user friendly, customized in terms of appearance, and, most important, matches their needs (Pino, Boulay, Jouen, & Rigaud, 2015). Despite these barriers, the projected market for service robots is great. For example, international sales of service robots for personal and domestic use (including care robots used by older adults) increased by 24 percent from 2015 to 2016 and now totals approximately 6.7 million units (International Federation of Robotics, 2017). These numbers are relatively small but are obviously growing quickly. In the future, care robots may be less expensive and more accepted and eventually may become "care as usual."

CHAPTER SUMMARY

- The Internet is an increasingly important source of information, education, and support for older adults. As older adults become more familiar with online resources, this platform will grow in importance and utility.
- Gerontechnology refers to the use of a variety of monitors, sensors, and electronic devices designed to improve the lives of older adults and their caregivers.
- Smart home technology is the systematic use of gerontechnology in a residence to provide monitoring, surveillance, and assistance.
- Gerontechnology and smart home applications can help older adults remain in their home safely and relieve some of the burden experienced by caregivers.
- In response to growing numbers of older adults and a scarcity of caregivers, robots have seen rapid development over the past several years. Although ethical issues abound, caregiving robots may be the norm in the future in many industrialized societies.

DISCUSSION QUESTIONS AND EXERCISES

1. Review the statements in the Fact or Fiction? list near the beginning of the chapter. After reading this chapter, can you identify which are true and which are false?
2. In small groups, do Internet searches on the following terms:
   - COPD
   - Arthritis
   - Osteoporosis
   - Home health care

   What are some of the first sites that your searches return? What might this mean for an older adult or caregiver in search of information?
3. Go to the Facebook page for the Alzheimer's Association (https://www .facebook.com/actionalz/). As you look at the page, identify online resources that might be beneficial for older adults and family members dealing with this dementia.
4. Smart home technology holds great promise helping older adults live safely and well in the community. Envision yourself as an older adult. Would you welcome smart home technology into your own home? If not, why not? If so, to what degree?
5. To understand more about the capabilities of robots, check out the following Ted Talks:
   - Henry Evans & Chad Jenkins: Meet the Robots for Humanity
   - Cynthia Breazeal: The Rise of Personal Robots
   - Henry Brooks: Why We Will Rely Upon Robots

ADDITIONAL RESOURCES

AARP Technology: http://www.aarp.org/research/topics/technology/

AgeLab MIT: http://agelab.mit.edu

Commercially Available Robots: https://www.ald.softbankrobotics.com/en /cool-robots/pepper

International Society for Gerontechnology: http://www.gerontechnology.info

LeadingAge Center for Aging Services Technologies: https://www.leadingage.org /center-aging-services-technologies

National Parkinson Foundation: http://forum.parkinson.org/index.php?/forum/3
-open-forum

National Science Foundation Smart Home Video: http://www.nsf.gov/news
/special_reports/science_nation/eldertech.jsp

PARO Social Robot: http://www.parorobots.com/

Pew Research Center: Internet & Technology: http://www.pewinternet.org

REFERENCES

Anderson, K. A., Nikzad-Terhune, K. A., & Gaugler, J. E. (2009). A systematic evaluation of online resources for dementia caregivers. *Journal of Consumer Health on the Internet, 13*(1), 1–13.

Aronson, L. (2014, July 20). The future of robot caregivers. *New York Times,* p. SR4.

Bedaf, S., Gelderblom, G. J., & De Witte, L. (2015). Overview and categorization of robots supporting independent living of elderly people: What activities do they support and how far have they developed. *Assistive Technology, 27,* 88–100.

Boots, L. M., de Vugt, M. E., van Knippenberg, R. J. M., Kempen, G. I., & Verhey, F. R. (2014). Andrew Thompson A systematic review of Internet-based supportive interventions for caregivers of patients with dementia. *International Journal of Geriatric Psychiatry, 29*(4), 331–344.

Bornkessel, A., Furberg, R., & Lefebre, R. C. (2014). Social media: Opportunities for quality improvement and lessons for providers—A networked model of patient-centered care through digital engagement. *Current Cardiology Reports, 16,* 504.

Hamm, M. P., Chisholm, A., Shulhan, J., Milne, A., Scott, S. D., Given, L. M., & Hartling, L. (2013). Social media use among patients and caregivers: A scoping review. *BMJ Open, 3*(5), 1–9.

International Energy Agency. (2017). *Energy efficiency 2017.* Retrieved from http://www.iea.org/publications/freepublications/publication/Energy _Efficiency_2017.pdf

International Federation of Robotics. (2016). *Definition of service robots.* Retrieved from http://www.ifr.org/service-robots/

Kachouie, R., Sedighadeli, Khosla, R., & Chu, M-T. (2014). Socially assistive robots in elderly care: A mixed-method systematic literature review. *International Journal of Human-Computer Interaction, 30,* 369–393.

Liu, L., Stroulia, E., Nikolaidis, I., Miguel-Cruz, A., & Rincon, A. R. (2016). Smart homes and home health monitoring technologies for older adults: A systematic review. *International Journal of Medical Informatics, 91*, 44–59.

Morris, M. E., Adair, B., Miller, K., Ozanne, E., Hanson, R., Pearce, A., . . . Said, C. M. (2013). Smart-home technologies to assist older people to live well at home. *Journal of Aging Science.* Retrieved from http://www.esciencecentral .org/journals/smart-home-technologies-to-assist-older-people-to-live-well-at -home-jasc.1000101.pdf

Namkoong, K., DuBenske, L. L., Shaw, B. R., Gustafson, D. H., Hawkins, R. P., Shah, D. V., . . . Cleary, J. F. (2012). Creating a bond between caregivers online: Effect on caregivers' coping strategies. *Journal of Health Communication, 17*(2), 125–140.

Nikzad-Terhune, K., Anderson, K. A., & LaBey, L. (2015). The impact of the Internet and social media on caregiving. In J. E. Gaugler & R. L. Kane (Eds.), *Family caregiving in the new normal* (pp. 269–290). San Diego, CA: Academic Press.

Pew Research Center. (2013). *Peer-to-peer health care.* Retrieved from http://www .pewinternet.org/2013/01/15/peer-to-peer-health-care/

Pew Research Center. (2016). *Digital readiness gaps.* Retrieved from http://www .pewinternet.org/2016/09/20/digital-readiness-gaps/

Pew Research Center. (2017a). *Internet/Broadband fact sheet.* Retrieved from http://www.pewinternet.org/fact-sheet/internet-broadband/

Pew Research Center. (2017b). *Social media fact sheet.* Retrieved from http://www .pewinternet.org/fact-sheet/social-media/

Piau, A., Campo, E., Rumeau, P., Vellas, B., & Nourhashemi, F. (2014). Aging society and gerontechnology: A solution for an independent living? *Journal of Nutrition, Health & Aging, 18*(1), 97–112.

Pino, M., Boulay, M., Jouen, F., & Rigaud, A-S. (2015). "Are we ready for robots that care for us?" Attitudes and opinions toward socially assistive robots. *Frontiers in Aging Neuroscience, 7*, 1–15.

Robinson, H., MacDonald, B., & Broadbent, E. (2014). The role of healthcare robots for older people at home. *International Journal of Social Robotics, 6*, 575–591.

Schulz, R., Beach, S. R., Matthews, J. T., Courtney, K., De Vito Dabbs, A., & Person Mecca, L. (2016). Caregivers willingness to pay for technologies to support caregiving. *Gerontologist, 56*(5), 817–829.

Vallor, S. (2011). Carebots and caregivers: Sustaining the ethical ideal of care in the twenty-first century. *Philosophy & Technology, 24,* 251–268.

Wilson, C., Hargreaves, T., & Hauxwell-Baldwin, R. (2015). Smart homes and their users: A systematic analysis and key challenges. *Personal and Ubiquitous Computing, 19,* 463–476.

Yusif, S., Soar, J., & Hafeez-Baig, A. (2016). Older people, assistive technology, and the barriers to adoption: A systematic review. *International Journal of Medical Informatics, 94,* 112–116.

A Commentary on the Future of Home- and Community-Based Services for Older Adults

▸ JOSEPH E. GAUGLER, PHD, UNIVERSITY OF MINNESOTA

THIS EXCELLENT, COMPREHENSIVE BOOK PROVIDES one of the best overviews to date of the state of home- and community-based services (HCBS) in the United States and beyond. Perhaps as important, the book does so in a way that is relevant to scholars as well as practitioners. As all good work does, the preceding chapters provided me with much food for thought as I considered the state-of-the-art of HCBS as well as future opportunities to pursue knowledge in this critical domain of long-term care. With this in mind, I offer some of the key points and questions that the book raised for me as they pertain to HCBS and long-term services and supports (LTSS). LTSS are a spectrum of health and social services that includes HCBS, but also takes into account services that are provided in institutional settings. In the ideal, LTSS are a "system in which people with disabilities and chronic conditions have choice, control and access to a full array of quality services that assure optimal outcomes, such as independence, health and quality of life" (Centers for Medicare & Medicaid Services, n.d.).

THE REBALANCING OF CARE TO HCBS

The last three decades have seen a shift away from the bias of payments for long-term care to nursing homes and toward HCBS (Gaugler, 2016; Harrington & Kitchener, 2003; Kassner, 2011). This has occurred as states have used Medicaid funds in a more flexible fashion via waivers. Additional initiatives, spurred on in part by the 1999 Olmstead Act, emphasized the drive to rebalance LTSS toward community-based options and alternatives (Harrington & Kitchener, 2003; Stone & Benson, 2012). Included in the rebalancing effort since the turn of the century have been Aging Disability and Resource Centers to serve as "single points of entry" and information for older adults as well as "Money Follows the Person" grants to further decouple services and housing and result in more flexible use of LTSS, ideally in older adults' homes.

The driving influence on these changes is likely twofold: (1) by rebalancing to HCBS, the high costs of nursing home (NH) use is thought to be offset by these services, which cost less than daily NH costs; and (2) delivering LTSS in people's homes better achieves person-centered care by allowing older adults and their families the option to choose where they receive supportive services.

Surveys suggest there is considerable support among providers to rebalance long-term care toward HCBS delivery (Grabowski, Cadigan, Miller, Stevenson, Clark, & Mor, 2010). However, whether these efforts actually decrease long-term care expenditures overall is unclear, which leads to a question that Grabowski (2006; Grabowski et al., 2010) and others have posed: If rebalancing toward HCBS does not reduce long-term care costs and is not successful in flattening the cost curves of Medicaid, Medicare, or other payment sources, why should rebalancing receive support? Perhaps it relates to the second point related to why rebalancing to HCBS has occurred—it is what older people and their families both want and desire. A point that Grabowski and colleagues make that I find particularly powerful is their call for a de-emphasis on cost savings (for example, whether HCBS substitutes for NH care) and more emphasis on the cost-effective delivery of HCBS. Another compelling point Grabowski and colleagues (2010) make is that if indeed HCBS is found to reduce NH expenditures, then the budget streams from both NH and HCBS should be integrated so these cost savings go toward supporting and expanding more community-based long-term care services.

THE ASSUMPTION OF "SUBSTITUTION"

The more nuanced view of HCBS cost savings notwithstanding, I found it interesting that throughout the text and likely in the minds of many who advocate for continuing expansion of HCBS, it is assumed that community-based long-term services and supports are cost beneficial because they are cheaper to provide that daily nursing home care. Core to this assumption, however, is whether HCBS can actually substitute, or replace, residential long-term care services effectively. Such an argument is core to the efforts of transitioning older people from nursing homes or similar settings to home- and community-based environments with the necessary services and supports. Some estimates suggest that 40 percent of first-time nursing home admissions at ninety days have health and functional conditions that could support discharge from the NH to a community setting with the proper supports (Arling, Kane, Cooke, & Lewis, 2010). However, it also has been suggested that NH diversion efforts have benefited younger, developmentally disabled adults more than older adults.

One question has animated my work on residential long-term care placement and family caregiving: is it really a question of replacement of one service (nursing homes) with another (HCBS), or is it more an issue of appropriate targeting and timing of services to best meet the needs of older adults and families at their particular juncture of a chronic illness or condition? How well current assessments operate to match the needs of older adults and their families with a given long-term care service is not well understood, although assessments abound to determine whether an older person is "nursing home eligible," and the development of care plans is often embedded in such assessments. More specifically, the need to effectively tailor existing LTSS to the individualized needs of older people and their caregiving families in a way that is effective and efficient is of great scientific and practical interest.

The expansion of HCBS may influence the timing of use of other services, which in some ways is the more critical question. Instead of hoping or assuming that HCBS can substitute for more expensive forms of care, perhaps the focus should be more on implementing mechanisms that allow for more efficient targeting and personalization of services that meet the needs of older adults and their family caregivers. It does not seem immediately apparent that current assessment approaches do so, with their emphasis more on eligibility for programs than on the generation of algorithms that target the more appropriate or most highly recommended LTSS for that given older person (Gaugler, Reese, & Tanler, 2016; Kane, Boston, & Chilvers, 2007).

THE STATE OF INTERPROFESSIONAL CARE IN HCBS

An intriguing perspective raised is the degree of interprofessional care in HCBS. Although tools and approaches to operationalize and assess interprofessional care domains in other care settings currently exist, they are noticeably absent for HCBS. The extent of interprofessional care in HCBS is unknown, as is what such care should like or if it is even desirable when delivering LTSS (intuitively, one would believe "of course it is," but nonetheless this is a question of interest that should be answered). As chronic disease care models in various health care settings have demonstrated, interdisciplinary teams focused on care management appear to have considerable potential. However, it remains unknown what interprofessional care does and how it "should" function in home- and community-based settings. To some degree, one could argue that HCBS should be seamlessly integrated with the aforementioned chronic disease care models that are delivered in primary or specialty care clinics rather than being seen as a separate entity. Alternatively, the integration of acute and chronic disease care can be housed within HCBS, as the Program for All-Inclusive Care for the Elderly (PACE) demonstrates and is so aptly described in this book. It could be argued that novel efforts to incorporate effective care models that integrate HCBS with innovative care models (such as dementia care management) within existing health care systems remains an area ripe for future research and demonstration to better enhance continuity of care for older people in need. Degree of integration is key in such models. Specifically, integration would likely entail much more than providing information and referral (which appears to be the norm, if even offered). Instead, integration should represent a more seamless way for an older person and his or her family to learn about, pay for, and if necessary utilize HCBS that are aligned with the care plans of a primary or specialty care provider.

WHAT DOES "EVIDENCE-BASED" MEAN IN THE CONTEXT OF HCBS?

A common concern across the chapters is the lack of "high-quality evidence" available to support the overall efficacy of HCBS, particularly when it comes to cost savings. As noted earlier, current research suggests a mixed bag, if not worse, when it comes to efficacy for HCBS.

However, it is possible that the gold standard of the randomized controlled trial (RCT) for evaluating efficacy of HCBS or similar programs is misguided. For example, Zarit and his colleagues have utilized novel quasi-experimental (nonrandomized designs) to examine the efficacy of adult day services on key health outcomes for dementia caregivers (Zarit, Kim, Femia, Almeida, & Klein, 2014; Zarit, Whetzel, et al., 2014), and he expounds on his reasons for doing so (see Zarit, Bangerter, Liu, & Rovine, 2017). Such methodological insights are of interest, but also led me to wonder how can we make the case not only to funders but to other aggregators/synthesizers of evidence (for example, Cochrane, AHRQ, other clearinghouses) to actually change the way evidence is "rated." Nonpharmacological approaches such as HCBS are already marginalized given the lack of attention they have received in RCT designs, and a further lack of RCT types of designs would risk them being excluded entirely from syntheses or considered "weaker." It is not immediately clear that conducting more nonexperimental, controlled studies (albeit with elegant designs) will immediately overcome such biases. When we discuss "paradigm" shifts of methods in this context, I argue that the actual advance is/will be in the deployment of big data/machine learning tools, which have the potential to fundamentally alter how all types of care are delivered. I suppose one could consider this a quasi-experimental design of a type, albeit on a much larger scale. However, for HCBS or similar types of programs to allow for such evaluations, process and outcome data that is integrated in health records or similar data aggregation tools is required to better ascertain the degree to which HCBS are effectively improving key outcomes of interest to these stakeholders.

THE POTENTIAL OF HCBS IN TRANSITIONAL CARE

Transitions are sentinel events in which acute care considerations and chronic/long-term care needs either conflict or are misaligned, leading to particular challenges for older adults and their caregiving families (Gaugler, 2016; Levine, Halper, Peist, & Gould, 2010). Home- and community-based services are well positioned, however, to enhance transitional care for older adults in need of community-based supports. Current evidence-based approaches have focused on transitions from hospitals to home for older adults (Coleman, Parry, Chalmers, & Min, 2006; Naylor et al., 1994,

1999), but the increased emphasis on transitioning older adults from nursing homes to the community has provided greater opportunities for HCBS to demonstrate their importance in supporting older people and their families. This has occurred with NH diversion programs and Money Follows the Person grants, as noted previously. Several barriers to effective delivery of these programs remain, however, including availability of HCBS and appropriate community housing for residents transitioning from NHs, a limited "point of entry" for these programs (for example, NH admission) that may limit their overall reach, staff training, and overall integration of these programs into long-term care funding streams that require ongoing attention to allow HCBS to effectively enhance transitional care for older adults and their families (Gaugler, 2016; Holup, Gassoumis, Wilber, & Hyer, 2016; Reinhard, 2010).

THE HCBS "DOUGHNUT HOLE"

When considering assisted living and many other HCBS programs, I am often left wondering if we cover the needs of caregiving families and older adults in need to the extent that we believe we should. The use of Medicaid waivers has helped broaden the extent of LTSS for underserved families, but the costs of HCBS mean that they are likely affordable only for wealthier families. What about the large number of families who cannot afford to utilize HCBS but do not qualify for Medicaid? In many conversations I have with middle-class families caring for relatives with memory loss, I know they remain frustrated not only at the lack of availability of HCBS in some instances but also their inability to pay for them for an extended period of time or on a regular basis. For example, the average cost of adult day services in the United States is around $70 per day, and it is highly unlikely that many families or older adults with middle-class or lower incomes could afford to pay for more than one day a week of such care, which is likely insufficient to allow adult day services to exert a meaningful benefit. The Affordable Care Act has offered flexibility to states via the Community First Choice Option to relax income eligibility criteria for Medicaid in order to deliver HCBS more flexibly and to provide spousal protections (Stone & Benson, 2012). However, finding additional ways to loosen eligibility to assist families who do not qualify for Medicaid waivers but at the same time cannot afford to fund HCBS out of pocket requires us to think creatively about how we can support the large majority of families caring for relatives in need with community-based services in a reasonable manner; that is, avoiding the "woodwork" effect (see Weissert & Frederick, 2013).

CONCLUSION

Due to a convergence of sociodemographic trends, health care realignment, and economic imperatives, HCBS are finally poised to take their place as integral components of effective chronic and long-term care. With this in mind, it is absolutely critical that we view HCBS as much more than what they are now—an adjunct set of services that exist outside of formal health care systems. Home- and community-based services require integration in both funding streams and care delivery planning with other acute and long-term/chronic disease services that go well beyond the traditional "information and referral" function often provided. Instead, coordination of information and services that flows across HCBS, primary care providers, and specialty or other long-term care providers is needed along with inclusion of HCBS providers in the care planning process where appropriate. Utilizing HCBS as a mechanism to enhance the often disruptive aspects of transitional care is another strategy to further advance how HCBS are used and delivered. In the end, one could make the argument that facilitating personhood as we age is not possible without vibrant, accessible, and coordinated HCBS, and we as scholars, providers, and practitioners would be well-advised to champion this message as we envision the future of HCBS.

REFERENCES

Arling, G., Kane, R. L., Cooke, V., & Lewis, T. (2010). Targeting residents for transitions from nursing home to community. *Health Services Research, 45*(3), 691–711. doi:10.1111/j.1475-6773.2010.01105.x

Centers for Medicare & Medicaid Services. (n.d.). *Long-term services and supports.* Retrieved from https://www.medicaid.gov/medicaid/ltss/index.html

Coleman, E. A., Parry, C., Chalmers, S., & Min, S. J. (2006). The Care Transitions Intervention: Results of a randomized controlled trial. *Archives of Internal Medicine, 166*(17), 1822–1828. doi:10.1001/archinte.166.17.1822

Gaugler, J. E. (2016). Innovations in long-term care. In L. K. George & K. F. Ferraro (Eds.), *Handbook of aging and the social sciences* (pp. 419–439). London, UK: Academic Press.

Gaugler, J. E., Reese, M., & Tanler, R. (2016). Care to Plan: An online tool that offers tailored support to dementia caregivers. *The Gerontologist, 56*(6), 1161–1174. doi:gnv150 [pii]

Grabowski, D. C. (2006). The cost-effectiveness of noninstitutional long-term care services: Review and synthesis of the most recent evidence. *Medical Care Research and Review, 63*(1), 3–28.

Grabowski, D. C., Cadigan, R. O., Miller, E. A., Stevenson, D. G., Clark, M., & Mor, V. (2010). Supporting home- and community-based care: Views of long-term care specialists. *Medical Care Research and Review, 67*(4 Suppl), 82S-101S. doi:10.1177/1077558710366863

Harrington, C., & Kitchener, M. (2003). *Medicaid long-term care: Changes, innovations, and cost containment.* San Francisco, CA: University of California, San Francisco.

Holup, A. A., Gassoumis, Z. D., Wilber, K. H., & Hyer, K. (2016). Community discharge of nursing home residents: The role of facility characteristics. *Health Services Research, 51*(2), 645–666. doi:10.1111/1475-6773.12340

Kane, R. L., Boston, K., & Chilvers, M. (2007). Helping people make better long-term-care decisions. *The Gerontologist, 47*(2), 244–247.

Kassner, E. (2011). *Home and community-based long-term services and supports for older people.* Washington, DC: AARP Public Policy Institute.

Levine, C., Halper, D., Peist, A., & Gould, D. A. (2010). Bridging troubled waters: Family caregivers, transitions, and long-term care. *Health Affairs, 29*(1), 116–124. doi:10.1377/hlthaff.2009.0520

Naylor, M., Brooten, D., Jones, R., Lavizzo-Mourey, R., Mezey, M., & Pauly, M. (1994). Comprehensive discharge planning for the hospitalized elderly. A randomized clinical trial. *Annals of Internal Medicine, 120*(12), 999–1006.

Naylor, M. D., Brooten, D., Campbell, R., Jacobsen, B. S., Mezey, M. D., Pauly, M. V., & Schwartz, J. S. (1999). Comprehensive discharge planning and home follow-up of hospitalized elders: A randomized clinical trial. *Journal of the American Medical Association, 281*(7), 613–620.

Reinhard, S. C. (2010). Diversion, transition programs target nursing homes' status quo. *Health Affairs, 29*(1), 44–48. doi:10.1377/hlthaff.2009.0877

Stone, R. I., & Benson, W. F. (2012). Financing and organizing health and long-term care services for older populations. In T. R. Prohaska, L. A. Anderson, &

R. H. Binstock (Eds.), *Public health for an aging society.* (pp. 53–73). Baltimore, MD: Johns Hopkins University Press.

Weissert, W. G., & Frederick, L. (2013). The woodwork effect: Estimating it and controlling the damage. *Journal of Aging & Social Policy, 25*(2), 107–133. doi:10.1080/08959420.2013.766073

Zarit, S. H., Bangerter, L. R., Liu, Y., & Rovine, M. J. (2017). Exploring the benefits of respite services to family caregivers: Methodological issues and current findings. *Aging & Mental Health, 21*(3), 224–231. doi:10.1080/13607863.2015.1128881

Zarit, S. H., Kim, K., Femia, E. E., Almeida, D. M., & Klein, L. C. (2014). The effects of adult day services on family caregivers' daily stress, affect, and health: Outcomes from the Daily Stress and Health (DaSH) study. *Gerontologist, 54*(4), 570–579. doi:10.1093/geront/gnt045

Zarit, S. H., Whetzel, C. A., Kim, K., Femia, E. E., Almeida, D. M., Rovine, M. J., & Klein, L. C. (2014). Daily stressors and adult day service use by family caregivers: Effects on depressive symptoms, positive mood, and dehydroepian-drosterone-sulfate. *American Journal of Geriatric Psychiatry, 22*(12), 1592–1602. doi:S1064-7481(14)00047-5

ADMINISTRATION ON AGING (AOA) A federal office on aging responsible for implementing the Older Americans Act. It is part of the U.S. Department of Health and Human Services.

ADULT DAY SERVICES (ADS) Services that support the health, nutritional, social, and daily living needs of adults with functional limitations in a group setting during daytime hours.

AFFORDABLE CARE ACT (ACA) A comprehensive health care reform law enacted in 2010 with three goals, including to offer affordable health insurance, to expand the Medicaid program, and to support medical care delievery methods designed to generally lower the costs of health care.

AGING AND DISABILITY RESOURCE CENTER (ADRC) A single point of entry for information, referral, assessment, and care transition planning not only for older adults but also individuals of all ages with disabilities.

AGING IN PLACE The ability of an individual to remain living in the community in spite of age and/or health-related changes that may make this difficult.

AREA AGENCY ON AGING (AAA) Regional planning and service areas and corresponding organizations to support elders locally.

ASSISTED LIVING (AL) A residential care setting that provides older adults with assistance and supervision with personal and health care as well as support with activities of daily living.

CARE PLAN A tool that identifies a resident's care needs/goals, and interventions to meet those care needs/goals.

CAREGIVER'S BILL OF RIGHTS Rights for caregivers, care recipients, and the public to recognize what family caregivers are entitled to while in the role of a caregiver.

CASE MANAGEMENT Care coordination, including activities such as scheduling services, monitoring care being provided, and providing information and referrals.

CASH AND COUNSELING Older adults and those with disabilities served by Medicaid can receive a cash allowance or voucher to pay for home- and community-based services.

CENTERS FOR MEDICARE AND MEDICAID SERVICES (CMS) Federal agencies responsible for administering programs for older adults, including Medicare and Medicaid.

CONGREGATE CARE Settings where older adults receive services as a group, such as a congregate meal site.

CONTINUING CARE RETIREMENT COMMUNITY (CCRC) Residential settings that provide a continuum of services from independent living, assisted living, and skilled nursing, to nursing home care within a single campus.

DEPENDENCY RATIO The number of older adults (65 and older) divided by the number of working age adults (18 to 64).

DIGITAL DIVIDE Disparities in access to or ability to use technology.

DUAL ELIGIBLE Older adults who qualify for both Medicare and Medicaid.

FAMILY-CENTERED CARE Care that is congruent with family preferences and that places the family (including the older adult) at the center of decision making.

GERONTECHNOLOGY Technology such as monitors, sensors, and electronic devices designed to improve the lives of older adults and their caregivers.

GREEN CARE FARMS (GCF) Working farms where adults with disabilities engage in activities ranging from feeding and caring for animals to harvesting vegetables and preparing fresh meals.

HOME- AND COMMUNITY-BASED SERVICES (HCBS) Health care and support services that are delivered in the residences and neighborhoods where older adults and their family caregivers live.

HOME-BASED PRIMARY CARE (HBPC) Medical care that is provided in individuals' homes, formerly referred to as "house calls."

HOME HEALTH CARE The provision of health care services to people of any age at home or in other noninstitutional settings.

HOSPICE A model of care that provides comprehensive services at the end of life with the goals of patient and family comfort, alleviation of pain, and support during and after the dying process.

INFORMAL CAREGIVERS Individuals who provide various levels of physical and emotional assistance to adults with functional or cognitive limitations, also referred to as "family caregivers."

INTERDISCIPLINARY AND MULTIDISCIPLINARY TEAMS Teams of health care professionals drawn from various disciplines, such as medicine, nursing, social work, pharmacy, and allied health.

INTERPROFESSIONAL EDUCATION (IPE) Education that focuses on teamwork, quality improvement, and cross-discipline competence.

LONG-TERM SERVICES AND SUPPORTS (LTSS) Services and support provided to older adults and their families in institutional and noninstitutional settings.

MEDICAID A federal health insurance program for low-income children, adults, seniors, and people with disabilities.

MEDICARE A federal health insurance program for people age 65 and older. Part A covers hospital care, hospice, and some transitional home care. Part B covers primary care provider services and outpatient care. Part C (Medicare Advantage) is a private contract that provides services covered under Parts A and B, with some additional coverage. Part D covers prescription medications.

NATURALLY OCCURRING RETIREMENT COMMUNITY (NORC) Communities not originally built for older adults but to which large numbers of older adults have either relocated or continued to live over time.

OLDER AMERICANS ACT (OAA) The first federal law (1965) to establish a network of comprehensive, organized, and coordinated services and planning to serve older Americans.

OMBUDSMAN PROGRAM A program authorized under the Older Americans Act that provides residents of long-term care facilities with advocacy and quality assurance services.

PALLIATIVE CARE Care that is administered to provide comfort at any time during the course of an illness.

PATIENT-CENTERED CARE Health care that establishes a partnership among practitioners, patients, and their families to ensure that decisions respect patients' desires, needs, and preferences.

PHYSICAL ACTIVITY ON PRESCRIPTION (PAP) Prescribed physical activity and fitness programs for health problems, often as an alternative or a supplement to traditional medical treatment.

PROGRAM FOR ALL-INCLUSIVE CARE FOR THE ELDERLY (PACE) Programs that provide home-and community-based services for adults age 55 and older who otherwise would require nursing home care.

RESPITE A break provided to family caregivers either by having someone come to the home or by serving the older adult in a setting outside of the home (for example, adult day services).

SAFE TECHNOLOGY Technology (such as cameras, motion detectors, alarms) that monitor safety and detect adverse events, such as falls.

SERVICE COORDINATORS Providers who assist residents of congregate housing with support and service coordination.

SERVICE-ENRICHED HOUSING Subsidized, congregate housing that provides health and social services to low-income older adults.

SMART HOME TECHNOLOGY The systematic use of gerontechnology in a residence to provide monitoring, surveillance, and assistance.

STRESS PROCESS MODEL A framework for examining the context, stressors, and outcomes of family caregiving.

VILLAGE A consumer-driven neighborhood membership program that coordinates and delivers services and support to older adults living in the community.

Andersen Health Behavioral model, 31,
45; criticism for, 36–37; determinants
of, 34, 35, 36; race and ethnicity and,
36–37
Angela (case study), 169
AoA. *See* Administration on Aging
Applebaum, Robert, 45; on Medicaid
HCBS funding, 44
Area Agencies on Aging (AAA), 20, 33,
45–46, 96, 247; application of, 37;
Elder Care Locater for, 39; Martha and,
40; Matura and, 40–41; services of, 39
Aronson, Louise, 219
assessment process: for AL, 154; family
caregivers and, 74–76, 75; for
interprofessional and interdisciplinary
education and practice, 58; NORC and
survey for, 115–16, 122
assisted living (AL), 8, 145, 165, 247;
Aegis Gardens and, 156–57; assessment
process for, 154; availability of, 148;
core components of, 147; cost of, 148;
dementia and, 146, 148, 152, 160;
discussion questions and exercises for,
160; fact or fiction questions and, 146;
funding for, 146; future of, 155, 159;
history of, 146–48; hospitality model
of, 151; Medicaid and, 146, 147, 148;
models of, 150–51; nursing home and,
146–48, 160; practice applications
for, 153–55; race and ethnicity and,
156–57; research and evidence for,
157–58; SAH as, 158; Serdinak on,
155–56; service coordinators for, 150,
157–58, 160; service plan for, 154–55;
services for, 148–49, 149; Sherman
and, 153; social workers and, 156; staff
requirement for, 151; Zimmerman on,
158–59
Assisted Living Workgroup, 148

baby boomer generation, 1
Balanced Budget Act, 130
Beer, Jenay, 225
Bruin, Simone de, 207–8
Bush, George W., 16

Callahan, Patty, 79
caregivers: of HBPC, 138; internet and,
222–23. *See also* family caregivers
Caregiver's Bill of Rights, 247
CareGiving: Helping an Aging Loved One
(Horne), 74
care plan, 247; for hospice, 191;
interprofessional and interdisciplinary
education and practice and, 58–59
care transitions, 59
case management, 20, 247;
interprofessional and interdisciplinary
education and practice and, 59; NORC
and, 117; social workers and, 53
case study: Angela as, 169; Mr. Garcia as,
56; Janet as, 187–88; Johnson, E., as,
114–15; Luuk as, 213; Madera as, 77–78;
Martha as, 40; Misaki as, 230; Nadif
as, 96–97; Sherman as, 153; Thomas as,
132–33
Cash and Counseling, 17, 248; benefits
of, 16
CCRC. *See* continuing care retirement
community
Centers for Medicare and Medicaid Services
(CMS), 248; Affordable Care Act and,
59; Final Rule for Medicaid HCBS and,
18–19; HBPC and, 133; HCBS policies
and, 18; home health care and, 95;
hospice and, 184; OAA and, 44
Choudhury, Habib, 1, 87
chronic conditions: aging population and, 4;
longevity and, 4; mental health and,
4–5
CHSP. *See* Congregate Housing Services
Program
CLASS. *See* Community Living Assistance
Services and Supports Act
CMS. *See* Centers for Medicare and
Medicaid Services
Community First Choice Option, 242
Community Living Assistance Services and
Supports (CLASS) Act, 13, 20
Congregate Care, 248
Congregate Housing Services Program
(CHSP), 152

of, 2–3; challenges for, 21–24; CMS and, 18; consumer involvement in, 16, 25; as cost-effective, 2, 238–39, 240; discussion questions and exercises for, 25; enabling and need variables for use of, 43–44; fact or fiction questions and, 13, 25; family caregivers and, 22–23, 70–71, 84; federal involvement in, 21–22; history of, 14–17; institutional care and, 19; interprofessional care and, 240; Medicaid funding for, 17–18, 24, 44, 237–38, 242–43; Medicare coverage and, 17, 24; middle class and, 242–43; models for, 25, 240; Money Follows the Person and, 17; nursing home care compared to, 2; OAA funding for, 38–39; personalization of care for, 239; policies and, 6–7, 17; practitioners involved in, 52–53; predictors of use of, 42–43; public policy and, 13; rebalancing toward, 237–38; recipients of, 13; recruitment and retention for employees of, 23; research and evidence for, 240–41; residual model of, 13, 24; service providers of, 46; transitional care and, 241–42, 243; unmet needs and, 22; women and, 23, 42. *See also specific topics*
home-based primary care (HBPC), 2, 8, 248; AAHCM and, 130; American Academy of Home Care Medicine and, 130; Balanced Budget Act and, 130; caregivers of, 138; CMS and, 133; cost of, 134; discussion questions and exercises for, 141–42; eligibility for, 133, 141; fact or fiction questions for, 128; fee-for-service models and, 129–30; funding for, 129, 134–35, 140; future of, 137, 139–40, *140*, 142; HCS and, 131, *131–32*; house call and history of, 127, 128, 129–30, 141; illnesses and homebound adults and, 133, *134*; interprofessional teamwork and, 128, 131; Leff on, 138–39; Medicaid and Medicare and, 134; Murphy on, 136–37; PACE and, 135; practice application for, 130–31; quality standards for, 139,

140; research and evidence for, 137–38, 141; services of, 128, 141, 145–46; social workers and, 132; Thomas and, 132–33; VA and, 135; veterans and, 135–36
homebound adults, 141; illnesses and, 133, *134*
home health care, 7, 87, 248; CMS and, 95; dementia and, 93; demographics of patients of, 91–92; depression management intervention and, 99; discussion questions and exercises for, 102; eligibility and funding for, 93–94; fact or fiction questions for, 88–89; funding for, 93–94; future of, 100–101, *101*, 102; goals of, 88; health conditions and, *92*; history of, 88, 89–90, 101; interprofessional teamwork and, 102; Lee on, 99–100; Medicaid and Medicare and, 90–91, 93–95, 99, 102; perspectives from the field for, 92–93; practice application of, 90–92; professionals delivering, 101; quality and location for, 89–99; race and ethnicity and, 95–96; rate for, 94–95, 102; research and evidence for, 97–99; services offered for, 91, *91*, 92; staffing for, 91; therapy and, 93, 99; visiting nurse programs and, 89
Horne, Jo, 74
hospice, 3, 8–9, 182, 248; care plan for, 191; CMS and, 184; cost of, 194–95; dementia and, 191; demographics of patients in, 191, 197; discussion questions and exercises for, 197; Douglas on, 192; eligibility criteria for, 186–87, 197; fact or fiction questions for, 183; for-profit, 189–90, *190*; funding for, 184–85; future of, 196; goals of, 183, 196; health conditions and, 191, *191*; history of, 183, 184–85, *185*; interdisciplinary and multidisciplinary teams for, 190–91, 192; Janet and, 187–88; LCDs for, 186; location of, 189, 197; Medicare and Medicaid and, 184, 185–86; palliative care and, 183, 186, 187; practice application for, 185–87; race